ADVANCE PRAISE FOR

Civic Engagement in Diverse Latinx Communities

"Centering Latinx communities and social justice partnerships, this book addresses issues, practices, and communities rarely explored in the literature on civic and community engagement. The focus on diverse Latinx communities creates space to consider how the communities where we partner, the students in our classrooms, the issues being confronted in community spaces, and the identities we claim as facilitators and conveners of these experiences can (and should) inform our praxis in community engagement. The aims of all of the partnerships explored in the text to advance justice and to transform the social concerns that perpetuate inequality are a powerful reminder of the possibility of civically engaged teaching and learning. *Civic Engagement in Diverse Latinx Communities* is a unique, important, and remarkable contribution."

—*Tania D. Mitchell, Associate Professor of Higher Education, University of Minnesota*

"The fundamental axis of this book is rooted in the intersection of Latinx experience and civic engagement from a social justice point of view. The authors carefully discuss the ways Latinx communities have knowledge and points of view that are important, as well as make a valuable contribution to debates and best practices about engaging communities. They provide empirical evidence that measures the hidden value and contribution of faculty of color in their commitment to social change, which are experiences emerging from U.S. minoritization and the product of a legacy of colonization and conquest."

—*Julia E. Curry, Associate Professor of Mexican American Studies, San Jose State University*

"This is one of the most exciting and important books on civic engagement in higher education in some time. It answers the call from the past decade of scholarship for critical frameworks and social justice approaches to service learning and community engagement. The scholars contributing to this book provide cogent examples of exemplary practices of engagement that enact authentic reciprocity in a context of social justice partnerships that form the basis for collaborative teaching and learning and new knowledge generation. Engagement with Latinx communities, by and with Latinix scholars and students, informs service learning and community engagement practices across disciplines and different sectors of higher education. This is exactly the book the field needs now. I will be including it as required reading in my civic engagement courses."

—*John Saltmarsh, Professor of Higher Education, University of Massachusetts, Boston*

Civic Engagement in Diverse Latinx Communities

Yolanda Medina and Margarita Machado-Casas
General Editors

Vol. 17

The Critical Studies of Latinos/as in the Americas series
is part of the Peter Lang Trade Academic and Textbook list.
Every volume is peer reviewed and meets
the highest quality standards for content and production.

PETER LANG
New York • Bern • Berlin
Brussels • Vienna • Oxford • Warsaw

Civic Engagement in Diverse Latinx Communities

Learning From Social Justice Partnerships in Action

Edited by Mari Castañeda
& Joseph Krupczynski

PETER LANG
New York • Bern • Berlin
Brussels • Vienna • Oxford • Warsaw

Library of Congress Cataloging-in-Publication Data

Names: Castañeda, Mari, editor. | Krupczynski, Joseph, editor.
Title: Civic engagement in diverse Latinx communities: learning from social justice partnerships in action / edited by Mari Castañeda & Joseph Krupczynski.
Description: New York: Peter Lang, 2018.
Series: Critical studies of Latino/as in the Americas; vol. 17
ISSN 2372-6822 (print) | ISSN 2372-6830 (online)
Includes bibliographical references and index.
Identifiers: LCCN 2017038338 | ISBN 978-1-4331-4726-5 (pbk.: alk. paper)
ISBN 978-1-4331-5014-2 (hardback: alk. paper)
ISBN 978-1-4331-4825-5 (ebook pdf)
ISBN 978-1-4331-5008-1 (epub) | ISBN 978-1-4331-5009-8 (mobi)
Subjects: LCSH: Community and college—United States.
Service learning—United States.
Social justice—Study and teaching (Higher)—United States.
Hispanic Americans—Social conditions.
Hispanic Americans—Study and teaching (Higher).
Classification: LCC LC238 .C59 2018 | DDC 378.1/03—dc23
LC record available at https://lccn.loc.gov/2017038338
DOI 10.3726/b11957

Bibliographic information published by **Die Deutsche Nationalbibliothek.**
Die Deutsche Nationalbibliothek lists this publication in the "Deutsche Nationalbibliografie"; detailed bibliographic data are available on the Internet at http://dnb.d-nb.de/.

The paper in this book meets the guidelines for permanence and durability of the Committee on Production Guidelines for Book Longevity of the Council of Library Resources.

29 Broadway, 18th floor, New York, NY 10006
www.peterlang.com

Printed in the United States of America

We dedicate this book to our *madres poderosas*, Guadalupe Hernández and Rose Acevedo Krupczynski, for teaching us how to engage in the world with courage and joy.

Table of Contents

Acknowledgements

We would first like to acknowledge the scholar-activist authors who contributed to this edited collection. It is their commitment, reciprocity, risk-taking, and love for Latinx communities that is transforming higher education, civic engagement, and community-based relationships. We are so honored to be part of your journey and we thank you for your willingness to be part of ours. Secondly, we want to recognize our wonderful colleagues and dearest friends at the University of Massachusetts, Amherst for their magnificent support and encouragement, especially in the Department of Communication, the College of Social and Behavioral Sciences, the Center for Latin American, Caribbean and Latina/o Studies, the College of Humanities and Fine Arts, the Center for Design Engagement, the Department of Architecture, and Civic Engagement and Service Learning. We also want to say *mil gracias* to NECLS (New England Consortium of Latina/o Studies) and the *mujeres* online writing group for continually reminding us that scholarly production is an important form of liberation and transformation. Similarly, thank you very much to Peter Lang Publishers, particularly Tim Swenarton and Sarah Bode as well as Yolanda Medina and Margarita Machado-Casas (series editors for *Critical Studies of Latina/os in the Americas*) for believing in this book project and ushering its existence. Last but not least, we want to give a big shout out to our *familias*, whose unconditional love and dedication to social justice movements energizes us every day. We especially want to thank our son, Miguel Angel Paredes, an emerging 21st century leader and community-oriented artist-activist (a.k.a. Tuzko), for always motivating and inspiring us to create the art and world we want to see!

With love, deep respect, and gratitude for all, Mari Castañeda and Joseph Krupczynski, Amherst, MA.

Introduction: Toward a Latinx Community-Academic Praxis of Civic Engagement

Mari Castañeda and Joseph Krupczynski

Latinx[1] communities are powerful sources of knowledge. Unlike the dominant media images, emboldened by the hateful rhetoric of the current U.S. administration, that portray these communities as sites of violence, degeneration or illegality, this book aims to show how faculty and students at a range of universities and colleges across the United States are learning from, and engaging with Latina/o communities through social justice partnerships, while concurrently disrupting the fallacious notions that circulate about people of Latin American and Caribbean descent. Cumulatively, the chapters in this book point toward a Latinx community-academic praxis that challenges how knowledge is created, how civic engagement is practiced, and the application of community service-learning in higher education, especially at a moment when racial/ethnic communities are persistently challenged politically, economically and socially. The U.S. Census predicts that by the year 2050, the diverse Latinx population will double in size and constitute nearly 30% of all people residing and working in the United States (Colby & Ortman, 2015). Presently, 1 out of 4 children born in the U.S. are of Latina/Hispanic descent. Demographic statistics and socio-cultural research confirm that the Latinx diaspora will undoubtedly impact the future of American politics, economics, cultural landscapes, and educational institutions (Kochhar, Suro, & Tafoya, 2005; Suro & Singer, 2002). Yet the nature and contour of that influence will be greatly dependent on the general population's perception and treatment of Latinos and the opportunities available to harness the social and cultural assets that will shape their participation in civil society and the public sphere.

Similarly, it is important to examine how the racial, economic, and cultural diversity of Latinx communities have affected the ways in which the population is (mis)understood and its contributions to public life are (un)acknowledged in the U.S. (Arreola, 2004; Diaz & Torres, 2012; Geron, 2005). In an effort to disrupt racist and problematic perceptions of U.S. Latinos while also collaborating with local communities to create opportunities for empowerment and engagement, the scholars in this collection have developed social justice oriented courses and research projects in a wide array of fields that link college student learning with civic engagement and transformative community movements. Working in communities is not a new practice for university faculty committed to social justice, especially those rooted in Latinx/Chicana studies, African American studies, and ethnic studies. These fields were in fact the result of community organizing and scholar-activists demanding that their institutions create spaces where issues and concerns of underrepresented populations could be taken seriously and critically examined (De la Torre, 1993; Lowe, 1996; Pérez, 1999; Rojas, 2007; Saldívar, 1997; Sandoval, 2000).

The surge in civic engagement and community-based learning at colleges and universities has created new pedagogies and creative opportunities to engage with communities of color. *Civic Engagement in Diverse Latinx Communities: Learning from Social Justice Partnerships in Action* brings together excellent examples of community-academic partnerships in Latinx communities that include social justice approaches to civic engagement and community service-learning in a wide variety of fields such as media studies, architecture, literature, education, sociology, anthropology and journalism. Their combined experience in community-based teaching as well as their exceptional understanding of social justice pedagogies makes this collection a trove of insights with lessons learned from diverse Latino communities that can also greatly inform student learning and local community partnerships. Building upon the best practices from scholarship in civic engagement, community service-learning, Latina/Chicana/o/x studies, indigenous studies, community studies, intersectional postcolonial/decolonial feminism, and communication/media studies, the authors demonstrate what is possible through civic engagement by drawing on a Latinx community-academic praxis.

In the past several years, several monographs have been published that address civic engagement and community service-learning as key themes for educational institutions, policy makers, community-based organizations and cultural/economic sectors seeking to connect and work with local and global communities as well as challenge historical social relations of exploitation (see Dostilio, 2017; Post, Ward, Longo, & Saltmarsh, 2016; Stoecker, 2016). Although we build on this past work, there are key differences between what those book volumes attempt to address versus what our collection is aiming to do through its emphasis on Latinx community-academic praxis. First, we firmly believe in the importance of highlighting Latina/o communities as specific sites of creative and dynamic civic engagement and thus build off similar work (see Pérez, Espinoza, Ramos, Coronado, & Cortes, 2010). This volume gives voice to social justice community-academic projects in order to learn from and bear witness to the lived (transnational) experiences of Latinos across the United States. It aims to shift the conversation about community-university partnerships as something where students "do good" for a community, towards a Latinx community-academic praxis that emphasizes social justice partnerships in action, which aim to critically engage with the multiple intersections of oppression (Castañeda, 2008).

Secondly, the scholar-activists in this collection are partnering with Latina/o communities, sometimes under extraordinary circumstances, in an effort to rethink civic engagement practices that center the decolonization of knowledge and a critique of the ways in which color-blind racism can affect student learning. By including elements of *testimonio*—personal narrative and autoethnography—into the essays, the authors lay bare their presence in a collaboration that aims to address the multiple issues diverse Latinx communities are facing. *Testimonio* also provides the opportunity to discuss theoretically and empirically the racialized and labor conditions of a pedagogically-based, social justice oriented civic engagement. Thirdly, as the political economy of academic institutions shift towards corporate-based models of teaching, in both explicit and subtle ways, it is critical to ascertain how community-academic partnerships will be affected by these structural-cultural changes. Many of the chapters include pedagogical solutions for creating more community engaged institutions of higher learning in order to change the exclusiveness of the Ivory Tower and support the communities that are changing the social and cultural life of the U.S.

Ultimately, this collection demonstrates that documenting personal experiences in the classroom and in communities is a powerful tool for the production of new knowledge and frameworks of understanding (Burciaga & Cruz Navarro, 2015). Lastly, by collectively emphasizing the possibilities of a critical civic engagement the authors are contributing to a social justice epistemology that aims to investigate and develop new praxis for how to engage with diverse communities in the 21st century. As the chapters in this volume demonstrate, Latinos are material and active subjects with historically specific experiences that must be understood and recognized within local and transglocal contexts. Diverse Latino communities are not stereotypical discursive reproductions, but embodied material and cultural agents who are producing knowledge and making history, albeit within conditions not entirely of their own making. Ultimately, collectively, we aim to ask, how do we make higher education more responsive to local and regional community needs through reciprocity and with respect to different ways of knowing and learning? In this vein, and in an effort to practice the principles of Chicana/Latinx feminist decolonial methods, many authors engage with the writing practice of *testimonio* in order to bear witness and develop insight and theoretical connections between their experiences as teachers in the classroom, partners in communities, and activists in civil society. Unlike some of the dominant narratives about civic engagement and service-learning within communities of color, we aim to challenge the deficit models often associated with Latina/o peoples and create new forms of understanding of what is possible when social justice partnerships are put into action.

With this in mind, we use the term Latinx as well as Latina/o, Latino and Latinos and other specific group names such as Chicana/o, Mexican-American and Puerto Rican throughout the book in an effort to be as inclusive as possible. These communities, as many others of color, have also historically experienced coercion with regards to sexual and gender identities. The term Latinx emerged from diverse Latina/o activists and educators arguing that despite mainstream narrow understandings of Latinidad, there needed to be a broadened inclusion of sexual and gender identities within racial, ethnic and cultural positionalities. Thus, this edited collection—*Civic Engagement in Diverse Latinx Communities: Learning from Social Justice Partnerships in Action*—includes a variety of terminologies currently used to describe diverse Latino communities, sometimes interchangeably, and highlights Latinx in the book title in order to build bridges between history, contemporary identities, and the transcultural and political power of global south communities to claim space and voice their engaged presence.

The Rise of Civic Engagement and Community Service-Learning

According to the Association of Colleges and Universities, "in this turbulent and dynamic century, our nation's diverse democracy and interdependent global community require a more informed, engaged, and socially responsible citizenry. Both educators and employers agree that personal and social responsibility should be core elements of a 21st century education if our world is to thrive" (AACU, 2016, n.p.). Indeed, preparing students and communities for the social transformations across the Americas and around the globe is an important part of higher education. The expansion of organizations focusing on service-learning and community-based research such Campus Compact, Teach for America, ServiceCorps, AmeriCorp, and PeaceCorps point to growing appeal of the civic engagement capacity of young adults. Communities can be positively impacted by the participation of emerging leaders while also developing a long-lasting engagement with civic life, especially within and beyond local communities (Saltmarsh, 1996, 1997). Yet it is important to note that not all forms of civic engagement, particularly at universities and colleges, are effective or transformative. Such limitations often occur when community partners are not included in the development of engagement projects. One way faculty members with more critical orientations towards service-learning and community engagement have addressed the tendency for such projects to only benefit students is to base civically engaged partnerships on social justice principles. In doing so, they consequently shift away from solely utilizing normative (ivory tower-centered) modes of engagement. Such critical orientations have emerged from much debate about who ultimately benefits from these kinds of partnerships, especially if the university fails to critically examine how such projects can sometimes reproduce inequities and negative stereotypes (Castañeda, 2008; Labonte, 2005; Parsons & Stephenson, 2005). Lacking critical frameworks or social justice approaches in university-centric community partnerships can end up hurting and exploiting communities, particularly those that are already experiencing marginalization. The neoliberal push towards revenue generation at many institutions of higher education also impacts such partnerships since universities now see communities as sources of revenue rather than as settings in which resources (human and otherwise) at the college can be utilized for transformative community and civic engagement in collaborative projects (Dowling, 2008). In fact, socially just community-university partnerships take as their center the need to make colleges accountable to the communities they work with as well as the development of connections that engender equitable reciprocity. Such partnerships are also consistently engaging in reflective practices that recognize the wealth of knowledge in communities and the importance of disrupting traditional notions of town-gown power relations as much as possible (Ash & Clayton, 2004).

Additionally, the practices of civic engagement through socially just community-university partnerships have the potential to create an environment in which students' prejudices and stereotypes can be interrogated. Through this process, community partners become co-creators of knowledge while also gaining the benefit of student/faculty participation in projects. Civic engagement efforts that are linked to socially just community-university partnerships also have the benefit of demonstrating to students how community environments are spaces in which relevant and meaningful knowledge production is taking place. Thus, college students, including their professors, become learners and publically engaged scholars who have much to appreciate from community members (see Dostilio, 2017; Post et al., 2016). Concurrently, community members are able to share their stories and humanize the challenges and triumphs facing the groups in their organization. This is especially important for communities of color, who are often demonized and misrepresented in the mainstream media outlets. Students sometimes enter into community settings with inappropriate stereotypes and negative representations, yet by participating in civic engagement through socially just service-learning partnerships, uninformed notions about people and places can be disrupted and even transformed. Such transformation has the potential to develop a positive ripple effect in students' future democratic (perhaps even radical) participation, especially if they engage with communities that challenge their normative understandings of race, class, gender, sexuality and citizenship.

By incorporating community-based and service-learning projects into college courses, students develop a range of civic engagement skill sets that are increasingly critical given the growing diversity in the United States. In fact, Astin, Vogelgesang, Ikeda, and Yee (2000) actually found not only positive outcomes across various measures such academic performance (critical thinking skills), values (commitment to activism), leadership (interpersonal skills), and plans to participate in service after college, but they also found that both students and professors "develop[ed] a heightened sense of civic responsibility and personal effectiveness through participation in service-learning courses" (pp. 3–4). In summary, the community partnerships included in courses, especially where reflection and discussion was a core of the pedagogical framework, mattered and made a difference for everyone involved. Bowman (2011) also found increased experiences with diversity when students participated in civic engagement projects and courses, which were not only curricular but also co-curricular and interpersonal. A reduction in racial bias was also detected in the study, and ultimately, Bowman (2011) noted, "the empathic bonds that occur primarily through interpersonal interaction—as opposed to simply 'engaging' with diversity abstractly through course work or workshops … lead to a greater importance placed on social action engagement and, ultimately, to civic action" (p. 23).

Additionally, Howard (1998, 2001) notes community-based and service-learning courses present the opportunity for students, professors and community actors to develop a synergistic and relational learning environment. Such an environment "encourages social responsibility; values and integrates both academic and experiential learning; accommodates both high and low levels of structure and direction; embraces the active, participatory student, and welcomes both subjective and objective ways of knowing" (Howard, 1998, p. 25). Such a synergistic experience is best attainable when best practices are applied to course structure and partnerships: (1) meaningful content, (2) voice and choice, (3) personal and public purpose, (4) assessment and feedback, and (5) resources and relationships (Melaville, Berg, & Blank, 2006). Ultimately, a well-planned civic engagement course has the potential to inspire students and community partners to appreciate reciprocity, lifelong learning, responsive engagement, and astute critical citizenship.

The inclusion of community engagement by the Carnegie Foundation furthered the efforts towards service-learning and civic engagement by developing a set of criteria and classifications that universities and colleges could aim towards (Carnegie Classifications of Institutions of Higher Learning, 2015). Such classifications have become badges of honor that communicate to the college community and its prospective students the value that a campus places on service-learning and civic engagement (Study Group on Civic Learning and Engagement, 2014). The growing emphasis of service-learning as community-based also reoriented the role of community members as central actors in community-university partnerships. In this capacity, community members could now work closely with faculty to develop the course structure, community projects, and assessment of not only student work, but also the overall partnership (Blouin & Perry, 2009; Ward & Wolf-Wendel, 2000). Service-learning has historically emphasized volunteerism and even charity approaches to community engagement, but the inclusion of critical, social justice frameworks has sharpened academic-community praxis by understanding how the intersections of race, gender, class and sexuality shape community and civic engagement (Mitchell & Humphries, 2007; Morton, 1995).

However, there remains a lack of diversity in terms of student and faculty participation in civic engagement and service-learning even while communities have become more diverse, in large because many institutions of higher education, especially research universities, do not reflect U.S. diversity. Although many academic fields are now incorporating community-based research and community service-learning, they still struggle to diversify participation, including those of community partners (Price, Lewis, & Lopez, 2014). There are many socio-political reasons why this is the case. In the context of students, college debt has made it difficult to participate in extracurricular activities that may take time away from supposedly real courses perceived as offering specific career skill sets (Bragg, 2001). We would argue that civic engagement and service-learning actually do prepare students for the workforce and democratic participation (Simons & Cleary, 2006). Also, more college students are working and attending school, which makes it difficult for students to participate in projects taking time away from their employment responsibilities. With regards to faculty, the growing pressure to publish peer-reviewed articles in the highest-ranking journals in the field, or produce books contracted with university presses, or secure large funds from public and private granting agencies, makes it more difficult develop civic engagement, community-based or service-learning opportunities for students and communities because of the time commitment they require (Abes, Jackson, & Jones, 2002; McKay & Rozee, 2004; O'Meara & Niehaus, 2009). However, as the chapters in this edited collection show, it is possible to combine research interests, student development, diverse socio-political strategies, and community engagement in ways that promote social justice, new knowledge formations, and collective academic spaces. The social justice partnerships discussed in this volume attempt to go beyond traditional notions of service-learning as merely volunteerism and charity work, and in fact demonstrate there is much to learn from partnerships with diverse Latina/x communities who are agents in their own historically and culturally specific realities.

The Emergence of a Latinx Community-Academic Praxis

This collection aims to transform the conversation about civic engagement and service-learning by showing the possibilities of social justice partnerships in action through a Latinx community-academic praxis. Such a framework takes as its guiding principle the idea that Latino communities engage in knowledge production and socio-political organizing on a daily basis, both within and outside of normative western modalities. The social justice orientation of this collection is not merely about pointing out or addressing injustices and misrepresentations, but also recognizing the cultural assets and funds of knowledge the community already embodies. Additionally, it is about acknowledging how these assets can potentially transform the ways in which civic engagement is practiced collaboratively over time. Lastly, this work is deeply influenced by the legacy of ethnic studies, especially Chicana/Latino studies and indigenous studies.

Scholar-activists have historically recognized the need to work with, and for, communities of color, particularly at times when mainstream academic spaces have pathologized communities of color (Collins, 2005; Kershaw, 2003; Torres, 2013). In many instances, these communities were not included in studies at all (Markus, Steele, & Steele, 2000). Ethnic studies scholars in the post-Civil Rights era aimed to turn such pathologizing on its head (Darder & Torres, 1998; Rosaldo, 1985). Many of these trailblazing scholar-activists also recognized the deep knowledge that was present in communities of color; communities that deserved to be recognized, included, and not dismissed. The critically important scholarship of Third World feminism furthered these efforts and broke down barriers by developing theoretical frameworks that took as its center the community—in all its complexity, contradictions, and possibilities (Sandoval, 1991). To be so closely engaged with communities was in many ways a political project given the emphasis on objective research in the academy as well as the historical racism and discrimination that was being felt across institutional, economic and political realms.

Despite the political and social progress since the Civil Rights era, the realities of changing demographics in the U.S. (and across the Americas) as well as the reemergence of white supremacy, is currently fueling a political sphere that demonize and scapegoat Latinx people, particularly those who are of Mexican-descent including undocumented, UndocuQueer and transgender identified people. In this political context, highlighting engaged scholarship that embodies a Latinx community-academic praxis is more important than ever as communities are under siege and attacked through discursive, symbolic and physical violence. Such violence damages self-esteem, reproduces economic inequities, and generates social responses that spur more audiovisual and interpersonal attacks (Chávez, 2013; Santa Ana, 2013). This collection demonstrates that rather than retreating to the Ivory Tower, we are witnessing increasingly more students and faculty (especially those of color and/or from working class backgrounds) engaging collaboratively with underrepresented communities in order to make visible these communities' precious knowledge and speaking up against the hate speech that attempts to delegitimize and cower Latina/o communities. Professors, students and communities are working together to challenge the social structures that aim to restrict community access to resources, including educational opportunities, media spaces, and the built environment.

Furthermore, civic engagement and community service-learning often operate from the principle of difference, but what happens when communities share affinities with students and their professors? Very little scholarship is written about academics of color working on civic engagement and service-learning with communities of color. Although issues regarding class and educational privilege persist, many of the authors in this collection identify as first generation college students, Latinx and indigenous, and acknowledge the intersectionality of their lived experiences and community partnerships. Their engagement with Latina/o communities is not an exotic experience, but one of real material and personal connection. These connections are also politically informed, which builds on the long legacies of scholar-activists and the decolonization of knowledge. It is important to note that the authors in this collection are committed to the interstitial spaces of academia in order to foster engagement, empowerment and communication of what is often made silent.

Lastly, the authors demonstrate how to work collaboratively with communities so that the reciprocity of knowledge and its creation can formulate new ways of being and thinking in the world. The embodiment of a Latinx community-academic praxis is more than simply doing good in a community setting. The framework aims to disrupt negative stereotypes of Latinx communities and work within the fissures to dislodge the barriers to opportunities that are constantly placed between communities of color and institutions of higher education. We also do not believe you have to be Latinx to do the work presented here, but we do hope to inspire other scholars to use their educational resources in meaningfully productive ways that can potentially create a scholarship of social justice engagement produced collaboratively by communities, students, and faculty. Partnerships between communities and universities/colleges do not have to be exploitive, and the growing scholarship of engagement that challenges notions of race, ethnicity, class, gender and sexuality as it is practiced in community-based learning is one example of how critical academic spaces can promote social justice, equity, and peace, despite the current era of turmoil and hate speech (Kajner, Chovanec, Underwood, & Mian, 2013; Mitchell, Donahue, & Young-Law, 2012; Shabazz & Cooks, 2014). We are in a neoliberal moment where we need to find ways to escape the trap of individuals and develop new approaches for working through the community and university divide.

Making visible what is often invisible is a key theme that drives the chapters in this collection. The chapters' orientations are influenced by Chandra Mohanty's comments about the beauty and impetus of the written word:

> Writing often becomes the context through which new political identities are forged. It becomes a space for struggle and contestation about reality itself. If the everyday world is not transparent and its relations of rule—its organizations and institutional frameworks—work to obscure and make invisible inherent hierarchies of power, it becomes imperative that we rethink, remember, and utilize our lived relations as a basis of knowledge. Writing (discursive production) is one site for the production of this knowledge and this consciousness. (2003, p. 78)

In addition to writing about civic engagement, service-learning courses, and community-based research projects, many authors also include the lived experience of social relations as a methodological and theoretical writing tool (Delgado Bernal, Burciaga, & Flores Carmona, 2012; Huber, 2009). This scholarly practice, in some cases embodied as *testimonio*, is a political effort to insert the voices of Latinx scholar-activists in the discussion of civic engagement and community service-learning. These voices are often absent in the civic engagement scholarship, and in many cases at the major academic conferences as well, thus this edited monograph brings Latina/o scholar-activist voices to the forefront of such conversations. The chapters in the book are organized under three themes: (1) rethinking community and civic engagement; (2) community voices and the politics of place; and (3) expanding the media and cultural power of communities.

The first thematic section of the book—"Rethinking Community and Civic Engagement"—addresses the ways in which faculty, students and community partners are rethinking the ideas and practices of community and civic engagement. The first chapter by Antonieta Mercado titled, "Civic Engagement: Learning from Teaching Community Praxis," addresses the incorporation of *tequio*, which means community work in Náhuatl language, within community based courses as a process for building bonds and trust with immigrant and indigenous communities. Next is a chapter by Joseph Krupczynski titled, "Imagining a *Nueva Casita*: Puerto Rican Subjectivities and the Space of the 'In-between' on an Urban Farm in Western Massachusetts," and he describes a project that helped develop a more complex understanding of cultural heritage in an effort to create a transnational and emancipatory space/place firmly rooted in Latina/o cultural subjectivities. Claudia A. Evans-Zepeda's chapter, "Subject-Heading or Social Justice Solidarity? Civic Engagement Practices of Latinx Undocumented Immigrant Students," offers reflections on the ways in which undocumented Latina/o college students participate in critical civic praxis to subvert the racist nativism prevalent in the dominant immigration discourse. The following chapter, "Keeping It Real: Bridging U.S. Latino/a Literature and Community Through Student Engagement," by Marisel Moreno demonstrates how applying community based learning pedagogy to the study of U.S. Latino/a literature provides unique opportunities for students to develop practices and dispositions that help to enhance their understanding of civic engagement and social justice. Lastly, the co-authored chapter by Clara Román-Odio, Patricia Mota, and Amelia Dunnell titled, "Public Humanities and Community-Engaged Learning: Building Strategies for Undergraduate Research and Civic Engagement," offers a case study to show how by linking the public humanities to community-engaged learning we can build meaningful strategies to strengthen both undergraduate research and civic engagement.

The second thematic section of the book—Community Voices and the Politics of Place—discusses the importance of community voices in shaping the reclamation and contestation of place and belonging. The section begins with Jonathan Rosa's chapter, "Community as a Campus: From 'Problems' to Possibilities in Latinx Communities," in which he points to the productive possibilities that emerge when we shift from viewing marginalized communities as static objects of academic analysis to dynamic sites of collaborative knowledge production. Following is the chapter titled, "Motherists' Pedagogies of Cultural Citizenship: Claiming Rights and Space in a Xenophobic Era," by Judith Flores Carmona and here she describes how Latina mothers enact pedagogies of the home and their responsibility to fight for basic social needs and the various forms of activism that take place through their participation in their children's education and educación in their community, school, and homes. The chapter by J. Estrella Torrez titled, "Responsibility, Reciprocity, and Respect: Storytelling as a Means of University-Community Engagement," presents three tenets—responsibility, reciprocity, and respect—extrapolated through work with Latino and Indigenous communities that can be used in developing collaborative relationships in predominantly white U.S. regions. The following chapter, "Arizona-Sonora 360: Examining and Teaching Contested Moral Geographies along the U.S.-Mexico Borderlands," by Celeste González de Bustamante suggests that when coupled with a critical borderlands pedagogy, the concepts of moral geography and counter-cartographies can be useful tools for understanding the dynamics of the Arizona-Sonora borderlands. Lastly, Ginetta E. B. Candelario's chapter, titled "*Saber es Poder*: Teaching and Learning about Social Inequality in a New England Latin@ Community," discusses the local Latino/a community of Holyoke, MA as a case study of Puerto Rican experience in the U.S. and the importance of Latino Studies' founding principle of community service and engagement for understanding the socio-politics of place.

The final thematic section—Expanding the Media and Cultural Power of Communities—shows the multiplicity of cultural production can work as valuable pathways for civic engagement and telling stories that prioritize community lives and knowledge production. The first chapter by Jillian M. Báez titled, "Media Literacy as Civic Engagement," calls attention to how media literacy, as a form of civic engagement, not only involves learning how to deconstruct media texts, but also understanding oneself as a player within the media system who can advocate and/or contest media production, ownership, and content. Following is the chapter, "'I Exist Because You Exist:' Teaching History and Supporting Student Engagement via Bilingual Community Journalism," by Katynka Z. Martínez in which she describes how student demands for a more relevant education and a more just society led to the emergence of a Latina/o newspaper that is still advocating for community rights, especially in the current era of gentrification in San Francisco. The third chapter, titled "Hashtag Jóvenes Latinos: Teaching Civic Advocacy Journalism in Glocal Contexts" by Jessica Retis describes the powerful impact that is produced when students include their personal experiences when creating stories by, with, and for young Latinos. Similarly, Sonya M. Alemán, in her chapter titled, "Chicana/o Media Pedagogies: How Activism and Engagement Transform Student of Color Journalists," chronicles the types of civic engagement and/or activism that was catalyzed as the result of a community-media partnership and the differentiation between activism and engagement this partnership had for students who belonged to racially and ethnically marginalized groups. The final chapter of this anthology is by Rogelio Miñana, and in "Lessons from Migrant Youth: Digital Storytelling and the Engaged Humanities in Springfield, MA," he examines the positive potential of digital storytelling as a space for self-expression for young migrants and the lessons that faculty and students learned from community members on the role of higher education in society as well as on the pedagogy and methodologies of the engaged humanities.

Together as a whole, these sections bear witness and convey meaningful stories of professors, student and community working together through social justice partnerships across diverse Latina/o communities. All the authors are scholar-activists striving to embody a Latinx community-academic praxis in their civic engagement and community service-learning work while also challenging the closed quarters of academia. We hope that readers will be inspired by the partnerships discussed in *Civic Engagement in Diverse Latinx Communities: Learning from Social Justice Partnerships in Action* and are open to the possibilities that a Latinx community-academic praxis can offer in their efforts toward social justice and transformative liberation.

Note

1. We use the term Latinx throughout this book in an effort to be inclusive and acknowledge the diversity of terms for people of Latin American and Caribbean descent. As noted by Castañeda, Anguiano, and Alemán (2017), "the term Chicana primarily refers to female persons of Mexican origin living in the U.S. and signify ideologies of self-determination, anti-racism, anti-sexism and anti-assimilation that emerged during the 1960s. The 'a/o' configuration counters the patriarchy embedded in the Spanish language that privileges the male identity in mixed-gender plural constructions. 'Mexican American' were primarily used to identify this ethnic community. Chicana, Chicanx, Latinx, Xicana have since evolved to include any woman [or person] of Latino origin who share similar anti-oppressive political philosophies and, when composed with an 'x' to deconstruct patriarchy and gender binaries" (p. 184).

References

AACU. (2016). *Civic learning.* Retrieved from https://www.aacu.org/resources/civic-learning

Abes, E. S., Jackson, G., & Jones, S. R. (2002). Factors that motivate and deter faculty use of service-learning. *Michigan Journal of Community Service Learning, 9*(1), 5–17.

Arreola, D. (Ed.). (2004). *Hispanic spaces, Latino places: Community and cultural diversity in contemporary America.* Austin, TX: University of Texas Press.

Ash, S. L., & Clayton, P. H. (2004). The articulated learning: An approach to guided reflection and assessment. *Innovative Higher Education, 29*(2), 137–154.

Astin, A. W., Vogelgesang, L. J., Ikeda, E. K., & Yee, J. A. (2000). *How service learning affects students.* Los Angeles, CA: Higher Education Research Institute, University of California.

Blouin, D. D., & Perry, E. M. (2009). Whom does service learning really serve? Community-based organizations' perspectives on service learning. *Teaching Sociology, 37*(2), 120–135.

Bowman, N. A. (2011). Promoting participation in a diverse democracy a meta-analysis of college diversity experiences and civic engagement. *Review of Educational Research, 81*(1), 29–68.

Bragg, D. D. (2001). Community college access, mission, and outcomes: Considering intriguing intersections and challenges. *Peabody Journal of Education, 76*(1), 93–116.

Burciaga, R., & Cruz Navarro, N. (2015). Educational testimonio: Critical pedagogy as mentorship. *New Directions for Higher Education, 2015*(171), 33–41.

Carnegie Classifications of Institutions of Higher Learning. (2015). *Facts and figures.* Retrieved from http://carnegieclassifications.iu.edu/downloads/CCIHE2015-FactsFigures.pdf

Castañeda, M. (2008). Transformative learning through community engagement. *Latino Studies, 6,* 319–326.

Castañeda, M., Anguiano, C. A., & Alemán, S. M. (2017). Voicing for space in academia: Testimonios of Chicana communication professors. *Chicana/Latina Studies: The Journal of MALCS, 16*(2), 158–188.

Chávez, L. R. (2013). *The Latino threat: Constructing immigrants, citizens, and the nation.* Stanford, CA: Stanford University Press.

Colby, S. L., & Ortman, J. M. (2015). *Projections of the size and composition of the U.S. population: 2014 to 2060, P25-1143.* Washington, DC: U.S. Census Bureau. Retrieved from http://www.census.gov/content/dam/Census/library/publications/2015/demo/p25-1143.pdf

Collins, D. E. (2005). The ivory tower and scholar activism. *Academe, 91*(5), 26–28.

Darder, A., & Torres, R. D. (Eds.). (1998). *The Latino studies reader: Culture, economy, and society.* Malden, MA: Wiley-Blackwell.

De la Torre, A. (1993). *Building with our hands: New directions in Chicana studies.* Berkeley, CA: University of California Press.

Delgado Bernal, D., Burciaga, R., & Flores Carmona, J. (2012). Chicana/Latina testimonios: Mapping the methodological, pedagogical, and political. *Equity & Excellence in Education, 45*(3), 363–372.

Diaz, D. R., & Torres, R. D. (Eds.). (2012). *Latino urbanism: The politics of planning, policy, and redevelopment.* New York, NY: NYU Press.

Dostilio, L. D. (Ed.). (2017). *The community engagement professional in higher education: A competency model for an emerging field.* Sterling, VA: Stylus.

Dowling, R. (2008). Geographies of identity: Labouring in the "neoliberal" university. *Progress in Human Geography, 32*(6), 812–820.

Geron, K. (2005). *Latino political power.* Boulder, CO: Rienner.

Howard, J. P. (1998). Academic service learning: A counternormative pedagogy. *New Directions for Teaching and Learning, 1998*(73), 21–29.

Howard, J. P. (2001). Principles of good practice for service-learning pedagogy. *Michigan Journal of Community Service-Learning, Summer*, 16–19.

Huber, L. P. (2009). Disrupting apartheid of knowledge: Testimonio as methodology in Latina/o critical race research in education. *International Journal of Qualitative Studies in Education, 22*(6), 639–654.

Kajner, T., Chovanec, D., Underwood, M., & Mian, A. (2013). Critical community service learning: Combining critical classroom pedagogy with activist community placements. *Michigan Journal of Community Service Learning, 19*(2), 36–49.

Kershaw, T. (2003). The black studies paradigm: The making of scholar activists. In J. L. Conyers (Ed.), *Afrocentricity and the academy: Essays on theory and practice* (pp. 27–36). Jefferson, NC: McFarland and Company.

Kochhar, R., Suro, R., & Tafoya, S. (2005). *The new Latino south: The context and consequences of rapid population growth.* Washington, DC: Pew Hispanic Center.

Labonte, R. (2005). Community, community development, and the forming of authentic partnerships: Some critical reflections. *Community Organizing and Community Building for Health, 2*, 82–96.

Lowe, L. (1996). *Immigrant acts: On Asian American cultural politics.* Durham, NC: Duke University Press.

Markus, H. R., Steele, C. M., & Steele, D. M. (2000). Colorblindness as a barrier to inclusion: Assimilation and nonimmigrant minorities. *Daedalus, 129*(4), 233–259.

McKay, V. C., & Rozee, P. D. (2004). Characteristics of faculty who adopt community service learning pedagogy. *Michigan Journal of Community Service Learning, 10*(2), 21–33.

Melaville, A., Berg, A. C., & Blank, M. J. (2006). *Community-based learning: Engaging students for success and citizenship.* Washington, DC: Coalition for Community Schools.

Mitchell, C., & Humphries, H. (2007). From notions of charity to social justice in service-learning: The complex experience of communities. *Education as Change, 11*(3), 47–58.

Mitchell, T. D., Donahue, D. M., & Young-Law, C. (2012). Service learning as a pedagogy of whiteness. *Equity & Excellence in Education, 45*(4), 612–629.

Mohanty, C. (2003). *Feminism without borders.* Durham, NC: Duke University Press.

Morton, K. (1995). The irony of service: Charity, project and social change in service-learning. *Michigan Journal of Community Service Learning, 2*(1), 19–32.

O'Meara, K., & Niehaus, E. (2009). Service-learning is … how faculty explain their practice. *Michigan Journal of Community Service Learning, 16*(1), 17–32.

Parsons, M., & Stephenson, M. (2005). Developing reflective practice in student teachers: Collaboration and critical partnerships. *Teachers and Teaching, 11*(1), 95–116.

Pérez, E. (1999). *The decolonial imaginary, writing Chicanas into history.* Bloomington, IN: Indiana University Press.

Pérez, W., Espinoza, R., Ramos, K., Coronado, H., & Cortes, R. (2010). Civic engagement patterns of undocumented Mexican students. *Journal of Hispanic Higher Education, 20*(10), 1–21.

Post, M. A., Ward, E., Longo, N. V., & Saltmarsh, J. (Eds.). (2016). *Publicly engaged scholars: Next-generation engagement and the future of higher education.* Sterling, VA: Stylus.

Price, V., Lewis, G., & Lopez, V. (2014). Service-learning with students of color, working class and immigrant students: Expanding a popular pedagogical model. *Currents in Teaching & Learning, 7*(1), 23–36.

Rojas, F. (2007). *From black power to black studies: How a radical social movement became an academic discipline.* Baltimore, MD: Johns Hopkins University Press.

Rosaldo, R. (1985). Chicano studies, 1970–1984. *Annual Review of Anthropology, 14*(1), 405–427.

Saldívar, J. D. (1997). *Border matters: Remapping American cultural studies.* Berkeley, CA: University of California Press.

Saltmarsh, J. (1996). Education for critical citizenship: John Dewey's contribution to the pedagogy of community service learning. *Michigan Journal of Community Service Learning, 3*(1), 13–21.

Saltmarsh, J. (1997). Ethics, reflection, purpose, and compassion: Community service learning. *New Directions for Student Services, 1997*(77), 81–93.

Sandoval, C. (1991). U.S. third world feminism: The theory and method of oppositional consciousness in the postmodern world. *Genders, 10*, 1–24.

Sandoval, C. (2000). *Methodology of the oppressed.* Minneapolis, MN: University of Minnesota Press.

Santa Ana, O. (2013). *Juan in a hundred: The representation of Latinos on network news.* Austin, TX: University of Texas Press.

Shabazz, D. R., & Cooks, L. M. (2014). The pedagogy of community service-learning discourse: From deficit to asset mapping in the re-envisioning media project. *Journal of Community Engagement and Scholarship, 7*(1), 71.

Simons, L., & Cleary, B. (2006). The influence of service learning on students' personal and social development. *College Teaching, 54*(4), 307–319.

Stoecker, R. (2016). *Liberating service learning and the rest of higher education civic engagement*. Temple, PA: Temple University Press.

Study Group on Civic Learning and Engagement. (2014). *Preparing citizens report on civic learning and engagement*. Boston, MA: Massachusetts Board of Higher Education.

Suro, R., & Singer, A. (2002). *Latino growth in metropolitan America: Changing patterns, new locations*. Brookings Institution, Center on Urban and Metropolitan Policy in collaboration with the Pew Hispanic Center.

Torres, E. E. (2013). *Chicana without apology: The new Chicana cultural studies*. New York, NY: Routledge.

Ward, K., & Wolf-Wendel, L. (2000). Community-centered service learning: Moving from doing for to doing with. *American Behavioral Scientist, 43*(5), 767–780.

Section I

Rethinking Community and Civic Engagement

1. *Civic Engagement: Learning From Teaching Community Praxis*

Antonieta Mercado

For indigenous Nahua philosophers, the purpose of a teacher in society was to help others acquire knowledge of the world in order to know themselves. A teacher "puts a mirror before others," to teach them prudence and cultivate a wise face and a true heart, teaches others "that which is human" (León-Portilla, 1963, p. 15). According to León-Portilla, "face and heart" are the equivalent of what we call personality (1963, p. 115), and it is the work of the teacher to help the youth to develop their own. I am a college professor, and a working-class immigrant from Mexico, and I teach communication classes with a focus on social justice at a medium-sized private Catholic university in Southern California. The school where I teach has a commitment to diversity, inclusion, social justice, and community engagement as its core mission, and it embraces the Catholic tradition of serving with compassion, fostering peace, and working for justice (Teel, 2014).

I understand that one of my main roles as a social justice educator in the field of communication is to make my students aware of the construction of mediated representations of themselves and others and to show how these representations affect the way they see the world and the people around them. It is almost impossible for all human beings to have direct contact with all of human experience, so for the most part; it is through mediation and communication practices that we learn about world problems and about our lives and those of different others. By different others I mean people who are not part of our immediate communities or families, ethnic, racial, or social groups. Usually, these mediated representations of others leave deep imprints in our minds, to the point that when we actually encounter others, we tend to think we know their experience in the world through the images and language we had been exposed to and have used to describe them (Swartz, 2006). While some mediated representations of the self and others may be accurate, most representations contain prejudices, over-simplified and essentialist pre-conceptions of the world and our communities. In our daily mediated experiences, we usually do not learn the historical circumstances of the lives of underrepresented people, such as African Americans, Latinos, Native Americans, immigrants, or the poor, so, it is difficult to gauge the context of their actions. Media also provide many of the epistemological and rhetorical instruments for us to think about ourselves and others and to ponder the impact of world problems on our communities. Social justice education from the point of view of communication thus focuses on the ways that "dominant discourses, social structures, patterns of interactions and the like produce injustice" (Frey, Barnett-Pearce, Pollock, Artz, & Murphy, 1996, p. 111).

However, social justice is a contested term and making students aware of unjust structures and historical trends should not be the only purpose of educators (Rodriguez, 2006; Swartz, 2006). Usually awareness by itself can backfire, leaving students with the theoretical knowledge to understand and criticize dominant discourses and representations, but disempowered to act, thinking that in order to fight injustice, they need greater powers to challenge an oppressive and unjust social system. While educating about injustice is an important step, commitment to act is also important for both achieving more just societies and educating future leaders. This process also makes them aware of their power to start acting differently and work towards bettering the world with the knowledge and inclination to foster both self-reflection and dialogue with others. Educating for social justice needs to involve a wider understanding of community and communication, not only as an instrument, but also as an ecology, where compassion and empathy can be fostered through rhetorical and discursive practices (Rodriguez, 2006). Communication involves a commitment to our immediate communities and to the world as well as a willingness to learn from them. It also includes understanding power imbalances that media and other institutions, such as the school and the legal systems, have created. These are some of the major aims of my pedagogy, and I am sharing some of its principles in this chapter, along with some examples of community service and experiential learning for social justice that I have implemented over the years as an educator and scholar.

Intersectional Roles: From the Community to the Classroom

I am a working-class immigrant that moved from Mexico to the United States two decades ago, and for years, I had been active in the immigrant Latinx community, working with different immigrant organizations having a transnational outlook. For almost a decade now, I have been working with an indigenous migrant organization named the Indigenous Front of Binational Organizations (FIOB). Initially, I started to work with FIOB in order to study their transnational practices of communication and civic organization. Working with indigenous immigrants from Mexico, I learned first-hand that people who are marginalized by the dominant culture of a political community, either in terms of a lack of fair-representation or access to material resources, have had to develop strategies to negotiate their own place in face of the so-called mainstream culture. Working with indigenous communities also helped me understand my own non-mainstream situation in both the Mexican and U.S. academia.

In the case of Mexican indigenous migrants in the US, this negotiation between dominant and non-dominant places multiplies for them, since they have been dealing with unfavorable dominant arrangements in their communities of origin in Mexico. When they migrate they also have to deal with a dominant society that does not distinguish them from other non-indigenous Mexicans when they move and settle in the United States. Consequently, peripheral and marginal groups in society have had to learn the ways of the mainstream in order to communicate and function within a pre-established social arrangement, while people who are situated at the center of the dominant culture usually do not feel the need to learn how to communicate with those in the periphery.

In my research, I have defined this capacity of coping and learning from different environments, social arrangements, and languages as "grassroots cosmopolitanism" because it entails a practical worldliness with important levels of sophistication in transforming the self in order to understand and function with those who are in the mainstream and may not feel the need to invest time or effort in understanding those at the margins. I define grassroots cosmopolitism as the individual and collective human engagement with the experience of others, a flexibility in accommodating and accepting diversity in individual and group life, and an adjustment, both physically and discursively, to different socio-cultural environments (Mercado, 2011, p. 400). Grassroots cosmopolitans have a willingness to increase dialogue and solve conflict across cultures, social classes, races, genders, and other differences without necessarily losing allegiances to a particular group, and while avoiding making those allegiances a source of conflict. This happens because grassroots cosmopolitans acknowledge hierarchies of power in communication with different others and seek to develop horizontal relationships as they go (Mercado, 2011, and 2015b).

For indigenous migrant communities who organize across borders, economic resources, although important for the survival of the organizations, are not the only crucial factor for their transnational success. Rather, these communities engage in a practice rooted in indigenous principles of community service called *tequio*. *Tequio* comes from the Náhuatl *tequitl*, which means community work and service, and it is a common practice in indigenous communities in Mexico, although it can be known by other names as well. This service usually entails the donation of work or money to complete a community project. Dedicating time to serve for the greater good usually conveys a higher social status and it is also a pre-condition for leadership positions in these communities (López-Bárcenas, 2004; Rivera-Salgado & Escala-Rabadán, 2004). People who donate their time or resources (knowledge, skills, talents, etc.) are highly respected by the rest of the community. In this way, belonging to a community is gauged by the capacity of people to serve others for the greater good.

Practices of *tequio* enrich both the cultural and social capital of indigenous communities, and are an important characteristic that indigenous migrants bring with them when they move to the United States. Many indigenous migrant organizations survive due to this system of cooperation and voluntary and semi-voluntary work (Mercado, 2015a). When I started working with FIOB, I was asked to contribute with my *tequio* to the organization. I did not know how I could be of use, since FIOB members have a high level of organizational sophistication, and I felt at times that I was wasting their time. However, with time, I started to integrate into the organization and helped them with what I knew: Writing press releases, designing flyers, documenting events, helping with speeches and presentations, bringing community knowledge into university contexts, and likewise university knowledge into the community. As my involvement in FIOB grew, I developed the commitment to seeing indigenous knowledge respected in academia, and I have been studying ways to identify and challenge prevalent colonial structures of knowledge and power that have affected indigenous groups and their representation in the public sphere. Thus, my involvement in FIOB has consisted in donating my time and communication skills to help the organization. I periodically teach leadership and media literacy workshops in the community, especially with the San Diego FIOB chapter. I still help with their media outreach whenever they need to promote local events, such as designing flyers and other materials. I also attend organizational meetings, and events, either in Southern California, Baja California and Oaxaca, such as conferences, assemblies, festivals, and celebrations, whenever possible.

Practices of Tequio *as Bridgework in the Classroom*

Having the experience of working with a transnational indigenous migrant community, I have slowly incorporated the principles of *tequio* and community engagement into my classroom, as I am gaining confidence and developing skills to take my students into the community. In the last couple of years, I have participated in the design and implementation of a senior survey assessing the abilities of my department's graduating students to critically engage in the analysis of media representations. While I was pleased that our students were able to identify media conglomerates, and the effects of oligopolies and monopolies in the public sphere, many of them were also feeling disempowered to act, since they did not know how to apply their critical knowledge towards real-life situations. Thinking about this disconnect, I decided to implement community engagement activities in most of my courses, either as fundamental part of the course or as an option, so students could see the relationship between communication and community, and understand that communication is not only an instrument, but also both a way of constructing the world and a practice of naming and making sense of self and others. Community engagement would allow students to see how knowledge is co-created in practice as well as understand that there are different epistemological practices in the community and the university.

Students generally come from an educational system that makes individual competition almost a given, so I re-emphasize principles of compassion, understanding of the self, and acceptance of others (which are also core principles of my university's mission). I also want my students to grapple with the conception of the classroom as a community that we all need to foster in order to make it better. One of my purposes of teaching communication and social justice classes, is to create what Kathryn Sorrells (2012) has named "intercultural bridgework," which means developing sensitivity, understanding, and empathy to create points of entry, contact, negotiation, and connection between different people to eventually understand that these differences are what constitute us as human communities (p. 168). I want to help students develop awareness about themselves, others, and hierarchies of knowledge and power, in many cases illustrated by the distance that social class, race, gender, sexual preferences, nationality, disability, and ethnicity have enacted between communities and individuals.

Another purpose, and probably the most pressing one, is that once students are aware of those social inequalities, they can feel the need to engage in action to ease the pain and suffering that those hierarchies have created among individuals and communities. Making my students aware of *tequio* as the indigenous principle of community building has also been an important step in teaching them about social action. Witnessing what indigenous migrant communities do to resist and find their place in often very hostile environments, helps my students regain confidence in direct action and connect them with experiential learning, which implies student active involvement in problem-solving and reflection (Dewey, 1938; Moore, Boyd, & Dooley, 2010). Learning occurs when experience is understood and transformed (Kolb, 1984).

Introducing indigenous practices of community building and understanding is also important in terms of teaching social justice, since reflecting upon non-dominant ways of organizing and solidarity-building is a crucial gateway towards engaging students in self-reflection and the acknowledgement of greater structures of power. For instance, one way is by unpacking the effects that colonialism has had on contemporary social, political, and epistemological hierarchies or knowledge and power. An example of this hierarchy is the discrepancy between the scientific knowledge produced in the university, and the existence of community funds of knowledge, which are defined as the accumulated and culturally relevant bodies of knowledge and practical skills necessary for households and individual functioning (Moll, Amanti, Neff, & Gonzalez, 1992). Often, these community practices and bodies of knowledge are not formally acknowledged by the university, and students are not trained to identify their importance. When introducing community engagement in my classes, I explain to my students the importance of situating ourselves as members of the community and doing self-reflective work as entry points into any activity. In my introductory and lower division classes, for instance, the experiential learning may be just the awareness of social injustice, unfair representation, and hierarchies of power in social institutions, and the fact that we are all embedded in unjust and hierarchical systems of power. Ultimately, I want my students to understand that many acts of injustice are not necessarily the decision of individuals, but are the products of unjust systems of social relations. In upper division classes, I ask my students to get involved in particular communities or local organizations and explore the possibilities of performing bridgework between the university and local organizations. The following, are some of the activities that I have introduced in my classes, to represent entry points for students into the community for both, action and self-reflection.

Friendship Park

Since I have the advantage of being located in San Diego, a border town, I introduced a trip to the US-Mexico border in both my upper division and lower division classes. When discussing issues related to nationalism, students visit a place called Friendship Park located at the point where the Pacific Ocean is divided by a U.S.-built double fence. Friendship Park was inaugurated by First Lady Pat Nixon in 1973, and the day of its inauguration she said that no fence should exist between two friendly neighbors, referring to the chicken wire fence that existed at that time separating both countries at certain points of entry, although not throughout the entire border. After a constant build-up of the fence since the 1994 launching of Operation Gatekeeper, there are places where it is possible to see an ever growing double or triple fence and multiple Border Patrol vehicles monitoring the area in between the fences. Although immigration from Mexico has decreased in the last few years, the display of border security and border protection rhetoric is ever growing, as we can see with the current Trump administration.

Many Mexican immigrants who live in California come to Friendship Park to see through the fence their relatives who live in Mexico. Some families travel for hours to be able to encounter their loved ones through a steel-wire fence, heavily patrolled by police and surveillance equipment. Access to the park on the U.S. side is also very restricted and difficult, since people have to walk a mile and a half each way to access Friendship Park. In general, the experience can be sobering, since there is so much that a tall and steel-reinforced fence accompanied by law enforcement officers and surveillance gear can tell us about friendship. On the Mexican side it is possible to see the normal street traffic, a big bull-fighting ring, a park, the beach, street vendors selling popsicles in pushing carts, and sometimes even musicians performing next to the border.

That fence speaks much more about the way the United States imagines itself as a community and how it sees other communities in the world; it is a clear illustration of the works of nationalism and fear of the other. After the visit to the park, my students generally make the walk back in silence, some of them conversing with each other or with me in deep reflection about the significance of the fence dividing two countries that are commercial partners due to the North American Free Trade Agreement (NAFTA) and that are not at war with each other yet have severe economic disparities. As a border town, San Diego has many opportunities to study international and transnational issues related to immigration and communication. I ask students to write a reflection on this trip, and the best student responses are published in our Department of Communication Studies newsletter, serving the double purpose of informing other students about what their peers are doing in the community and helping students publish their work.

Many students express that they want to write something almost immediately after visiting the park, since the experience of seeing the border, its militarization, and the families speaking through the ever-reinforced fence is deeply moving. Friendship Park does not have easy access, and it is open only half a day on Saturdays and Sundays. This is one of the rare moments when we can see the face of law enforcement and militarization constructed in a place with such a name evoking friendship, but separated by a double fence. After this trip, many students become interested in understanding and discussing the urgency of comprehensive immigration reform, and the implications of an outdated immigration system that criminalizes migrants due to economic or political disparities. Other students reflect on patterns of segregation in San Diego, and wonder why the self-image of America's Finest City includes the beaches, but does not include the border, or immigrants from Latin America living and working in the city. This single field trip makes my students reflect upon how the image of the city is constructed for the benefit of the tourism industry to highlight only some of its inhabitants. Students also reflect on how local and national media contribute to making geographies and people either dangerous or invisible for others, such as this part of the border with a difficult and controlled access for the general public.

Day of the Dead Altar

As a Mexican immigrant in California, and as an active member of an indigenous migrant organization, observing the celebration of the Day of the Dead has been an important part of my upbringing. The Day of the Dead is a complex celebration with many points of entry, from the spiritual that joins Catholic and Indigenous syncretism, to the political and journalistic aspect, since this tradition has been used as a communication device and a channel for socio-cultural expression of marginalized communities as well as for political criticism both in Latin America and in the United States (Marchi, 2013). The journalistic tradition can be linked to political cartoonist José Guadalupe Posada, who in the late 19th and early 20th centuries in Mexico published his drawings of skeletons (*catrines*) elegantly dressed to criticize the extreme economic and social polarization that led to the Mexican Revolution in 1910. This tradition has prevailed and grown in recent times, making the Day of the Dead a time when artists, journalists and the public write satirical poetry and draw cartoons about the rich and famous to satirize their deeds and imply that they have been taken by *la muerte* (grim reaper/death) as punishment for their misbehavior (Mercado, 2015c). During the Day of the Dead, it is also common to exchange candies in the form of sugar skulls as a sign of friendship.

For the past four years, for both my introduction to media studies and upper division intercultural communication classes, I have asked students to organize and set-up a Day of the Dead Altar, usually on the last day of October, or the first in November. Students analyze readings about the multiple significance and mix of traditions, both spiritual and secular, linked to this celebration, and they also contribute with an artistic piece ranging from a painting, drawing, small shrine in a cardboard box, papier mache skull, poem, satirical verses, short story, or any artistic contribution they can imagine might represent their point of entry into this celebration. The idea of the activity is to demonstrate that it is possible to achieve the communication of messages through culture, and that journalism is not restricted to the reporting of hard news. Festivals and celebrations, such as the Day of the Dead have been a staple of many marginalized communities as a way of representing themselves in the public sphere when mainstream journalism has ignored them. Some authors have called this "the cultural public sphere," which includes literary works along with forms of representation of feeling and drama. Jim McGuigan (2005) has defined it as "the articulation of politics, public and personal, as a contested terrain through affective (aesthetic and emotional) modes of communication" (p. 435).

The tradition of arranging altars for the dead has been slowly adopted in the United States, especially in California and other states with a strong Latinx community presence, combining indigenous traditions of honoring the dead with other traditions brought by immigrants from Latin America, different members of the Latinx community, and the general public. In the past decade or so, there have been multiple public celebrations honoring this day and its many meanings for the different cultures that have adopted it in the U.S. In 2013, the Disney Corporation unsuccessfully attempted to copyright the Day of the Dead, and since 2007, they have an exhibit about the day in their amusement park in Anaheim, California. Many criticized this move as pure cultural appropriation with the intent to make money out of what is considered by many a sacred holiday and a cherished community tradition. I explain to my students that it is important for us as scholars of communication to understand the processes of cultural adaptation, cultural appropriation, and the creation of culture industries, such as in the case of Disney Corporation commodifying the attractive artistic imagery of this indigenous holiday for their own economic gain. Other companies such as Nestle have also used the images of festive skulls in their bottles of water and other canned products. These companies are so powerful, that this appropriation is akin to cultural imperialism, where the so-called imagination industries look for creative clues in struggling indigenous communities.

Inspired by my colleague Alberto Pulido (2002) and his project of making little shrines or *cajitas* and reflecting upon the diversity of palettes we as individuals may have to express our thoughts, I challenge my students to produce an artistic representation of the holiday as a creative point of entry to understand the many meanings of this celebration. Students then are asked to help me put together the altar, arranging *cempazúchitl* (marigold) flowers, along with their art pieces into a space in the University, and inviting members of the larger campus and the outside community (such as immigrant organizations that some of my students have worked with previously) to visit the altar. During the exhibit day, students hand out flyers to visitors and explain the multiple meanings of the Day of the Dead, from the sacred to the political and the commercial, that they have previously discussed in class. I also invite a speaker from the indigenous migrant organization I belong to in order to share the sacred and political aspects of the tradition, and how the Latinx and Indigenous migrant communities in San Diego have used the altars to make political claims about fair representation and access to resources, and to make their presence noticed in an environment that often makes them invisible.

Both the university and the local communities have responded positively, visiting the altar and asking questions about the multiple meanings of the Day of the Dead. Each year, I incorporate suggestions made by students about how to make this experience better for future students, and some of them have expressed that they want the altar to be on display more days, so more members of the community can see it. Students who were not familiar with this celebration, often said that, at first, they were not sure about what were they learning, or why was I asking them to engage in creating an altar, but then it became clear to them as they were explaining the complexity and significance of the holiday to visitors and community members. Sometimes students would comment in class that they were asked to speak about the Day of the Dead in other classes, since others learned about their artistic projects and involvement in preparing the altar for my classes. It is very common that in the self-reflection students mention that they felt accomplished and part of something very complex that they were able to explain to others using communication concepts, such as the cultural public sphere. This exercise promoted a critical self-reflection and willingness to acknowledge the importance of these spaces, especially for underrepresented communities, such as indigenous migrants or Latinx in California, to have access to dignified representation.

Students also comment that they knew about the celebration because of its commercialization and they usually associated it with Halloween, sometimes painting their faces imitating *catrinas*, but that they mostly ignored the historical, sacred, and political sides of it. Having community representatives coming in and talking to students as authorities also puts community knowledge at the same hierarchical level as academic knowledge. The presence of community speakers can be linked back to classroom discussions about funds of knowledge, the development of expertise, representation, and the effects of colonialism in epistemological hierarchies of knowledge and classification. This experiential learning has provided my students with significant spaces to think about media representation, alternative forms of media, commodification of culture, cultural imperialism, the role of the sacred and the political in the public sphere, and the role of invisible structures of colonialism in keeping entire populations outside of public representation. Linking the complexity of the multiple adaptations of this tradition as it crosses cultural and national borders, students can also reflect upon the need to decolonize what we know as universal forms of knowledge, and recognize that the knowledge generated in the community, while many may not recognize as valuable or accurate, is very important. Even corporations, such as Disney and Nestle, are attempting to co-opt and commercialize community knowledge, extirpating the political side of the Day of the Dead and selling only its aesthetic side.

The commercialization of the holiday and my personal engagement with community activism through art has been a big motivation for me to include this activity in my classes every Fall and I see myself continuing it for the foreseeable future. Students also seem to learn a great amount from an experience that teaches them to engage in explaining complex issues rather than simplifying them, as is favored by commercialism. Students actually take pride in learning its complexity and nuances, and feel accomplished when they can explain that complexity to others and to themselves. The university has also provided a place for community members to come and participate as co-creators of the altar and to share their knowledge of the celebration with students.

Community Advocacy

I teach an upper division course on *Public Relations and Community Advocacy* which I designed the idea that students should have the opportunity to engage directly with local community organizations to either start or expand media outreach programs. This is not a conventional PR class, and I do not provide an instrumental view of communication as a set of tools that can be used for an end. I am instead interested in teaching a critical perspective on the public relations industry and its influence in shaping public discourse and media, especially the lobbying industry that affects policy making. The course offers a critical, historical, and practical perspective on the U.S. and global public relations industry. It examines the current and historical dependency of news media outlets on the PR world as sources of information for the public. It also includes a critical examination of the techniques used by public relations practitioners, and their impact on the public interest, citizenship, social movements, sustainability, diversity, and consumption.

While the course offers a critical view of corporate public relations, it also offers concrete skill-building opportunities for students who may be interested in working to promote social justice through critical public relations and activism. The practical side of the class focuses on the use of communication theories and techniques, as well as public relations strategies for advancing social justice causes, such as fair representation of minorities in media, immigration reform, community development, ethical consumption, and the environment, fair access to resources, etc. Students who take the class dedicate one hour per week working for a local community organization, helping either to design or enhance their communication and public outreach programs, their social media presence, and in general to better their outreach to community, government, or the media.

While I provide my students with a critical view of the instrumental use of public relations for the corporate world, I also center many class activities and discussions on the *tequio* (service) practices that students are providing to the community. As with the other activities, students engage in bridgework between the university and the community. Since I teach communication courses, most of the time I am asked by local community organizations to help them with their communication or media outreach work, so this work is driven by community needs of self-representation and a willingness to learn how to navigate a highly-mediated world. For the most part, I have worked with organizations that dedicate their work either to immigration reform or to providing some kind of service to immigrants. Taking this into consideration, students engage with the organization to provide social media programs, open or improve the online presence of the organization, and help immigrants to streamline their business in case they are working with immigrants who are creating their own micro-business. At the end of the semester, each group of students give back to the community partner a portfolio with recommendations, reflections, and the completed work they developed in cooperation with the community partner during the semester.

One of the needs that I have identified in community organizations, especially in indigenous migrant communities, is to document the knowledge of elder members that have participated in social justice struggles and who have been the founders of many binational organizations such as FIOB. This knowledge not only keeps the organization alive, but it is also connected to indigenous forms of organization, direct democracy, systematic accounts of medicinal plants properties, the cultivation of food, and sustainable living practices that may be beneficial for everyone. I have taught this class at different institutions, and I am working towards better integrating classroom knowledge with community service (*tequio*). It is challenging to make students reflect on their work in the community, while at the same time teaching them about the impact of the public relations industry. Integration of knowledge and practice is an ongoing challenge while doing community engagement, while students go to the community with the willingness to provide their *tequio*, it is necessary to remind them that learning in the community is often not as structured as in the classroom and they will have to adjust to the rhythms of the organization and perform their role as advisors and consultants for the media outreach or social media project. Experiential learning can be confusing at times, and in particular some students may find it difficult to develop the understanding of social structures affecting the community they are working with in the length of one semester. This is one of the main challenges, for this class, to make it substantial and critical, but engaging and in some way useful for both the community partner and the students.

Conclusion

One of my commitments as an educator and a communication scholar working with indigenous immigrant communities is to introduce principles of decolonization, media representation, and awareness of power imbalances linked to hierarchies of knowledge so my students can bring these questions with them when working as professionals and engaging in social justice work. Respecting community knowledge, practicing self-reflection, and having a commitment to action by engaging in *tequio* practices for community organizations are some of the goals I have for my students while they take my courses, move through class discussions, and experience civic engagement with community partners. It is important to contextualize the need to work in the community so students can position themselves and reflect upon power and knowledge hierarchies as well as upon the position and role of the university as a center for the creation and dissemination of certain kinds of knowledge. It is also important that my students comprehend the importance of indigenous knowledge, that it can be at the center, respected, and preserved, instead of tossed aside as non-scientific or useless.

The community engagement activities that I have developed are important entry points into community life and their struggles for access to resources and fair representation. Meeting and working with indigenous migrants, students are thus able to start questioning desires of homogenization and appreciate the value of diverse cultures, languages, and community knowledge. As their relationship with the community develops, students also come to understand how these communities have been marginalized despite having much more knowledgeable experience about mainstream society than is imagined. Additionally, we engage in class discussions about different conceptions of cosmopolitanism, such as the concept of grassroots cosmopolitanism discussed in this chapter. Students meet people in the community and engage in conversations and mutual projects around *tequio* practices, and value their knowledge and expertise. Therefore, it is not an issue of bringing university knowledge to the community, but of establishing a reciprocal exchange and awareness of positionalities.

Exploring issues of social justice using communication as a starting point to make students aware of how hierarchical structures work and affect the way certain groups and their practices are represented in the public sphere, helps to make community engagement a more reciprocal act. Instead of being simply passive observers, students co-participate and co-create solutions to particular problems and support community projects that need their expertise and knowledge of mediated representation, such as the establishment or improvement of media and social media outreach programs. Students are in constant communication with community members, so they are aware of the particular needs of the organization. Community organizations also benefit, since they establish and sustain cooperation programs with the university, and have the chance to benefit from sustained student cooperation and productive exchange.

References

Dewey, J. (1938). *Experience and education*. New York, NY: Simon and Schuster.

Frey, L. R., Barnett-Pearce, W., Pollock, M. A., Artz, L., & Murphy, B. A. O. (1996). Looking for justice in all the wrong places: On a communication approach to social justice. *Communication Studies, 47*(1–2), 110–112.

Kolb, D. A. (1984). *Experiential learning: Experience as the source of learning and development*. Newark, NJ: Prentice-Hall.

León-Portilla. M. (1963). *Aztec thought and culture: A study of the ancient Nahuatl mind*. Norman, OK: University of Oklahoma Press.

López-Bárcenas, F. (2004). Los sistemas indígenas de cargos en la Mixteca. In A. Hernández Núñez & F. López Bárcenas (Eds.), *La Fuerza de la Costumbre: Sistema de Cargos en la Mixteca Oaxaqueña*. Oaxaca, MX: COAPI.

Marchi, R. (2013). "Doing democracy" via public day of the dead rituals. In N. S. Love & M. Mattern (Eds.), *Doing democracy: Activist art and cultural politics* (pp. 75–95). Albany, NY: SUNY Press.

McGuigan, J. (2005). The cultural public sphere. *European Journal of Cultural Studies, 8*(4), 427–443.

Mercado, A. (2011, May 28). *Subtractive citizenship or grassroots cosmopolitanism: Transnational communication and citizenship practices among indigenous Mexican immigrants in the United States.* Paper presented at the International Communication Association Annual Conference, Boston, MA.

Mercado, A. (2015a). El Tequio: Social capital, civic advocacy journalism and the construction of a transnational public sphere by Mexican Indigenous migrants in the US. *Journalism, 16*(2), 238–256.

Mercado. A. (2015b, January). Medios Indígenas Trasnacionales: El fomento del Cosmopolitismo desde abajo. [Transnational Indigenous Media: Fostering Grassroots Cosmopolitanism]. *Comunicación y Sociedad* 23: 171–193.

Mercado, A. (2015c, October 28). Day of the dead: When indigenous practices meet spiritual traditions. *San Diego Free Press.* Retrieved from http://sandiegofreepress.org/2015/10/day-of-the-dead-when-indigenous-practices-meet-spiritual-traditions/

Moll, L. C., Amanti, C., Neff, D., & Gonzalez, N. (1992). Funds of knowledge for teaching: Using a qualitative approach to connect homes and classrooms. *Theory into Practice, Qualitative Issues in Educational Research, 31*(2), 132–141.

Moore, C., Boyd, B. L., & Dooley, K. E. (2010). The effects of experiential learning with an emphasis on reflective writing on deep-level processing of leadership students. *Journal of Leadership Education, 9*(1), 36–52.

Pulido, A. (2002). The Living Color of Students' Lives: Bringing Cajitas into the Classroom. *Religion and Education*, 29 (2), 69–77.

Rivera-Salgado, G., & Escala-Rabadán, L. (2004). Collective identity and organization strategies of indigenous and Mestizo Mexican migrants. In J. Fox & G. Rivera-Salgado (Eds.), *Indigenous Mexican migrants in the United States* (pp. 449–466). La Jolla, CA: Center for U.S.-Mexican Studies, UCSD/Center for Comparative Immigration Studies, UCSD.

Rodriguez, A. (2006). Social justice and the challenge for communication Studies. In O. Swartz & Health Services Center at the University of Colorado (Eds.), *Social justice and communication scholarship* (pp. 21–34). Newark, NJ: Lawrence Erlbaum Associates.

Sorrells, K. (2012). *Intercultural communication: Globalization and social justice.* Los Angeles, CA: Sage Publications.

Swartz, O. (2006). Reflections of a social justice scholar. In O. Swartz & Health Services Center at the University of Colorado (Eds.), *Social justice and communication scholarship* (pp. 1–19). Newark, NJ: Lawrence Erlbaum Associates.

Teel, K. (2014). Getting out of the left lane: The possibility of white anti-racist pedagogy. *Teaching Theology and Religion, 17*(1), 3–26.

2. *Imagining a* Nueva Casita: *Puerto Rican Subjectivities and the Space of the "In-between" on an Urban Farm in Western Massachusetts*

JOSEPH KRUPCZYNSKI

Agustin Lao-Montes (2001), in describing the potential for Latina/o radical democratization in New York notes, "the right to the city means the right to freedom, to explore and invent new and more fluid ways of life and self-definition, and to create new and to re-create older forms of political community out not only of need but also from desire" (p. 145). This essay explores the nature of this this creative call to action. It examines how this paradigm to "invent new and more fluid ways of life and self-definition" is enacted within a community engaged architectural project located on an urban farm known as *La Finca* in Holyoke Massachusetts. Owned and operated by *Nuestras Raíces* (Our Roots), a grass-roots organization that promotes economic, human and community development through projects relating to food, agriculture, and the environment, *La Finca* becomes a site where a unique material and imagined community is established. One where the complex liminal conditions of Holyoke's diasporic Puerto Rican community are elaborated, and that responds inventively with economic, environmental and cultural resourcefulness. The site's unique position (both literally and metaphorically) as an ethnic farm on the edge/margin of a New England city is an important factor for the counter-hegemonic production inherent in their strategy of alternative development.

This occurs on multiple levels: economically, through *Nuestras Raíces*' innovations in community economies that develop successful alternatives to mainstream economic practices; environmentally, as the symbolic and practical agrarian traditions of New England and those of Puerto Rico find sustainable, and surprisingly familiar affinities; and culturally, through cultivating the spatial construct of the "in-between" that parallels the adaptability and resilience inherent in Puerto Rican subjectivities in the diaspora. The architectural project proposed for the site negotiates an array of social, cultural and political territories in an effort to creatively parallel the innovative cultural practices occurring on the farm. It is a modest effort to find a spatial articulation responsive to a more complex understanding of cultural heritage, beyond the exoticization of cultural difference, in order to create a transnational, sustainable and emancipatory space/place firmly rooted in Latina/o cultural identities. Through a series of theoretical frameworks that examine Latino/a, post-colonial and community economy theories, a performative, symbolic and socio-cultural approach to socially engaged architecture is emphasized.

Theorizing Engagement as "In-between"

Implicit in this emerging project were questions of how to create an appropriate architectural/spatial response to the economic, environmental and cultural innovation *Nuestras Raíces* supports. How one might escape the simplistic idea of a singular Puerto Rican identity and/or an essentialist Latina/o social imaginary, as well as avoid the tropicalized or clichéd nostalgia that are deployed as uncritical strategies for some architectural projects in Latina/o communities, became key questions to explore. Within my undergraduate architectural studio, my students and I established a critical approach to our design work by first researching urban *casitas.* These impromptu shed-like houses evoke a rural Caribbean character and are constructed in vacant lots in Puerto Rican neighborhoods, particularly in New York and other Northeastern cities. These material structures embody an imagined left behind countryside and a nostalgic idyllic rural life that, in the context of its urban environments, are transformed into complex vehicles for Puerto Rican community identity.

Urban *casitas* are modeled after their traditional antecedents on the island, small structures that were easily transported by rural farmers as they moved from place to place, either under forced evictions or to follow a lead to new work. In their diasporic urban settings, they have a similar (but updated) context where their makeshift construction ironically eludes to the pressures of development and gentrification faced by its builders and the surrounding community as once abandoned lots become hot properties for development. The presence of the urban casita is heightened by its position in the space/

void of a vacant lot surrounded by lived-in (and abandoned) buildings. They are stubborn provisional figures in a once densely populated urban condition, emboldened by a re-orienting Caribbean vernacular. This contrasting urban environment is vital to one of the casita's primary symbolic functions—the creation of a space for the Puerto Rican community in a context that historically has acted with indifference or hostility to their presence.

Luis Aponte-Pares (1995) observes that, like the Puerto Rican flag, the casita "becomes a vehicle through which their builders articulate and defend their national identity, their imagined community, their innate essence determining who they are in the urban milieu" (p. 14). *Casitas*, and the urban gardens in which they are sited, are fraught by their fragile and contested locations, where the limited resources of those engaged in maintaining their spatial rights and cultural identity are often in active opposition to the powerful forces of neo-liberalism and their attendant negative community effects. In contrast, *La Finca* outside of a dense urban context and wholly owned by *Nuestras Raíces*, suggests a spatial context not only of opposition, but a site "from which to see and create, to imagine alternatives, new worlds" (hooks, 1990, p. 150). Hence, another emblematic function of the casita (one reflective of the transformative promise of the site) links the renewal and resilience of Puerto Rican diasporic cultural practices sustained by circulatory migration and citizenship.

Aponte-Pares (1995) clearly connects the development of the casitas to this liminal cultural understanding when describing the fluid exchange of ideas and images that generations of travelers between island and mainland have cultivated. He observes that "unlike immigrants of yesteryear, and as 'colonial citizens,' Puerto Ricans circulate freely between two spaces: colony and metropolis; thus, circumventing or destroying traditional barriers associated with borders, or *fronteras*" (Aponte-Pares, 1995, p. 15). Juan Flores (2000), as well, elaborates on this insight when he writes, "beyond its practical and symbolic functions for the community in which it is located, the casita stands as a highly suggestive emblem of contemporary Puerto Rican culture, and of diasporic vernacular culture in general. For peoples caught up in the circulatory, back-and-forth migratory motion and thereby subject to the constant renewal of personal and historical ties, culture is experienced as dramatic movement and change, adaptability and resilience. … Borders, however vigilantly patrolled, are transversable and ultimately collapsible" (pp. 74–75. Borders are liminal spaces of changing relations, and as the complexity and contradiction inherent in the flows of globalization demonstrate, simple dualistic descriptions undermine their intrinsic dynamic potential. Since Gloria Anzaldúa (1999) defined the borderland as "a vague and undermined place created by the emotional residue of an unnatural boundary" Latino/a and Puerto Rican diasporic theoretical discourses have engaged this idea in a number of ways (p. 25). Primarily describing the translocal complexity Latino/as inhabit as they negotiate the translations and translocations inherent in their cultural practices.

Another key text within our design studio was Juan Flores' (2000) essay, "Broken English Memories: Languages in the Trans-Colony." Flores elaboration of the translocal complexity of Puerto Rican memory and identity as it moves back and forth between its geographical, linguistic and behavioral boundaries, generated much discussion in our studio. Additionally, it's explicit spatial metaphor of the "in-between" at the center of this text became influential for myself, my students, and our emerging design work on *La Finca*. In Flores' discussion of the here and there inherent in Puerto Rican lives, the post-colonial theorist Homi Bhabha concept of the third space informs his approach. He notes Bhabha's reflection on "the possibility of being, somehow, in between, of occupying an interstitial space that is not fully governed by recognizable traditions ... a space that produces another, a third space ... a space that is skeptical of cultural totalization, and of notions of identity which depend for their value on being pure" (p. 55). A paradigmatic space that Bhabha identifies as having "great political and poetic and conceptual value" and that Flores finds deeply familiar to Puerto Ricans in the US, and thus harboring the possibility of an "intricate politics of freedom and resistance" (p. 55). Such an insight became an important operating principle for the spatial organization of the projects we developed for *Nuestras Raices*, and allowed us to move from the exoticization of cultural difference to explore more complex issues of cultural heritage, discursive formations and evolving diasporic subjectivities.

Contextualizing Holyoke, MA

Holyoke, Massachusetts is a small city of just under 40,000 residents that encompasses both an inner city urban center and a surrounding suburban and exurban landscape. The division between the city's primarily low-income downtown neighborhoods (in which the population is over 80% Latino) and its relatively more affluent areas (in which the White population is over 95%) shapes Holyoke's political and socio-cultural dynamic in fundamental ways. During the last thirty years, Holyoke's Latino—mostly Puerto Rican—population has expanded by over 10,000, marking a 170% increase. In 2010, the Latino population comprised of 47% of city residents compared to 14% in 1980. Although the Latino population in the state is only 10.5% as opposed to the

US total of 17.1% and Hamden county has 22.6% Latinos, the city of Holyoke has a total Latino population of 47.4%; and within the downtown areas is 85% Latino. Thus, Holyoke has one of the largest Puerto Rican populations in the US, percentage-wise, relative to the number of total residents in the city.

Holyoke has been called Paper City because it was once a center of the world's paper industry. Its strong industrial economy provided employment for generations of immigrants, but today its downtown core is subject to the same contradictory conditions of many of today's post-industrial cities. It embodies the delicate balance between socio-economic disenfranchisement that is characterized by abandoned buildings, deteriorated infrastructure and the lack of adequate job opportunities, and the socio-cultural promise of a beleaguered, but resilient, community. An important presence that is often overlooked in a pure demographic analysis of the city is the strong array of grassroots and community-based organizations that support residents and provide needed services and spaces for community development. Besides *Nuestras Raices*, some of these organizations are: Nueva Esperanza, a Community Development Corporation working to build a stronger community in the urban core of Holyoke through the rehabilitation of approximately 400 units of housing for low to moderate income families; The Community Education Project, which provides essential programs in literacy and Adult Basic Education; Enlace de Familias de Holyoke, who provides family support through a licensed day care center for infants and toddlers, a Fathers Nurturing Program and is the founder of the Holyoke community charter school. In recent years, *Nuestras Raíces*' work to promote economic, human and community development through urban agriculture has become a crucial driver for Holyoke's Latina/o community interventions within the urban realm.

Urban Agriculture in Holyoke

In 1992, the low-income Latina/o residents of the neighborhood of South Holyoke cleared the bricks and rubble from a vacant lot to form *La Finquita* (the little farm) community garden. The following year *Nuestras Raíces* was founded to manage the garden and work towards a greener and healthier Holyoke. Since then, *Nuestras Raíces* has grown a network of community gardens throughout the city and a powerful array of innovative projects around food and the environment, the most recent being the development of *La Finca*, an urban farm off the Connecticut River. This twenty-acre site is being developed to support a variety of initiatives around sustainable, productive farming activities. These projects include: a beginning farmer training program and new business incubator; an environmental conservation and stewardship project; a youth development initiative and the development of new facilities for community celebrations, cultural exchanges, and educational and commercial activities—all growing holistically from the cultural and human assets of the community.

Urban agriculture has proven to be an effective way to promote community development because it offers a way for the Latina/o residents of downtown Holyoke to maintain a connection to the agrarian roots of their culture while putting down new roots in their adopted home. Many *Nuestras Raíces*' members grew up on the farms of rural Puerto Rico and some first came to the Northeast as migrant farm workers in the 1960s. Though they may live in the city now, they are farmers at heart, and have lifetimes of experience in agriculture that remains a deep part of their heritage. Projects based on agriculture, such as markets and community gardens, build on the skills and knowledge that participants already have, and are proud to have the opportunity to use to improve their community and to teach to a younger generation. Hence, *Nuestras Raices*' efforts involve a framework of economic experimentation and improvisation that seeks to build a community economy with a clear relationship to the social well-being of their community.

Julie Graham and Janelle Cornwell (2009) have described *Nuestras Raices*' approach to economic development as, "not a narrow project of capitalist growth but a broad endeavor addressing every dimension of social well-being—health and fitness, food and nutrition, environment, education, arts and culture, useful work, personal growth, community" (p. 12). Graham and Cornwell continue to explain how "stigmatized" and so-called "anti-development" practices such as, self-provisioning, gifting, and volunteer labor figure prominently in the organization's development strategies. This is a key component of their evolving "diverse economy," which emphasizes not just ends, but means and measures that aim to increase social well-being by "not just building human capital to suit the narrow requirements of the local labor market but reframing the undervalued skills of older men, youth, and women as wealth-generating assets" (Graham & Cornwell, p. 12). This construction of an alternative economic model is intrinsically linked to *Nuestras Raices*' community organizing and capacity building efforts. *La Finca* creates a unique agricultural attraction that not only celebrates the heritage of the community, but also recognizes the deeper cultural invention possible through cultivating a "social economy as a space of experimentation, where familiar concepts are redefined and novel visions are enacted" (Graham & Cornwell, 2009, p. 30).

The Nueva Casita *Project With* Nuestras Raices

In recent years, I have been working with *Nuestras Raices* (with both students and in my own studio) to design new buildings on their farm. At first, the organization was interested in developing a small building at the entrance of the farm for greeting visitors, holding farm meetings and providing for tool storage. Over time the project evolved into an assembly of small structures organized around a farm store, meeting space and *Lechonera*, a pig roasting restaurant and cultural site that has a ubiquitous and important presence across the island of Puerto Rico. The evolution of the spatial program from a free-standing structure used primarily by *La Finca's* farmers, to an assembly of culturally significant, income generating buildings with both farm functions and public interaction, reflects *Nuestras Raices* efforts to expand and strengthen their community economy through social entrepreneurship and cultural affirmation.

In addition, the introduction of this new program enhances and complicates the project's ethnographic function, inviting, as many ethnic restaurants do, a more complex interplay between cultural insiders and outsiders. As Lisa Maya Knauer (2001), in her analysis of ethnic restaurants, notes, "the (ethnic) restaurant has a multifaceted ethnographic project: cultural preservation, transmission and translation" (p. 431). For Holyoke's Puerto Rican community, *La Lechonera* would provide for another compelling cultural referent and refuge from dominant culture (intrinsically tied to the community's economic well-being), while for non-Latina/o visitors to the farm it becomes "a specialized kind of tourist production," but one outside the mainstream instinct for sameness and conformity; and for both Latina/os and visitors alike, a performative site for intercultural encounters (Knauer, 2001).

Early in our design process, I noticed students using bright colors on their models and drawings in ways that they had not before. Their explanation for this was simply that they were working in a Latino/a community and they wanted to reflect the "community." As the semester progressed it was clear that the readings, reflections and time that students had spent in the community provided an opportunity for them to critically assess their assumptions and arrive at, and design for, a more complex spatial understanding of community. As we developed our first design for the farm we began to call the project the *Nueva Casita* in recognition of the early research on urban casitas that informed our work. As that research intersected with our growing understanding of the concept of the "in-between" we moved towards a design that did not replicate the image of a traditional casita, but instead relied on its performative, symbolic and socio-cultural characteristics. Following the trajectories of our research we began to conceive of a space of permeable and flexible boundaries where open wooden screens modulate interior/exterior spaces to become concrete representations of the "change, adaptability and resilience" (Flores, 2000, p. 74) crucial to Puerto Rican subjectivity and culture. Our first design (for the smaller entry structure) consisted of a cube-like single room that was wrapped with a lighter enclosure of wooden slats. Besides providing a green strategy for needed solar shading, this room within a room produced an extended threshold for those entering the building and was one way we sought to spatialize our findings regarding *casitas*. These ideas were further explored by the design of a large shifting front wall and attached porch that created the necessary entrance to the building and articulating a spatial language of sliding and shifting planes—another formal strategy used throughout the structure. As the project evolved into multiple buildings (a *Lechonera*, farm store, and meeting room) we continued to develop this formal language of shifting and overlapping screens of varying opacities as an inventory of spatial strategies that articulated both environmental and cultural meanings.

In addition, we began to re-think the use of color in strategic and discursive ways, primarily on the inner walls of our double skinned structures. Since the outer screen walls were visually and tectonically similar to local farm buildings (particularly tobacco barns with their porous open facades), this development began to complicate the structures metaphoric meaning, which now extended to a formal and tectonic dialogue between notions of Caribbean and New England architecture. As such, the spaces "in-between" not only carried the potential for reflective articulation of diasporic Latino/a subjectivity, but also point towards the links and bridges between Puerto Rican and New England agrarian traditions (also one of the key characteristics of *Nuestras Raices* innovative stewardship). Hence, the design creates a contemporary/diasporic *casita* as an active place where the past and the future meet in a dialogue with its site, and where cultural identity is fully engaged in becoming as well as in being.

A prominent challenge that emerges from this project is to determine how *Nuestras Raices'* model of alternative practice, constructed on the outskirts of the city, would be able to be re-produced within the more contested space of the city's center, where the frameworks of power that reproduce inequalities are the most active. This question highlights *La Finca's* role as an incubator of alternative possibilities, one where the socio-political dimensions of Puerto Rican cultural practices are re-imagined as trans-representational and, more importantly, transformative in everyday life. What happens when this emerging idea is set firmly in the urban sphere where alternative constructs are

View of Nueva Casita Proposal

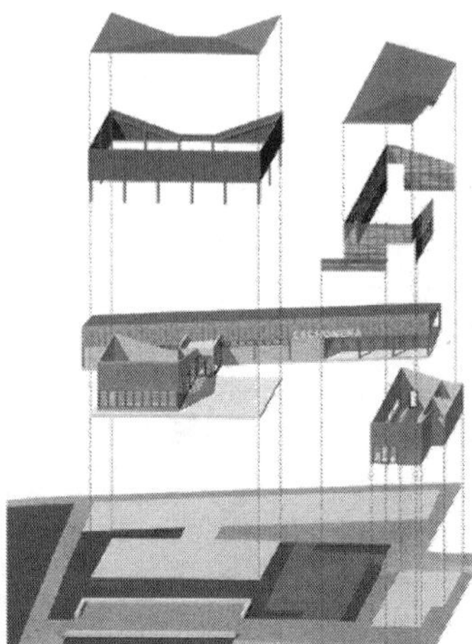

Expanded View of Lechonera

View at Lechonera Courtyard

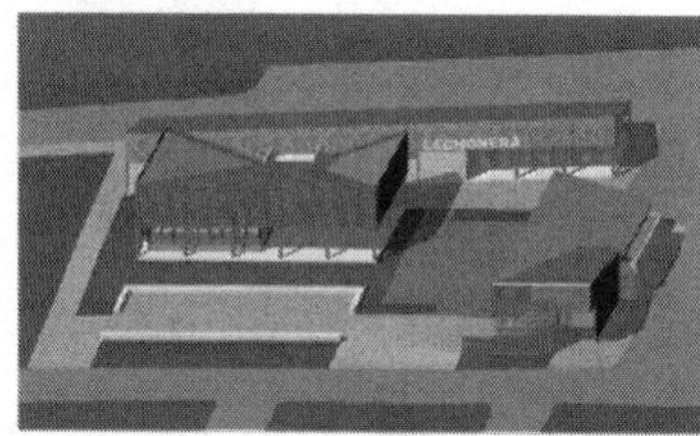

Overall View of Lechonera

View of Lechonera from La Finca

Figure 2.1. Nueva Casita and Lechonera Projects.
Source: Joseph Krupczynski (2008–2010).

expected to work only in resistance? What kinds of space/places are possible for Latinas/os in the city when this emerging idea takes root at the city's core? In the context of a growing recognition of the need for sustainable cities—inventive and open to a free balance between the social, environmental and economic factors—discovering the answers to these questions becomes an imperative need.

Conclusion

Globalization, and the virtual city of disembodied mobility may have reset the terms of engagement between material and virtual space in U.S. cities, yet that re-configuration has also heightened the need for, and value of, physical spaces that negotiate and validate the formation of cultural identity—especially, as another agent in the transformative dynamic of U.S. cities are their growing Latina/o populations. What is exciting about *Nuestras Raices'* recent initiatives are the ways they chart a clear path from a "politics of resistance and representation to a politics of transformation and liberation" (Lao-Montes, 2001, p. 142). In the hot-house of *La Finca*, this realizable utopia has planted the seeds on the outskirts of the city. How those rhizomatic shoots of transformation and liberation take hold to contest inequities and invent new ways in which Latina/o subjectivities can become firmly rooted in the city has yet to be fully explored.

A similar challenge may be directed at the educators, architects, designers and artists working within contested urban communities, and thus it is useful to return to the implications of the "in-between" as a spatial metaphor that supports critical spatial dialogues within and between a broad range of political, economic and social contexts. In a sense, the "in-between" is representative of the space of shifting, conflictive forces; a space, that as Flores (2000), quoting Homi Bhabha, notes "is skeptical ... of cultural totalization, and of notions of identity which depend for their value on being pure" (p. 55). As such, it can act as an operative and aesthetic model whose mutability can work in a number of ways to develop alternative projects and processes. It may provide frameworks for examining typical community engagement and design processes, encouraging creative work that moves beyond models of consensus to models of tactical collaboration, reciprocal cooperation and creative conflict, processes that are aimed at recognizing that the community is intrinsically linked to the production of its space (Miessen, 2007; Till, 1998). The "in-between" may well be that very structure necessary to thwart normative models of development and redirect the hegemonic designs of globalization through local agency.

As the architect and urban theorist Teddy Cruz (2005) has noted, these, and other approaches that might emerge under this critical lens, are hybridic, self-organizing and complex, and are best measured not by the forms created by architects and artists, but through the social formations provoked and supported by spatial practitioners working as cultural agents. Art and design practices that are capable of countering the alienating spectacles and divisive social processes that are endemic to our cultural landscape can work nimbly in this expanded field of the "in-between." Especially within cities like Holyoke, which are so burdened by disenfranchisement and social exclusion, and where there is a great potential and urgent need for catalyzing the material, symbolic and cultural capital that lies just below the surface. One can hope that evolving critical practices in architectural education could work to create spaces that reveal, instigate and challenge dominant social and political structures: and within those spaces, acknowledge the fluid and multiple characteristics that make up our public sphere and support a continuous process of social transformation and change.

References

Anzaldúa, G. (1999). *Borderlands/La frontera: The new mestiza* (2nd ed.). San Francisco, CA: Aunt Lute Books.

Aponte-Parés, L. (1995). What's yellow and white and has land all around it? Appropriating place in Puerto Rican *barrios*. *Centro: Journal of Centro de Estudios Puertorriquenos, 7*(1), 9–20.

Cruz, T. (2005). *Border postcards: Chronicles from the edge*. Retrieved from http://www2.cca.qc.ca/stirling/download/Cruz_Stirling_Lecture.pdf

Flores, J. (2000). *From bomba to hip-hop: Puerto Rican culture and Latino identity*. New York, NY: Columbia University Press.

Graham, J., & Cornwell, J. (2009). Building community economies in Massachusetts: An emerging model of economic development? In A. Amin (Ed.), *The social economy: International perspectives on economic solidarity* (pp. 1–41). London: Zed Press.

hooks, b. (1990). *Yearning: Race, gender, and cultural politics*. Boston, MA: South End Press.

Knauer, L. M. (2001). Eating in Cuban. In A. Lao-Montes & A. Dávila (Eds.), *Mambo montage: The latinization of New York* (pp. 425–447). New York, NY: Columbia University Press.

Lao-Montes, A. (2001). Niuyol: Urban regime, Latino social movements, ideologies of Latinidad. In A. Lao-Montes & A. Dávila (Eds.), *Mambo montage: The latinization of New York* (pp. 119–158). New York, NY: Columbia University Press.

Miessen, M. (2007). The violence of participation: Spatial practices beyond models of consensus. *Eurozine*. Retrieved from http://www.eurozine.com/articles/2007-08-01-miessen-en.html

Till, J. (1998). Architecture of the impure community. In J. Hill (Ed.), *Occupying architecture: Between the architect and the user* (pp. 61–75). New York, NY: Routledge.

3. *Subject-Heading or Social Justice Solidarity? Civic Engagement Practices of Latinx Undocumented Immigrant Students*

CLAUDIA A. EVANS-ZEPEDA

In the higher education process, where oftentimes diversity and race issues are conspicuously absent from discussions about learning, the practice of civic education is a key link to re-centering such issues to the educational and civic mission of higher education (Hurtado, 2007). Increasing educational equity for students of color—including Latinx undocumented students—is a priority that social justice educators in higher education should strive to achieve.[1] Social justice education, after all, is made up of teacher activists in political and social movements working to bring about changes in educational policies and institutional structures those educators perceive to be unjust (Montaño, 2002). Within current U.S. discourses of race and ethnicity, one such issue that demands focus is the inequities and disadvantages experienced by undocumented students: a population made up of 49% of undocumented young people ages 18 to 24 who have completed high school and have enrolled in or attended an institution of higher education (Perez, 2014).

Current nativist culture in the U.S. can render undocumented youth invisible. Institutionalized oppression coupled with anti-immigrant laws can make college an environment with xenophobic spaces (Kishner, 2015). Thus, access to postsecondary education and benefits for undocumented youth play an important role in colleges and universities. In addition, college can be a place where Latinx students can be offered educational tools that serve functional purposes and help build understanding of their marginalized experiences—a place for intellectual connections around the subject matters that impacts them. This research then, heeding the need to focus a communicative approach to the social justice learning for Latinx students, is a way to equip our undocumented students to navigate anti-immigrant spaces on campus and in their communities.

Motivated by questions about the relationship between co-curricular civic engagement, immigration activism, and linguistic change, this chapter explores examples of activism in college campuses. Secondly, I reflect on how undocumented Latinx college students participate in critical civic praxis to subvert the racist nativism prevalent in the dominant immigration discourse. Following Anguiano and Castañeda's (2014) call to promote critical Latina/o communication theorizing, this framework is utilized to explore the advocacy efforts of undocumented immigrant youth, and how through engagement with the Drop-the-I campaign, students expanded the purview of rights and belonging at a predominantly white normative college campus. The reflexive analysis builds on the individual and collective capacity for social justice by concentrating specifically on the recursive curricular and co-curricular efforts of the Dartmouth Coalition for Immigration Reform, Equality and DREAMers (CoFIRED) student group. I depict the group's success in petitioning for the Library of Congress to change the structure of its subject-heading policy in its cataloguing system. After a brief literature review, I discuss the students' activism in their efforts to highlight the word undocumented instead of the dehumanizing term "illegal alien," often used to perpetuate xenophobic ideologies when describing immigrants. The chapter concludes by re-conceptualization the ways these civic engagement efforts (both in and out the classroom) allow Latinx undocumented youth to resist linguistic hegemony and transforms their student identities towards ones that support their educational success.

Connecting Critical Pedagogy, Civic Engagement, and Latina/o Critical Communication

The general literature on integrative learning, which includes civic engagement literature, is vast and innovative. Studies in multiple venues have explored best campus practices and the known benefits of civic engagement in increasing student knowledge, values, and skills (Finley, 2011). Since service learning can potentially provide a context for students to rehearse and affirm white privilege, therefore what distinguishes (or should distinguish) critical civic engagement from (liberal) pedagogies designed to involve students in the teaching and learning process is a continual focus on challenging unequal relationships of power (Enders & Gould, 2009; Freire, 1993; Giroux, 2004). The layout of critical pedagogy scholarship paints two educational components—one structural, the other developmental—as students are entangled within a persistent racial caste system in the United States; entangled because the racial hierarchies operate in the contemporary society can become a double bind for particular students of color. They are a double bind for students of color, as scholars like Cammarota and Romero (2006) astutely point out, as studies warn that if both components are not addressed, "culturally-based explanations can contribute to racist ideology because they do nothing more than point to the putative 'foibles' in certain races while avoiding the real systemic problems of racism"; that is, "of white supremacy and white privilege" (p. 17). Consequently, instructional scholars like Warren and Fassett (2011) have offered the fundamental, interconnected commitments of their vision for critical communication pedagogy, which have been taken up by number of communication teachers, some of these efforts involving service-learning components (see Allen, 2011; Britt, 2012; Enders & Gould, 2009; Nakayama & Martin, 2007).

Critical pedagogies are complementary part of civic engagement that can work concomitantly with youth activism in higher education. Youth activism reflects young adults as immersed in civic participation and community involvement and its implication for increased understanding of policy and the role of citizens (Quijada, 2008). Research findings consistently demonstrate that through activism and civic engagement, social capital is gained, increased from the cultural and peer involvement during college. This involvement is a particularly useful way for students to acquire the additional cultural capital that helps them succeed academically and cognitively. Moreover, Kishner (2015) clearly argues societal institutions are strengthened when young people, particularly those most disadvantaged by educational inequity, turn their critical gaze to such education systems and participate in efforts to improve them.

Unfortunately, Latinx student populations are still the most disadvantaged yet stand to gain most from such holistic integrative educational efforts (Contreras, 2009; Hurtado, 2007). More and more we see that engaging Latinx students in civil rights struggles have the impact that makes experiential learning worth the challenges. For example, Latinx students who attend an urban university and who are involved in community service-learning courses showed greater gains in leadership development including their commitment to civic responsibility and desire to become community leaders than similar students not involved (Cress & Duarte, 2013). In a predominantly white institution, Castañeda (2008) applied the work on critical pedagogy by featuring how community-based learning in Latina/o media studies elicited a number of benefits, including: deconstruction of the status quo and the transformation of the public sphere. Cammarota and Romero (2006) similarly posit how essential it is that we implement an education for Latinx students and foster critically compassionate intellectualism by drawing on three prongs: critical pedagogy, authentic caring, and social justice content.

More specifically, Latinx immigrant youth live at the intersection of a number of key struggles and ideologies heralded against youth of color and immigrants (Seif, 2009, p. 4). And while there are fewer studies regarding the civic engagement of Latinx undocumented students, they are no less important. The nexus of age, race, and immigration status makes it particularly hard to identify and study immigrant youth, especially when they are undocumented since their educational membership and exclusion from other social arenas is complicated. Seif (2009, 2011) argues for inclusive definitions of "immigrant youth civic engagement," and for acknowledgement of the challenges and the varied ways in which their civic practices are enacted. Her research demonstrates that it is important to link learning with the civic missions of higher education to achieve greater coherence in undergraduate preparation (p. 186). Additionally, scholars like Pérez, Espinoza, Ramos, Coronado, and Cortes (2010) have examined the positive impact of the civic engagement of undocumented Mexican students and results on higher attendance, grade point average, self-esteem, academic self-efficacy, involvement in extracurricular activities, and motivation to learn. The finding that a majority of noncitizen college-going Latinx youth are participating in American civic life is significant in serving as predictor that such civically involved youth will continue to do so as adults.

Activism about and/or by undocumented youth is also relevant to the topic of Latinx civic engagement. Since the legislation was first introduced in 2001, the DREAM Act (Development, Relief and Education for Alien Minors Act) has been inextricably tied to the undocumented immigrant youth movement.[2] Numerous publications in the last several years add to our knowledge of immigrant youth involvement in activism and community building/organizing by youth working towards a pathway for citizenship. Such interdisciplinary attention to the topic is not surprising considering the burgeoning young generations of Latinx activism. In fact, undocumented youth have shown immense resistive capacity by engaging in activism, using a range of material and discursive strategies that have, in turn, equipped them with the ability to confront the political system respond to nativist, allies, and legislators (Anguiano, 2015). DREAM activists are also very involved in the discourse that is being produced about them; noteworthy is the work collectively written by undocumented students themselves, such as by the Students

Informing Now (SIN) Collective (2007), a student organization created at the University of California, Santa Cruz. Student leaders in organizations like this one work toward educational justice and immigrant rights. They have also constructed counter-narratives by featuring their grassroots actions and lived experiences (Dominguez et al., 2009).

Within the topic of critical pedagogy of undocumented youth there also exists other noteworthy efforts toward liberatory approaches for undocumented students in higher education. This includes innovative organizations like Freedom University, inspired by the legacy of the Southern Freedom School tradition. Their efforts function to provide a number of resources for undocumented students banned from public higher education such as "Georgia tuition-free education, college application and scholarship assistance, [and] tangible movement skill building" (Freedom University Georgia, n.d.). Other cutting-edge courses to underscore the central role of undocumented youth as social change agents and protagonists of the issue come from organizations like the uLEAD (University Leaders for Educational Access and Diversity) Network, an "online community of university leaders committed to broadening postsecondary access and support for all students, regardless of immigration status" (n.d.). Their website offers curriculum like uLEAD Module: Immigrant Youth Activism, which applies non-traditional ways of using critical pedagogy and civic engagement to support this population of students.

Despite the clear sense that theory can play a key role in advancing diversity from a place in the margins to the center, examination of the different dimensions of civic engagement and activism of Latinx undocumented youth remains a largely underdeveloped area in communication studies (Anguiano & Gutiérrez Nájera, 2015). In the next section I apply Latina/o Critical Communication theory (Anguiano & Castañeda, 2014) in order to centralize the Latina/o communicative issues and further address the nuances of contemporary Latina/o issues without having to continuously legitimize Latina/os' struggle for equality in the U.S. The Latina/o critical communication framework (LatCritComm) is centered to efforts "to move away from the fragmented examinations of Latina/os as racialized subjects," and rather emphasize a cross-functional bridge that connects theoretical tenets about Latina/o subjectivities and racialization in communication studies (Anguiano & Castañeda, 2014, p. 113). In what follows, I feature the particular benefits and reflections of integrating a LatCritComm perspective to the instructional sphere. Given the aim of the theory to simultaneously explain and critique racialized communication phenomena as it pertains to multiracial/multiethnic experiences, I apply the core tenets of LatCritComm theory and argue for this framework as relevant to the pedagogical commitment to investigate inequality and change based on meaningful civic engagement.

Creating CoFIRED

In January 2014, at the request of two undocumented students, along with Professor Lourdes Nájera Gutiérrez, I became a co-advisor to a student group. This student group sought to effectively function as a support network, advocacy group, and voice for undocumented students in the northeastern U.S. Created in Winter 2014, the organization became the Coalition for Immigration Reform, Equality and DREAMers (CoFIRED) a non-partisan organization dedicated to advancing the rights of undocumented students on campus and across the nation. At their founding, they effectually became a group who would pursue the following specific purposes and objectives:

1. organizing and strengthening alliances across the [Dartmouth] communities for a comprehensive approach to immigration reform;
2. uniting and collaborating with organizations, student groups, legal service providers, and advocacy groups outside the [Dartmouth] communities to provide a support network for [Dartmouth's] undocumented students;
3. supporting and guiding students whose immigration status deprived them of equal opportunities and access to higher education and other human rights;
4. advocating for equal representation of undocumented immigrants in higher education and administration;
5. demanding the increase of contemporary immigration reform classes that reflect the current situation of immigrants and immigration system;
6. increasing awareness in the [Dartmouth] community about the undocumented experience and the immigration system;
7. maintaining and providing updated information on immigration policies that affect the youth of the United States through education, family, social, economic policies.[3]

The first general officer meeting was held on February 5, 2014 with attendance of about ten members. By the end of that first term, CoFIRED had not only established itself as formally recognized group, but hosted events with other student groups and sparked meaningful dialogue across campus that had prior seldom happened. CoFIRED became the only undergraduate institutional representative for undocumented students. Under our guidance and advising, the programming created by the students was congruent with LatCritComm. Students were empowered to consider the problematics of the language in the public sphere and made efforts to dismantle the lack an awareness in the following: (a) the decentralized Latinx experience; (b) the racism faced by the Latina/o community; (c) the literacy-colorblind language/rhetoric toward Latina/os; (d) the use of decolonizing methodological approaches; and (e) the activism needed for social justice change.

Centralizing the Latino Experience

Besides helping individual students, CoFIRED transformed itself into a platform for activist policy and institutional change, especially when it came to raising campus awareness of the difficulties facing Latinx undocumented students (Wolfe, 2014). Aligned with the goals stipulated in their constitution, the group generated demands for recognition and advocated to increase the quality of services and available resources for undocumented students. An immediate consequence of the group coming together was giving a voice to the Latinx undergraduate students, increasing outreach and counseling of current and prospective undocumented students, built partnership with the Office of Visa and Immigration Services to help more students fill out the Deferred Action for Childhood Arrivals (DACA) paperwork, as well as connecting with local immigration lawyers for legal assistance through a DACA Day. Moreover, the group established a centralized place to meet to share information on topics as wide-ranging as understanding of the unique needs of undocumented students need for financial aid, admissions information, job hunting, and travel authorization. This is especially meaningful given it was taking place at an institution where these conversations were ordinarily silent, and thus, supporting students with weekly meetings to discuss such issues created cultural congruency. These discussions resulted in an improved campus climate that centralized and made visible their experiences and gave voice to these students.

Acknowledge and Address the Racism Faced by the Latina/o Community

CoFIRED set ambitious goals for their second semester as a group. They sought to host an event in conjunction with the online Drop the I-Word campaign. On a broad level, the national campaign promotes both individual and media responsibility for eliminating the word "illegal" from common usage. Race Forward and Colorlines, the daily news site it publishes, spearhead the online campaign, allowing visitors fill out a pledge against the use of the word illegal to describe a person without immigration status. After weeks of planning, the first event was executed and featured a lecture on the topic regarding the rhetorical power of language. Launching the Drop the I-Word campaign on campus effectively helped meet the principles of the group: to support programming focused on a communicative approach to increasing immigration equity. Through story sharing and reflective prompts, the co-curricular pedagogical efforts fostered a unique learning environment that encouraged the participating students, faculty, and staff members to explore issues of identity, diversity, and inequity while building skill for and commitment to social justice responsibility and action. The focus on language as the featured mode of activism was conceived after incorporating discussions about the rhetorical impact of words on social justice efforts.

In particular, the group met to discuss the persuasive role of changing the terms of the debate. In doing so, members discussed the word as having been shown to be a powerful rationalization tool to justify harsh treatment and restrictive immigration policy (Ngai, 2004). After all, the terminology of illegal alien has garnered significant attention by law and humanities scholars, all which note the prominence of this legal description in emphasizing criminality and foreignness (Ackerman, 2014; Anguiano, 2015; Chomsky, 2014). However, the strategy of changing the terminology on campus was not just to create a replacement term for illegal alien. These strategic efforts were designed to create a sense of self qua undocumented, and thus to demand linguistic changes be implemented at a campus level. This worked in conjunction with a petition for the campus community to sign pledges they'd stop using the I-word, and rather, would use terms that more accurately described a person's legal situation (e.g., undocumented immigrant, unauthorized person, or migrants without papers). CoFIRED ran a successful flier campaign on and off campus aimed at promoting awareness and dispelling myths about undocumented immigrants on campus. The student involvement in this operationalized civic engagement was transformative in that it re-shifted the conversation to foster self-labeling as a way to counter the negative consequences of the epithet illegal alien.

Resist Literacy-Colorblind Language/Rhetoric Toward Latina/os

Another way CoFIRED leaders and supporters enacted the LatCritComm framework was in taking a holistic perspective to eliminate the use of the illegal not just the college but nationwide. In Spring 2014, the students collaborated with Library Administration for support from college staff librarians and the reference bibliographer. The collaborative group of board members organized their efforts to remove illegal immigrant and all variations thereof from library subject headings. By inciting the college library's use of undocumented rather than illegal in reference to immigrants, CoFIRED encountered a policy that suggested that the college did not have the power to change categories—reference librarians do not have access to the cataloging (editing) system. The campus library, which follows a system of subject headings set by the Library of Congress, would need to submit a subject-heading-change proposal to the Library of Congress, to change the subject heading language across all U.S. libraries adopting the Library of Congress Subject Heading system.

The drafted proposal required extensive research gathered by the students. Under the direction of Jill Baron, the Librarian for Romance Languages & Literatures and Latin American Studies, and John C. DeSantis, Cataloging and Metadata Services Librarian, with guidance of both advisors, putting the proposal together was an integrative learning process that facilitated student interaction with faculty, staff and off-campus library personnel. This holistic and collaborative process was important because face-to-face interaction with faculty and staff is a crucial piece of engaged learning that positively supports social identity groups (Hurtado, 2007). The retention of students, in general, and of students from underrepresented groups, in particular, increases with more faculty- student contact (Kuh, 2005). The campaign also promoted a broad-based set of multilayered thinking and socio-cognitive skills for making a long-standing change to the problematic language used in both educational and larger public spheres.

Deploy Decolonizing Methodological Approaches

Through the fostered mentorship within the co-curricular programming, the students came together and affirmed a postcolonial reflexivity. Postcolonial reflexivity, or rejecting the constitutive logic of settler colonialism, is at the core of LatCritComm. One of the key tenets that compliment civic education is the need to extend educational focus beyond the white western pedagogical tools and theories educators often rely on, and to instead cultivate more productive intercultural campus culture (Gorski, 2008; Nakayama & Martin, 2007). Overall, this application of LatCritComm extends the definition of student *citizenship*, as many of these undocumented students are progressively changing the landscape of what postsecondary inclusivity for undocumented students means. As Giroux (2004) explains, crucial pedagogy is related to issues of democracy, citizenship, and the struggle over the shaping of identities and identifications. These factors need to be taken up as part of the broader campus politics—as part of a "larger attempt to explain how learning takes place outside of schools or what it means to assess the political significance of understanding the broader educational force of culture" (p. 61).

Participation in the CoFIRED group called and allowed for each individual to harness his or her opinions through activists' efforts, it encouraged metacognition about the role of language to counteract anti-immigrant sentiment. Building on the foundations of LatCritComm theory and research in communication studies, these student efforts integrated a decolonizing approach in challenging the student body to consider discontinuity of nativism against undocumented students. The active thinking processes that took place among students, moved them to consider alternative ways to address the structural and systematic aspect of their own embedded worldviews to those of another (and their peers).

Promote a Social Justice Dimension

In response to the initial CoFIRED's petition, the Policy Standards Division of the Library of Congress, which maintains Library of Congress Subject Headings, opposed the constituent request initiated by the students. Taking the CoFIRED's lead, the American Library Association critiqued their decision with a resolution arguing for them to reconsider their rejection, resulting in the LOC reconvening on this matter and announcing the heading would be changed. The executive report acknowledged that use of illegal alien—entrenched in existence as one of the oldest headings in Library of Congress Subject Headings since 1910—had become pejorative and therefore would be cancelled as a bibliographical term. While the LOC did not implement the recommended "undocumented immigrants" as the new terminology, the approval effectively meant a replacement of all records by two headings, noncitizens and unauthorized immigration; the revision of existing bibliographic records to commence in May 2016.[4]

Indeed, the students two years of petitioning and persistence in challenging of status quo resulted in the groundbreaking result that created a much-needed change within the structures of power held by this institution. This, I posit, creates long-lasting positive effects that impacts all the libraries and urges the communities using them to reconsider how we think about this topic. What CoFIRED demonstrated is part of what we hope to accomplish with LatCritComm, to yield benefits from a holistic approach that equips students of color. Other positive outcomes included the students' leadership ability and capacity to host the 6th Annual Collegiate Alliance for Immigration Reform conference.[5] The successful execution of this conference in November

2015 meant the participating Latinx CoFIRED students remained active, persisted with its campaign, and became a group that earned acclaim for its social justice successes. Even prior to the LOC victory, their success was proclaimed by CAIR conference participants, but also by the greater campus and was further evidenced when awarded the 2015 Martin Luther King Jr. Social Justice Award at Dartmouth College for student groups (SJA Winners, 2015). Following the LOC heading announcement, CoFIRED effectively made it so that undocumented students' presence was expanded, thus creating support networks that developed both long-term and continuous relationships within and beyond other member of the Ivy-League undocumented community.

The coalitions created at the collegiate level for immigrant rights is just one of the ways Latinx students created a more visible and concerted need for institutional support as well as a more inclusive environment for undocumented youth and the larger fight for immigration reform. CoFIRED immigrant youth confronted and resist inequities. This resulted in the adopted motto of group, "undocumented and unafraid," which serves as a testament to their willingness to embrace being undocumented despite the hostile climate. In turn this tactic furthered their advocacy endeavors, and example of the many remarkable acts of confronting the political system forged through the constant navigation of their purported illegality (Costanza-Chock, 2014; Negrón-Gonzales, 2013). Students' engagement in these various types of interactions and activisms by groups such as CoFIRED act as a support system and advocacy channel for undocumented college students; they are examples of youth of color building political power in a context of inequality and exclusion.

Reflections on Operationalizing LatCritComm on Campus

In conclusion, the application of a Latina/o critical communication framework suggests the tenets can be operationalized to support the pursuit of institutions and individuals striving to achieve educational equality for all students. It is important to look at the implications of these civic engagement efforts (both in and outside the classroom) and the tremendous impact specific to communication studies which focus on communication as the articulation of meaning through words. The efforts described in this chapter reveal how Latinx undocumented youth can resist linguistic hegemony and transform their student identities to support their educational success.

First, the potential of applying this theory goes beyond the classroom and into co-curricular spaces. We aim for students to connect with community organizations, local struggles, and larger national movements. A key component of cultivating effective politically centered civic engagement is the potential of explicitly linking both curricular and co curricular campus civic engagement efforts (Finley, 2011, p. 15). This confirms both the need and benefit of institutional support for problem-based and interdisciplinary efforts that include some combination of civic engagement, service learning, and faculty-student research (Commins, 2013). As this CoFIRED case study demonstrates, the efforts to revoke the "illegal alien" subject heading, in assistance by the American Library Association, implies that learning and change takes place across a spectrum of social practices and settings. Specifically, this validates previous studies that demonstrate how student engagement with diverse interactions on campus and in the classroom, are more likely to confront notions of prejudice, be inclusive of views different from their own, and embrace social justice (Hurtado, 2007; Montaño, 2002).

Second, critical Latina/o communication is integral to the education that makes civic engagement relevant as both a skill to develop in students *and* as a tool for teaching and learning, especially if we hope to expand the possibilities of a democratic politics, the dynamics of resistance, and the capacities for social agency (Britt, 2012; Jackson, 2008). As social justice remains a focus for Latinx undocumented students, I argue that dialogic methods, such as the ones used with and by CoFIRED, engaged students in an examination of power structures and discriminatory practices of society based on language and immigration status. As students participated in numerous activities related to their work in this activist organization, they acquired rhetorical and discursive skills that enabled them to respond strategically to the events and circumstances of their college education and effectively promote the goals of the organization (Montaño, 2002, p. 268). The engagement I describe here, then, has the potential to improve cognitive development by enhancing reflective thinking capacities and ultimately helping to produce graduates that are able to further insert their critical competencies in an effective and transformative matter (Eyler, 2002).

Third, this points to the possibility of students embracing the differences encountered in higher education through activities that increase cultural knowledge—both in educating the campus population to reject the pejorative language that describes immigrants, and in empowerment to reject the oppressive nature of anti-immigrant sentiment. It validates our understanding that departments and programs with diverse activities can both inform students' identities, and also help them understand their identities in relation to societal issues. Importantly, while the efforts were initially mostly constrained to the college campus, the issues raised by the students developed into topics of interest for both the local and national community; their activism was first only featured as local news story then the landmark decision to cancel the subject heading garnered them national mainstream media attention (Qian, 2014; Seaman, 2014; Wang, 2014; Wolfe, 2014). To be clear, this feat takes place within a harsh political milieu; students are drawing indignation from conservative anti-immigrant sentiment that reject such efforts.[6] However, the coverage and extended impact of subject headings index used by libraries around the world signal the indomitable spirit of students and the promise of such engaged pedagogies in action. As such, these insights reveal the need to continue to create spaces for such struggles by embracing critical pedagogies in higher education and the unquestioned belonging of Latinx students.

Finally, the actions presented in this chapter serve as example of building bridges for the type of on-campus and co-curricular political advocacy that make the struggles of undocumented Latinx students more visible on college campuses. In doing so, I affirm the need to foster civic engagement by showing the possibilities of participatory engagement and ways Latinx youth are broadening our understanding of culture, identity, and power. Moreover, such involvement demonstrates why the work of Latinx youth, who have engaged in co-curricular civic learning and in anti-racism actions, are having huge victories, transforming institutional and public consciousness by fighting for more inclusive campus environments and society at large. As social justice educators, we want all voices and experiences to be valued justly at our institutions, and thus this kind of work is necessary if we want our students and communities to be transformed in the long run.

Notes

1. I use the gender-neutral term, Latinx, as the primarily identifier in this chapter in an effort to encompass genders outside of the limiting man-woman binary. As argued by Scharrón-del Rio and Aja (2015), including the x as the final gender-determining syllable is a purposeful move that makes Latino (normally a masculine identifier) a more inclusive term that goes beyond the scope of the masculine and feminine gender and sexual identities. For the remainder of the manuscript I use that label as interchangeable with the more commonly used terms for describing those grouped under the pan-ethnic identity, including, Latina/o and the more distinct Latin@.
2. While I focus on Latinx students, it is important to note that there is evidence of hidden diversity of undocumented students as Asian American and Pacific Islander community represents a rising number of the DREAM-eligible youth.
3. Their stated objectives also included: (1) building consciousness around the issues that undocumented youth face in both private and public institutions of learning; (2) to cultivate the seeds for a more inclusive Dartmouth community; (3) to spread awareness of the complexities, social, psychological, and spiritual, of the undocumented experience; (4) to increase the number of administrators and staff that have expertise about immigration reform, undocumented immigrants and immigrants; and

(5) to unite forces that support a comprehensive immigration approach at Dartmouth College.

4. For full announcement with rationale for the revisions to LCSH published by the Library of Congress, see: http://www.loc.gov/catdir/cpso/illegal-aliens-decision.pdf
5. Previously called the CAIR Summit, these gathering aims to unite collegiate organizations, community organizers, students, activists, scholars and leaders towards progress in the immigration reform movement, see: http://cofired.weebly.com/6th-annual-cair-conference.html
6. Most notably Rep. Diane Black (R-TN) introduced the Stopping Partisan Policy at the Library of Congress Act in action against LOC change, see: http://black.house.gov/sites/black.house.gov/files/FINAL_BLACK_061_xml.pdf

References

Ackerman, E. (2014). "What part of illegal don't you understand?" Bureaucracy and civil society in the shaping of illegality. *Ethnic and Racial Studies, 37*(2), 181–203.

Allen, B. J. (2011). Critical communication pedagogy as a framework for teaching difference and organizing. In D. K. Mumby (Ed.), *Reframing difference in organizational communication studies: Research, pedagogy, and practice* (pp. 103–125). Thousand Oaks, CA: Sage.

Anguiano, C. A. (2015). Dropping the "I" word: A critical examination of contemporary migration labels. In J. Hartelius (Ed.), *The rhetorics of U.S. immigration: Identity, community and otherness* (pp. 93–111). Pennsylvania, PA: Penn State University Press.

Anguiano, C. A., & Castañeda, M. (2014). Forging a path: Past and present state of critical Latina/o communication studies. *Review of Communication, 14*(2), 107–124.

Anguiano, C. A., & Gutiérrez Nájera, L. (2015). Paradox of performing exceptionalism: Complicating the deserving/undeserving binary of undocumented immigrant youth in elite institutions. *Association of Mexican American Educators Journal, 9*(2), 45–56.

Britt, L. L. (2012). Why we use service-learning: A report outlining a typology of three approaches to this form of communication pedagogy. *Communication Education, 61*(1), 80–88.

Cammarota, J., & Romero, A. (2006). A critically compassionate intellectualism for Latina/o students: Raising voices above the silencing in our schools. *Multicultural Education, 14*(2), 16–23.

Castañeda, M. (2008). Transformative learning through community engagement. *Latino Studies, 6*(3), 319–326.

Chomsky, A. (2014). *Undocumented: How immigration became illegal.* Boston, MA: Beacon Press.

Commins, M. M. (2013). Teaching immigration: Informing and elevating the debate. *Norteamérica, 8*, 173–190.

Contreras, F. (2009). Sin papeles y rompiendo barreras: Latino students and the challenges of persisting in college. *Harvard Educational Review, 79*(4), 610–631.

Costanza-Chock, S. (2014). *Out of the shadows, into the streets! Transmedia organizing and the immigrant rights movement.* Boston, MA: MIT Press.

Cress, C. M., & Duarte, R. (2013). Pedagogía comunitaria: Facilitating Latino student civic engagement leadership. *AUDEM: The International Journal of Higher Education and Democracy, 4*(1), 54–78.

Dartmouth Coalition for Immigration Reform, Equality and DREAMers. (n.d). *About.* Retrieved from http://cofired.weebly.com/about.html

Dominguez, N., Duarte, Y., Espinosa, P. J., Martinez, L., Nygreen, K., Perez, R., & Saba, M. (2009). Constructing a counternarrative: Students informing now (SIN) reframes immigration and education in the United States. *Journal of Adolescent & Adult Literacy, 52*(5), 439–442.

Enders, D., & Gould, M. (2009). "I am also in the position to use my whiteness to help them out": The communication of whiteness in service learning. *Western Journal of Communication, 73*(4), 418–436.

Eyler, J. (2002). Reflection: Linking service and learning—Linking students and communities. *Journal of Social Issues, 58*(3), 517–534.

Finley, A. (2011). *Civic learning and democratic engagements: A Review of the literature on civic engagement in post-secondary education.* Washington, DC: Association of American Universities and Colleges.

Freedom University Georgia. (n.d.). *About.* Retrieved from http://www.freedomuniversitygeorgia.com/

Freire, P. (1993). *Pedagogy of the oppressed.* New York, NY: Continuum.

Giroux, H. A. (2004). Cultural studies, public pedagogy, and the responsibility of intellectuals. *Communication and Critical/Cultural Studies, 1*(1), 59–79.

Gorski, P. C. (2008). Good intentions are not enough: A decolonizing intercultural education. *Intercultural Education, 19*(6), 515–525.

Hurtado, S. (2007). Linking diversity with the educational and civic missions of higher education. *The Review of Higher Education, 30*(2), 185–196.

Jackson, L. (2008). Dialogic pedagogy for social justice: A critical examination. *Studies in Philosophy and Education, 27*(2–3), 137–148.

Kishner, B. (2015). *Youth activism in an era of education inequality.* New York, NY: NYU Press.

Kuh, G. (2005). *Student success in college: Creating conditions that matter.* San Francisco, CA: Jossey Bass.

Montaño, T. (2002). Teachers as activists: Teacher development and alternate sites of learning. *Equity & Excellence in Education, 35*(3), 265–275.

Nakayama, T. K., & Martin, J. N. (2007). The "White problem" in intercultural communication research and pedagogy. In L.M. Cooks & J.S. Simpson (Eds.), *Whiteness, pedagogy, performance: Dis/placing race* (pp. 111–137). Lanham, MD: Lexington Books.

Negrón-Gonzales, G. (2013). Navigating "illegality": Undocumented youth and oppositional consciousness. *Children and Youth Services Review, 35*(8), 1284–1290.

Ngai, M. M. (2004). *Impossible subjects: Illegal aliens and the making of modern America*. Princeton, NJ: Princeton University Press.

Pérez, W., Espinoza, R., Ramos, K., Coronado, H., & Cortes, R. (2010). Civic engagement patterns of undocumented Mexican students. *Journal of Hispanic Higher Education, 20*(10), 1–21.

Perez, Z. J. (2014). *Removing barriers to higher education for undocumented students*. Retrieved from https://www.americanprogress.org/issues/immigration/report/2014/12/05/

Qian, M. (2014, April 1). "Drop the I-Word" event highlights students' stories. *The Dartmouth*. Retrieved from http://www.thedartmouth.com/2014/04/01/drop-the-i-word-event-highlights-students-stories/

Quijada, D. A. (2008). Marginalization, identity formation, and empowerment: Youth's struggles for self and social justice. In N. Dolby & F. Rizvi (Eds.), *Youth moves: Identities and education in global perspective* (pp. 207–221). New York, NY: Routledge.

Race Forward. (n.d.). *Drop the I-word campaign*. Retrieved from https://www.raceforward.org/practice/tools/drop-i-word-campaign

Scharrón-del Río, M. R., & Aja, A. A. (2015, December 5). The case FOR "Latinx": Why intersectionality is not a choice. *Latino Rebels*. Retrieved from http://www.latinorebels.com/2015/12/05/the-case-for-latinx

Seaman, S. K. (2014, September 10). Students petition Library of Congress to "drop the I-word." *Dartmouth Now*. Retrieved from http://now.dartmouth.edu/2014/09/students-petition-library-con

Seif, H. (2009). The civic life of Latina/o immigrant youth: Challenging boundaries and creating safe spaces. *Research Paper Series on Latino Immigration Civic and Political Participation, No. 5*. Retrieved from http://wilsoncenter.org/migrantparticipation

Seif, H. (2011). "Unapologetic and unafraid": Immigrant youth come out from the shadows. *New Directions for Child and Adolescent Development, 134*, 59–75.

SIN Collective. (2007). Students informing now (SIN) challenge the racial state in California without shame … SIN verguenza! *Educational Foundations, 21*(1–2), 71–90.

Social Justice Award Winners. (2015). *Dartmouth MLK social justice awards*. Retrieved from https://www.dartmouth.edu/~mlk/awards/2015sja.html

University Leaders for Educational Access and Diversity Network. (n.d). *About*. Retrieved from http://uleadnet.org/

Wang, T. (2014, March 31). Never rested: Undocumented life at Dartmouth. *The Dartmouth*. Retrieved from http://thedartmouth.com/2014/03/31/never-rested-undocumented-life

Warren, J. T., & Fassett, D. L. (2011). *Communication: A critical/cultural introduction*. Thousand Oaks, CA: Sage Publications.

Wolfe, R. (2014, October 5). Undocumented at Dartmouth College: New student group offers support for immigrants. *Valley News*. Retrieved from http://www.vnews.com/home/13668516-95/undocumented-at-dartmouth

4. *Keeping It Real: Bridging U.S. Latino/a Literature and Community Through Student Engagement*

Marisel Moreno

I will never forget the first time I realized the impact that Community-Based Learning (CBL) could potentially have on my students. It was a simple sentence in a final course reflection for my first CBL-U.S. Latino/a Literature course. In it, the student admitted that the course had changed his political views, especially on the topic of immigration. My first reaction was one of disbelief: how could this be if we don't openly address politics in the course? But the more I thought about it, the more it made sense to me. For an entire semester, this student had "listened" to the voices of U.S. Latino/a authors and poets and had also listened to the stories of the Latino/a children whom he tutored and mentored at *La Casa de Amistad*, our CBL community partner. The student's first-hand experience interacting with children of immigrant families allowed him to question and get past the stereotypes that Latinos/as face in this country, and which inform and distort the discourse on immigration. It was at that moment, when I realized the power that the combination of U.S. Latino/a Literature and CBL has to transform minds and hearts—to awaken students' desire for social justice and to become agents of transformation—that I decided that CBL must remain a central element of my courses. In this essay, I share a blueprint for those who are considering teaching CBL courses at the university level, or those who are looking for additional ideas on how to implement this pedagogy. I offer advice based on my experience teaching CBL-U.S. Latino/a literature courses because I have witnessed how this pedagogy has led to my students' increased civic engagement and quest for social justice.

It seems ironic to me given the impact on my students I have witnessed through my CBL-U.S. Latino/a Literature courses that I came across this transformative pedagogy by chance. I had never heard about service-learning (SL) or CBL until 2009, when I was asked to be part of a search committee for a faculty position for Spanish Community-Based Learning. The more I read about the field and researched other universities' CBL programs, the more curious and interested I became in adopting CBL in my own courses. What I read in the scholarship produced on CBL and teaching Spanish resonated with me, and the learning goals I had for my students. I noticed, however, that most studies focused on intermediate and advanced Spanish language/culture courses. As someone who teaches U.S. Latino/a Literature within the context of a Department of Romance Languages and Literatures (Spanish section), I was eager to find models on how to integrate CBL to advanced U.S. Latino/a literature courses, which usually address topics such as race, ethnicity, poverty, immigration, and transculturation. The anthology *Construyendo Puentes (Building Bridges): Concepts and Models for Service-Learning in Spanish* (Hellebrandt & Varona, 1999) provided me with a solid background, but most of the chapters in the collection focus on language and intermediate level courses, rather than advanced literature ones. Therefore, I began to piece together the best elements and ideas that I found on how to incorporate CBL, regardless of the discipline (see Castañeda, 2008; Plann, 2002). Early on, I learned that there's not *one* way to do CBL—there's not a one-size-fits-all model—but rather many ways and degrees to incorporate it into your teaching.

One of the main reasons why I felt compelled to integrate CBL into my U.S. Latino/a literature courses was because I wanted my students to experience "literature coming alive," and to understand its power to promote social justice. In addition to gaining a deeper appreciation for literature, I felt that student engagement with the local Latino/a community would allow my students (who are mostly non-Latino/a) to learn from and about this population, to connect with it in ways that literature also tends to promote. Although teaching U.S. Latino literature is fulfilling, I'm not oblivious to the fact that there is a significant social and cultural distance between most of my students and the material I teach. Because I work at an institution where the majority of the student body identifies as white middle/upper class, I thought that one way to bridge the gap between them and the course contents would be through CBL and the opportunity it would afford them to experience a weekly immersion in the local Latino/a community. Personal interactions, I believe, have the potential to open the eyes of my seemingly sheltered students—as many of them have qualified themselves over the years—to the issues and challenges affecting the local and national Latino/a community, as well as to their values and cultural norms.

Because of the demographic profile of most of my students, I came to see CBL as the missing link in my U.S. Latino/a literature classes. I envisioned it as a self-regenerating cycle where course materials would inform my students' experiences with the local Latino/a community, and where their experiences would in turn provide a deeper meaning to the material read for the course. After ten consecutive semesters of teaching upper-level CBL-U.S. Latino/a literature courses, and with over 5,000 hours of student service/engagement with the local Latino/a community, I am convinced that in the majority of cases, this pedagogical approach leads to more profound student learning and a deeper sense of civic engagement.

How to Set Your CBL Course Up for Success

When I decided to teach my first CBL course more than five years ago, the fact that I had not found a specific model that I could apply to my U.S. Latino/a literature courses was initially a source of anxiety. As a pre-tenured professor, I knew I was taking a significant risk by devoting hours to a type of course that was highly time-consuming. In fact, there are multiple studies that demonstrate the various factors that deter and motivate faculty to adopt service-learning methodologies, such as Abes, Jackson, and Jones (2002), Butin (2006), McKay and Rozee (2004), O'Meara (2003), and Ward (1998). However, as a Latino Studies scholar, I was aware that the field itself had developed in close relation to the challenges and experiences of Latinos in the United States, and it was important for me to remain true to that mission (Butin, 2006; O'Meara, 2003). That's why I embarked on what felt like a new academic adventure. While I felt somewhat anxious not having an already-made model for teaching upper-level U.S. Latino/a literature courses within a Spanish department—since most models I found for Spanish were for beginner and intermediate language levels—I did count on the support and expertise of colleagues well versed in CBL at my own university (where we have the Center for Social Concerns, an institute dedicated to community outreach).

Throughout the years, there has been one piece of wisdom that has been crucial for the development of my CBL-U.S. Latino literature courses: there is not one right way to do CBL. Keeping this important statement in mind, I share some of the advice I have based on my experience teaching CBL courses for the last five years.

Reflect on Your Course and How It Would Benefit From Linking It to the Community

Basically, ask yourself: What is this course about? What are some of the short and long-term goals I have for my students? Why and how would this course benefit from establishing a direct connection to the local community? While I believe that courses in a broad range of disciplines can potentially benefit from adopting a CBL approach, certain areas, by their very natures, lend themselves to this pedagogy more than others. For instance, because the service in CBL/CSL tends to take place at centers and organizations that serve underprivileged groups, courses in fields that address issues related to these groups (ethnic, Latino/a, African-American, Latin American, gender, and minority studies) are likely to benefit the most from a CBL approach. This is so because the experience of working with the community has the potential to awaken the student's consciousness about the types of inequalities faced by minorities.

In my own courses, where students learn about various Latino/a groups through a multidisciplinary lens that combines literature with history, anthropology, gender and ethnic studies, tutoring and mentoring students at an organization that serves U.S. Latino/as has opened their eyes to the structural disparities faced by many in our community. From realizing the extent of the education gap that affects Latino/a children, to witnessing the impact that poverty, unemployment, and language barriers have on the wellbeing of a family, to better understanding the effect that fear produces among families with mixed citizenship statuses—students usually express their discontent/disbelief about the lack of social justice experienced by those families and are often moved to become agents of change. Some examples of how many of my students have become agents of change include their continuing commitment to *La Casa de Amistad*, or other community organizations, beyond their semester in my class; their activism on campus to raise awareness about immigration issues; and an interest in pursuing graduate studies in fields that will allow them to serve the Latino/a community in the future, such as education and immigration law.

Be Selective When Choosing a Community Partner

When determining which center or organization to partner with for your CBL course, it is important to see the potential for mutual benefits for both parties. Ask yourself: How could partnering with this organization help my students meet their learning goals for this course? And equally important, how can my students help meet the needs of the organization? What can we do to maximize learning opportunities? Does the mission of the community partner align with the course objectives in any way? Simply put, how can all sides benefit from this partnership?

In my case, my community partner for five years has been *La Casa de Amistad* (http://www.lacasadeamistad.org/), an organization that serves the local Latino/a community through a range of programs (tutoring, mentoring, college preparation, citizenship classes, food pantry) that promote education and literacy. *La Casa's* focus on the education of underprivileged Latino/a children, as well as its focus on cultural literacy, aligns seamlessly with the goals of my courses for my own students. When my students work there, they are not only tutors and mentors, although this is a crucial aspect of their engagement with the organization, considering that they give the children the academic help that their families are often not equipped to provide (due to language barriers, time constraints, and/or the parents' lower education level). They are also role models and are expected to engage in conversations about the future and the value of education with the grade-school, middle- and high school students that they tutor. But above all, they are there to learn. As Castañeda (2008) explains, "Unlike volunteerism, CSL and CBL are forms of experiential learning in which both students and community partners equally benefit during the duration of the community-university partnership. … In this model, students are not merely volunteering their time, and the community partners are not simply receiving free labor. On the contrary, both students and community partners, along with the faculty member, are developing a meaningful CSL/CBL partnership that aims for reflection, transparency, accountability, reciprocity, and a transformative experience for all" (p. 320).

While some models of CBL allow students to select a volunteer site from several options, I have found that having all of my students working at the same site (although at different times/days) can provide additional benefits to our class and to the community partner. Having my students volunteer only at *La Casa de Amistad* every semester allows for my students to share experiences as a class. In other words, it provides a source of cohesion and bonding among them. From the fifteen-minute ride to the site every week, to class discussions about their experiences with CBL (which we have several times every semester), my students often experience a sense of camaraderie with each other based on this common experience that they share. From the perspective of *La Casa de Amistad*, having all of my students volunteer there translates into being able to run its after school programs. Meeting the needs of the community partner, as I explained above, is highly important.

In the case of *La Casa*, this organization relies almost exclusively on their volunteers. Having greater numbers of my students there provides a degree of consistency throughout the semester that is sometimes difficult to achieve with volunteers who are not involved in CBL (in which volunteering is formally tied to a course).

And finally, because keeping the lines of communication open between the community partner and the class should always be a central priority, working with only one organization makes this job more manageable for the instructor, who is the link between his/her students and the organization where they volunteer. The longer the relationship is cultivated—ideally over a period of several years—the stronger the connection developed between the community organization and the university/college. Scholarship addressing the central role of community organizations in CSL include Jacoby (2003), Mitchell (2008), and Ward and Wolf-Wendel (2000). In other words, such partnerships can help to diminish the town-gown divide because the best way to chip away at the ivory tower is to get students into the community.

Prepare Your Students and Help Them "Connect the Dots"

Another lesson I've learned over the years is the crucial role that student preparation and sustained dialogue can play in the success of the course (academic as well as in relation to the community organization). There are two central ways to think about student preparation. The first has to do with enhancing the students' knowledge about the specific communities with which they will be interacting. For example, because the local Latino/a community that *La Casa de Amistad* serves is predominantly of Mexican descent, and most of my students are non-Latino/a (largely white), we spend a great deal of time reading and discussing the historical background of this population in the United States. The literature they read in this first unit on "Mexican-Americans" also serves to provide them with a strong basis of cultural knowledge that allows them to better understand their experiences.

Some of the works we cover are: Rodolfo "Corky" Gonzáles' "I am Joaquín" (1967); Tomás Rivera's *… y no se lo tragó la tierra / … And the Earth Did Not Devour Him* (1987); Helena María Viramontes' *Under the Feet of Jesus* (1995); poems by Luis Rodríguez, Sandra Cisneros' *House on Mango Street* (1984) as well as the first two parts of Rosales' documentary series *Chicano! The History of the Mexican American Civil Rights Movement* (1996). Both *Chicano!* and "I am Joaquín" provide a historical background to the struggles faced by Mexican-Americans today. Rivera's, Viramontes,' and Cisneros' first person accounts—told from the perspective of children—effectively convey the hardships faced by immigrant farm workers (in the case of Rivera and Viramontes), and by Latinoa/o children in urban areas. In my experience, teaching a combination of these works has helped my students to engage in their work at *La Casa de Amistad* with some of the background knowledge and cultural sensitivity that is necessary in order for them to succeed in fomenting mutually respectful and reciprocal relationships with the children.

Another way to think of student preparation has to do with their personal attitudes about their roles at the community organization. In my case, I constantly warn my students to avoid the "savior syndrome/complex." I remind them that they are not working at *La Casa de Amistad* to "save" anyone, so any sense of superiority and privilege (based on class, race, ethnicity, level of education, nationality, citizenship status, etc.) must be checked at the door. Early discussions of scholarship addressing the difference between volunteerism and experiential learning has always proven key to their successful CBL experience (see Castañeda, 2008; Plann, 2002). Put in a different way, we talk about the difference between "doing with" versus "doing for" the community, addressed by Ward and Wolf-Wendel (2000) when they state: "Mutuality and reciprocity are the cornerstones to service learning that is focused on doing with" (p. 769). As they suggest, the foundation of a productive CBL partnership is the simple understanding that both sides can teach and learn from one another.

Throughout the year, it is also important to remind students that they need to be active agents in their own learning process. Because so many factors come into play when doing CBL, it's not guaranteed that students will always notice a direct connection between the course contents and their experiences at *La Casa de Amistad* although I am diligent and intentional by guiding them throughout the semester. Over time, I have noticed a significant difference in terms of learning outcomes when comparing students who expect those connections to be evident and those who observe carefully and are able to see the bigger picture. For this reason, I remind them to try to see beyond the surface, to reflect on some of the key concepts we are studying (such as migration, transnationalism, poverty, racism, xenophobia, sexism, *marianismo*, discrimination, education gap, etc.). I also ask them to think of how their experiences at *La Casa de Amistad* have allowed them to gain a more nuanced understanding.

I have found that providing reflection prompts for their course journals, as well as other classroom practices that I will discuss below, has improved their capacity for observation and critical thinking skills. Since I have implemented this CBL best practice, I have noticed that students are better able to "connect the dots." There is research that demonstrates how this practice makes a big difference in students' critical understanding of historical and sociopolitical conditions (Collier & Driscoll, 1999). In addition to the more sophisticated understanding of certain concepts and issues, many of my students tend to mention (on their final course reflections) important life lessons learned through their CBL experience, including: gaining compassion, patience, understanding, perspective, and a deeper notion of their own privilege. These experiences are at the root of their transformation into agents of social change as they move towards promoting social justice.

The world is our classroom. While students may memorize definitions for immigration, immigrant, migrant farm worker, second-generation, racism, sexism, achievement gap, etc., those pale in comparison to how they are able to understand these concepts after taking a CBL course. These words gain a much deeper meaning because the concepts become personalized. An immigrant is not only a statistic anymore—or a threat to the U.S.—but rather the little boy they have been helping all semester with his math homework, someone who they see struggling with English, eager to earn good grades and be a doctor someday. All of a sudden, the negative perception of illegal immigrant is now the sweet and soft-spoken mother of the siblings they have been mentoring, someone they come to admire when they learn how she risked her life escaping unimaginable violence in her country in order to give her children a chance at life. It's about humanizing those who have become dehumanized in this society and it works not only for majority (white) students, but also for minorities. Even my Latino/a students—who usually come from Texas or California—have expressed the impact that learning about other Latinos (Latino/a is an umbrella term that erases many differences based on nationality, race, ethnicity, class, gender, etc.) has had on their education; it's not the same to grow up in a Latino neighborhood in Los Angeles as it is to grow up Latino in a small Midwestern city, where Latinos are truly a minority.

Remind Yourself That There's Not One "Right" Way to Do CBL

When I first started teaching courses with a CBL component I found myself facing challenges that I was not used to in the academic setting, namely, unpredictability. Yes, we can argue that this is part and parcel of teaching (we can't determine who our students are, their mood, their academic drive, etc.), but introducing an outside element (CBL community partner) into the mix adds another degree of unpredictability, especially if the agency you work with is a small non-profit. Some of the challenges my students and I have faced include (a) difficulty with transportation to site such as lack of student drivers and/or cars, (b) unexpected site closings such as due to weather or emergency repairs, (c) securing funding and/or help for special events or projects, and (d) my students' lack of experience teaching children or dealing with special needs students. When facing such challenges, it is not uncommon for students to voice their frustrations, or for us, professors, to feel the same. To address these challenges, we try to have a backup transportation plan for each day, have asked for funding from units at the university that support CBL, and maintain an ongoing dialogue with students about the challenges they are facing at *La Casa de Amistad* in order to help them navigate those obstacles. Above all, I have learned, with time, that one of the requirements of teaching a CBL course implies dealing with a certain degree of unpredictability. Learning that not everything is under our control and that one needs to go with the flow, so to speak, has been crucial in my experience. Learning to cope with setbacks is also a powerful life lesson for students and gracefully navigating unplanned situations also helps build a stronger partnership.

Along the same lines, the idea of being willing to make adjustments also applies to the way in which we envision and design our CBL courses. Over the years, the contents of my courses have changed. I have added new texts and adjusted contents in order to expose students to materials that I consider to be more in consonance with the types of experiences my students are bound to have at *La Casa de Amistad*. This has meant that I have designed units on Mexican-American literature and culture (including the works I mention above) as well as Central American letters, despite the fact that my primary research area is Latino/a Caribbean letters. Some of the texts and films discussed in this unit include William Archila's *The Art of Exile* (2009), Victor Montejo's *Sculpted Stones* (1995), Quique Avilés' *The Immigrant Museum* (2003), and the film *Voces Inocentes* (2007). Other times, it has meant tweaking the syllabus to cover topics related to the local Latino/a community and/or organizing Latino/a neighborhood visits (i.e., mini-immersions) for my students. These visits have always been organized by our community partner in order to help our students learn more about the community beyond the walls of *La Casa de Amistad*. The staff at *La Casa* sees this as a tool to enhance the connection between my students and the children, since most live in the surrounding area. It also has the purpose of aiding to revitalize that area, since students learn about restaurants and businesses that they can—and many do—visit in the future. Overall, as our community partner puts it, it's a win-win situation because my students learn about the neighborhood, and *La Casa* benefits by promoting the area and fomenting interaction between the university and the community.

And finally, being willing to make adjustments has also meant for me to allow more room for creativity in terms of my students' work. For instance, for the first three years I taught CBL courses, my students produced a final project in groups, and with the help of children at *La Casa*. These included bilingual creative projects that showcased poems, essays, and/or artwork by *La Casa's* children. Their objective was to encourage creativity and literacy among the children at *La Casa* (therefore working to advance the mission of the organization). Other students produced what we called research briefs, short investigative projects focused on topics proposed by *La Casa's* staff—and based on their students' and families' needs—that they thought would be helpful to the local Latino/a community. Over the years, my students produced dozens of these research briefs on a wide range of topics, including: race and ethnicity in the local Latino community, health, opportunities for higher education for undocumented students, Afro-Latinos, Central American Latinos, bilingual education, and even one on the history of *La Casa de Amistad*.

Over a year ago, following a conversation with *La Casa's* staff (it's important to communicate frequently), I decided to adopt another model. Now, my students interview a student throughout the semester and write their profile. These documents are also shared with *La Casa* and they in turn use them in their grant applications as supporting materials. The experience has been invaluable to my students, who have learned a great deal about the students they have worked with at *La Casa*, and have developed a deeper connection with them and their families. This type of project is an example of a best practice in CBL partnerships because as Lemieux and Allen (2007) explain, "Community service emphasizes students' contributions to the community and the development of students' civic responsibilities" (p. 310). Every semester I meet with *La Casa's* staff to give each other feedback and think of strategies that can help both sides the following semester. Most of these types of projects are not what we consider the standard literature paper. However, I believe that a significant aspect of engaging in a CBL partnership is giving a final tangible product that is useful to the community partner. This can take the shape of a class, group, or individual project and the nature of it should be determined by the community partner's needs as well as your own learning goals for your students.

Best Practices in the Classroom

Over the years, I have come to the conclusion that a successful CBL course—in any discipline—should include these four pillars: CBL readings, class journals, built-in CBL discussion times, and final course reflections. Every semester, the first assignment my students have is to read a couple of academic articles about CBL. Not only do these clarify what CBL entails and its repercussions in the classroom, they also allow them to reflect on their own expectations. It's productive to have students hold on to written reflections about their expectations at the beginning of the semester because it is always fun and instructive to compare them to those at the end of the semester. Journaling, both about course contents and my students' experiences at *La Casa de Amistad*, has been instrumental in their learning process. I usually include journal prompts in my syllabus so that they have some sort of direction in case they need it. Such prompts include questions such as:

1. How have the materials read enhanced your service experience?
2. How has your service experience deepened your understanding of texts studied in class?
3. How is your experience at *La Casa* helping you gain a deeper and more nuanced understanding of key concepts such as: poverty, discrimination, education gap, racism, internal colonialism, transnationalism, sexism, machismo, Latino/a, etc.?
4. What social issues do you see reflected in the literature and at *La Casa*?
5. What social problems are you discovering that need to be addressed?
6. How can you be an agent of change in our common search for social justice?

Without journaling about their experiences, students are more likely to go through the motions without seriously reflecting on the impact that CBL is having on their education and personal growth. Group discussion about their experiences at *La Casa de Amistad* is also a core component of my courses.

Just as students are expected to carve out a space to reflect on their experiences, and how those connect to the course content, it's also important to process them as a group. Class discussions about CBL allow students to share what they have learned and to ask questions to each other about how to approach certain situations. I often witness my students bonding as they share memories of certain children at *La Casa* or of specific memorable moments. It is a space for students to teach each other based on their personal experiences and to share their learning process. Another important piece in a CBL course is a final reflection (something my students complete in addition to a final paper based solely on literary analysis of a Latino/a literary work). The aim of these brief reflections (4–5 pages) is to give the opportunity to students to formally reflect on the connection between the course contents and their CBL experience.

Similar to their journals, I provide students with a set of prompts that allows them to structure their reflection. This is honestly one of my favorite aspects of my courses since these reflections often provide concrete evidence of my students' personal growth and increased sense of civic engagement (especially in relation to the Latino/a community). Comments such as CBL "made me feel part of the local community," "made me more engaged academically," "made me a better person," "allowed me to gain perspective and appreciate the opportunities I've had," effectively capture a range of learning outcomes. Year after year, one of the messages that stands out from my students' reflections and/or course evaluations is that without the experience at *La Casa de Amistad*, the course material would not have had the same degree of impact, because CBL has promoted a deeper comprehension of the issues addressed in class. And the community benefits from this partnership as well. At the most basic level, like many small organizations that depend almost exclusively on volunteers to run their programs, being able to count on the consistent presence of 15–20 of my students each semester has helped those programs run more efficiently.

In addition, over the years, staff members at *La Casa de Amistad* have noted how their young students have made significant improvements in their academic performance. The rate of retention of students at *La Casa's Crece Conmigo* and *Adelante América* programs (in which my students volunteer) has improved. There has also been a culture change in terms of their students' plans to pursue higher education. *La Casa* has put more resources into preparing middle and high school students for college, and my students' encouragement and help in this area has contributed to this success. This is a significant achievement given that six years ago, when our partnership was established, most students did not consider attending college. *La Casa's* students and families, my students, and myself, have benefited greatly from this partnership, and we will work to continue in a spirit of reciprocity.

Conclusion

CBL is a pedagogy that mixes the knowledge learned in the classroom with the knowledge that students acquire while performing volunteer service at a community organization. There is not one standard definition for CBL, the same way that there's not a one-size-fits-all model. Students in a course could all work at the same organization or disperse among various community organizations; there could be a minimum hour requirement (say ten hours per semester), or it could be a semester-long commitment, etc. Academic rigor should never be compromised, that is, CBL is not meant to substitute for class time. A central concern should be to maintain a balance between the needs of the community partner/organization (for instance, the need for tutors) and the needs of the students and the professor based on the learning goals of a particular course. Most importantly, students are not going to the organization to allegedly save anyone. They volunteer there in order to learn by complementing the knowledge they gain in the classroom.

One of the most powerful ways to combat racist and negative stereotypes about U.S. Latinos/as, or any group for that matter, is to learn about and interact with that particular community. CBL offers the opportunity to combine these two key aspects: the personal and the intellectual. It's not the same, although it is important, to learn about a people or group "from the outside"—limited to the four walls of a classroom—than to work and interact with that group. One aspect fortifies the other; what you learn in the classroom helps you understand the experiences at the community partner's organization, while at the same time your experiences there inform your understanding of the academic material. Students' eyes tend to open up to all sorts of biases and structural barriers that affect the lives of minorities in this country, not just Latinos/as. Usually, their sense of perspective is amplified. As one of my students once said about my CBL course, "It's all about things that I would never think about on my own because I'm a little white girl." With this newfound knowledge comes a great sense of responsibility, and students are often moved to do what they can to make a difference. Isn't this what academia should strive for?

It is precisely because of how transformative it has been for me to teach U.S. Latino/a literature with a CBL component, and because I can see the incredible potential we have before us, that I want to encourage (especially) faculty teaching minority literatures, to consider adding CBL to their courses. When you read a student's journal reflection where s/he states that, "if more people could study this literature and get to know kids like those at *La Casa*, there would be more peace and understanding in this world," you know that this is something worth sharing. CBL can be easily implemented in all disciplines, but I think those of us in literature have an advantage. We can use the stories, poems, and novels we teach to open our students' eyes. But, we can also provide them the opportunity to break out of their comfort zone and become, if only temporarily, part of the community they're learning about. U.S. cities and towns are replete with community centers and non-profit organizations serving U.S. Latinos, African-Americans, Asian-Americans, Native Americans, the undocumented, and many other groups whose stories we need to hear. Let's make those stories come alive by keeping it real—in and outside the classroom.

References

Abes, E. S., Jackson, G., & Jones, S. R. (2002). Factors that motivate and deter faculty use of service-learning. *Michigan Journal of Community Service Learning, 9*(1), 5–17.

Archila, W. (2009). *The art of exile.* Tempe, AZ: Bilingual Press/Editorial Bilingüe.

Avilés, Q. (2003). *The immigrant museum.* Mexico: Sol & Soul.

Butin, D. (2006). The limits of service-learning in higher education. *The Review of Higher Education, 29*(4), 473–498.

Castañeda, M. (2008). Transformative learning through community engagement. *Latino Studies, 6,* 319–326.

Cisneros, S. (1984). *The house on Mango Street.* New York, NY: Vintage.

Collier, P. J., & Driscoll, A. (1999). Multiple methods of student reflection in service learning classes. *The Journal of General Education, 48*(4), 280–292.

Gonzáles, R. (1967). *I am Joaquin: Yo Soy Joaquin.* Publisher not identified.

Hellebrandt, J., & Varona, L. T. (Eds.). (1999). *Construyendo puentes (building bridges): Concepts and models for service-learning in Spanish.* Washington, DC: American Association for Higher Education.

Jacoby, B. (Ed.). (2003). *Building partnerships for service-learning.* San Francisco, CA: Jossey-Bass.

Lemieux, C., & Allen, P. D. (2007). Service learning in social work education: The state of knowledge, pedagogical practicalities, and practice conundrums. *Journal of Social Work Education, 43*(2), 309–325.

McKay, V. C., & Rozee, P. D. (2004). Characteristics of faculty who adopt community service learning pedagogy. *Michigan Journal of Community Service Learning, 10*(2), 21–33.

Mitchell, T. (2008). Traditional vs. critical service-learning: Engaging the literature to differentiate two models. *Michigan Journal of Community Service Learning, 14*(2), 50–65.

Montejo, V. (1995). *Piedras labradas* (*Sculpted stones*). Evanston, IL: Curbstone Press.

O'Meara, K. (2003). Reframing incentives and rewards for community service learning and academic outreach. *Journal of Higher Education Outreach and Engagement, 8*(2), 201–220.

Plann, S. (2002). Latinos and literacy: An upper-division Spanish course with service learning. *Hispania, 85*(2), 330–338.

Rivera, T. (1987). *... y no se lo tragó la tierra / And the earth did not devour him.* Houston, TX: Arte Publico Press.

Rosales, F. A. (1996). *Chicano!: The history of the Mexican American civil rights movement* [DVD]. Houston, TX: Arte Público Press.

Viramontes, H. M. (1995). *Under the feet of Jesus.* New York, NY: Penguin.

Voces inocentes. (2007). [DVD]. Los Angeles, CA: Warner Home Video.

Ward, K. (1998). Addressing academic culture: Service learning, organizations, and faculty work. *New Directions for Teaching and Learning, 1998*(73), 73–80.

Ward, K., & Wolf-Wendel, L. (2000). Community-centered service learning: Moving from doing for to doing with. *American Behavioral Scientist, 43*(5), 767–780.

5. *Public Humanities and Community-Engaged Learning: Building Strategies for Undergraduate Research and Civic Engagement*

Clara Román-Odio, Patricia Mota, and Amelia Dunnell

A significant body of literature assessing the impact of community-engaged learning (CEL) on mastery of academic content, career choice, and civic engagement suggests that linking CEL to academic study is an effective and valuable pedagogy (Boss, 1994; Castañeda, 2008; Cohen & Kinsey, 1994; Danielson & Fallon, 2007; Mathieu, 2005; Wu, 2007).[1] As Linda Adler-Kassner, Robert Crooks, and Ann Watters (1997) assert, "service learning in the context of Composition can increase students' conception of the social far more effectively than either textbooks or experience alone" as students address the "causes of social problems and not just the symptoms" (p. 5). Other scholars claim the ethical and civic promise of CEL because it can foster democratic and social justice values and encourage students to take on the perspectives of others (Cushman, 1999; Warren, 1998; Weah, Simmons, & Hall, 2000). Yet, reflecting about the role of the university as a public good, some scholars ask, what exactly is CEL and what is its place in colleges and universities, particularly those near communities in need? For Sonia Nieto (2000) "at the heart of these questions is the issue of difference, meritocracy, unequal access to power, and the very purpose of education" (p. ix). Hence, she asserts that we should view service learning through a "critical multicultural lens" through which we could see the notion of civic responsibility within a context of "a pluralistic but unequal society" (Nieto, 200, pp. ix–x). Characterizing the task of universities as "urgent," Nancy

Cantor (2004), former chancellor of the University of Illinois at Urbana-Champaign, further argues that:

> Universities can fulfill this mission by offering contexts for the exchanges of people and ideas that are sustained, rather than one-shot efforts over a day, a week, or even a semester. These exchanges must appeal to people of different expertise and backgrounds. They should allow for open-mindedness, permit the suspension of everyday norms and judgments, and give standing to everyone, across generations. (p. 20)

Cantor (2004) offers the arts as a prototype for this type of exchanges because in her words, "the arts stand to the side of daily life, and they allow the expression of self and social tension in a safe way" (p. 20).

Following Cantor's insight, in this chapter we explore the intersection of the public humanities and community-engaged learning as a powerful strategy to open up new spaces for social dialogue. We argue that at their best, public humanities and community-engaged learning can strengthen undergraduate research and create, as Cantor suggests, a context for the exchange of peoples and ideas that maintain the university as a public good. We will examine a case study, Latinos in Rural America (LiRA), to illustrate ways in which the university can help shape environments where people from different backgrounds, races, ethnicities and generations can engage as equals in conversations that can bridge the gown-town divide. The chapter will discuss the process of putting the project together from logistics to curation of materials, and the development of the CEL component to the exhibit. The last section of the chapter addresses student surveys and the community response to LiRA. Overall, outcomes show that public humanities and community-engaged learning can promote not only intercultural development but also civic responsibility and commitment to social justice work.[2] Before describing LiRA, we will briefly digress to clarify terminology and how the public humanities inform this project.

The public humanities, like the arts, enable interpretation of the past and envisioning of the future. Particular to the public humanities is their emphasis on the analysis and exchange of stories, which can help us to engage more thoughtfully with our surroundings, including diverse cultures. Community—engaged learning, for its part, can be broadly defined as a pedagogy that builds on partnerships between institutions of higher education and surrounding communities to identify and work with public issues that have both academic and public life dimensions. CEL is change-oriented and finds research questions in the needs and knowledge of the community. It aims at preparing students for an active civic life by combining classroom learning objectives and skill development with social action geared at empowering community groups. As a public humanities project emerging from community-engaged learning, LiRA aims at intercultural development, a way of imagining a shared future that includes the interaction of different ethnic, linguistic, and racial groups based around a shared appreciation of place—in this case, Knox County, Ohio.

In order for this work to be done effectively, it is important to tell the story of the place and the stories of its people, with the focus here on the small but growing Latino population. We need new models of intercultural development to ensure a rural sustainability that includes Latinos as valued community members. The public humanities can play an important and strategic role in cultural brokerage, by telling new stories of distinctive rural communities and the people who live there. LiRA extends the public humanities goal of telling richer and more nuanced stories than those offered by mass media culture, which typically portrays Latinos in rural areas as only migrant farm workers, unattached to place. While our project includes the migrant farm worker experience, it also gathers a wide range of personal stories from diverse individuals to offer a window into the life of the Latino/a population in Knox County.

Latinos in Rural America: Stories of Cultural Heritage, Values, and Aspirations

Latinos in Rural America (LiRA) is a public humanities project that seeks to broaden knowledge, engagement with and understanding of the Latino/a experience in rural Ohio.[3] Rooted as it is in an oral history approach, it bears both the limitations and benefits that this entails. Of necessity, it is restricted to sharing the experiences of only a few of the members of this growing community. As such, it is not, nor does it pretend to be, representative in a statistical sense. Rather, its key merit is that it is rooted in interviews and direct personal interactions with members of the community that represent diverse areas of activity, social and economic conditions, stages of life, and aspirations within the broad social fabric of Knox County.[4] LiRA required hundreds of hours of research, interviews, transcriptions, and translations by Clara Román-Odio, Professor of Spanish and Director of Latino/a Studies at Kenyon College, and two undergraduate Spanish majors and Latino/a Studies concentrators, Patricia Mota '16 and Amelia Dunnell '17.

The project culminated in a public bilingual exhibition that traveled locally and throughout Ohio, December 2015 April 2016.[5] LiRA also resulted in two other community-engaged learning projects developed by students in one of Román-Odio's Spanish courses, Introduction to Chicano/a Cultural Studies

(SPAN 380), in Fall 2015: a pamphlet to serve as a primer on cross-cultural interactions, and a class at the Salvation Army in Mount Vernon, Ohio to help local Latino/a youths prepare for college.[6] The flier about Latino/a culture, values, and communication norms was distributed at the county Health Department, in local schools, and at social service organizations. At the college-prep class requested by Latino parents, Kenyon students are currently helping high-school and middle-school students familiarize themselves with the application process, research potential schools, and study for the SAT and ACT.[7] The LiRA exhibit is displayed permanently online through Digital Kenyon, a repository for the College's scholarly work.[8]

The project emerged from questions brought by a member of a Knox County community organization. She asked, "Where are the Latinos in Knox County? How can we reach them?" We took it as a challenge to answer these questions and launched the project aiming to:

1. increase knowledge, engagement with, and understanding of the Latino/a experience in rural Knox County;
2. develop intercultural exchange and relationships between the local Latino/a community and other Knox County and Ohio residents;
3. increase awareness of Latino/a contributions to the life of Ohio;
4. offer Latino/a youth new opportunities to interpret their past and articulate their future and, in this way, better gain access to relevant educational and social goods;
5. establish partnerships with local and state organizations and researchers to support intercultural development between Latinos and other state residents.

We wanted to learn about the history of the Latino/a population in Knox County, their journey stories (the past), what and where is home (the present). We wanted to hear about their values and cultural norms, about personal and community aspirations, and about their perceptions of diversity and inclusion. We conceived the project within the framework of the public humanities hoping to create an opportunity for intercultural dialogue and social justice engagement.

The exhibit that resulted from this effort consisted of ten panels with text in both English and Spanish that presented the content of the interviews. The exhibit also contained a video with captions in both languages, presenting the participants in conversation. Viewers could interact with the project by providing feedback after having seen the exhibit; a critical component of LiRA given that such reflection would, we hoped, lower intercultural barriers by encouraging viewers to engaged with their own perceptions of Latinos and how, if at all, these were changed or influenced by the exhibit. As part of the exhibit, we included two brochures (in English and Spanish). One presented selected images and bibliographical information from the exhibit. The other was a primer, in pamphlet form, to provide background knowledge and information on cultural roots and communication norms for successful interactions with Latinos, including tips to better bridge cultural gaps. The process of putting the project in place—from logistics to curation of materials to design, production, and the development of the community-engaged learning component to the opening of the exhibit—took approximately eighteen months. In what follows, we describe four key elements of this process.

Funding

External funding was indispensable to the creation of the exhibit. Hence, we sought to identify agencies that would have interest in the project. The primary funding of the work came from the Columbus, Ohio-based nonprofit organization Ohio Humanities, which supported the two main stages of the project: the community-based research phase (summer and fall 2015) and the dissemination of the project (fall 2015 and spring 2016). The Andrew W. Mellon Foundation Digital Scholarship program provided additional funding to digitize and archive collected materials. We also sought and obtained institutional support from Kenyon College to provide a permanent home for the collection at Digital Kenyon, a repository of research, scholarship, and creative exchange. In addition, the Kenyon College Summer Scholars program enabled student summer research and training.

Institutional Requirements and Training

The Institutional Review Board (IRB) at Kenyon College is careful to avoid unnecessary risks, particularly when engaging with vulnerable populations like children. Even though *LiRA* is based on oral history methodologies, which in some instances are exempted from IRB requirements, the LiRA research team received CITI training for research with human subjects. The training sensitized the team to the importance of protecting the privacy and preferences of participants. For example, to respect the preferences of those who did not wish to be videotaped or to disclose his or her identity, we created bilingual consent forms for interviews, video, audio files, and photos. We also created bilingual release forms that would enable the donation of interviews, as well as bilingual assent forms for the youth. Such forms framed the interview process in fairly standard and friendly ways. Additionally, we undertook training in oral history, the use of video cameras, and elements of video documentation.

Community Outreach

Community outreach was a key initial step that took approximately a couple of months. In order to connect with the local Latinos, we identified community leaders who served as a node of interaction for local Latinos. In our case, this was the manager of the Mexican restaurant in town, Fiesta Mexicana. We also engaged with the local Catholic Church to request their support for our outreach effort. This resulted in an initial meeting attended by approximately forty community members, confirming their enthusiasm for the project. Through a survey distributed at this meeting, we learned how Latinos wanted to participate, their particular interests and areas of concern, and the ways in which Kenyon students and faculty could engage with the community. To them, LiRA would offer a way to achieve important communal goals, such as improved access to educational opportunities for their youth as well as making known, in the public sphere, their goals and aspirations. This was important because Latinos in the area had experienced disparities in educational opportunities and, in some instances, a sense of isolation. Likewise, local social organizations that regularly interact with Latinos expressed concerns about language and cultural barriers keeping Latinos away.

Participant Interviews and Analysis of Materials

Research and the creation of materials involved a number of logistical steps. First, there was the selection and enrollment of participants. Guidance from the Oral History Institute (Kenyon College, June 4–6, 2015) suggested inclusion of about a dozen interviews to facilitate curation of materials in a reasonable amount of time. Given this limitation, we established an interviewee profile that would allow us to be as inclusive as possible; this included age, gender, nationality, ethnicity, occupation and economic condition as critical categories for final selection. After identifying participants, we defined the intended audiences for the project: Latinos (both rural and urban in Knox County and Ohio), organizations that interact with Latinos regularly such as social services organizations and local schools with an emerging Latino population, broader-based regional and/or national organizations with a common interest in bringing visibility and cultural presence to Latinos in the United States. We, then, identified venues for the exhibit and discussed schedules and facilities.[9]Finally, we sought advice from academic experts for the design of the online/on-site reflection surveys. This element aimed at developing opportunities for community building and relationships among Ohioans, including Latinos. The questionnaire would help participants to reflect about their own beliefs, values, and community aspirations, and to understand and engage with the diverse local Latino culture. We were interested in measuring attitudes toward, and knowledge about, the Knox County Latino population, as well as perceptions of diversity and inclusion. The questionnaire was bilingual (English and Spanish) and presented both online and on paper to accommodate visitor preferences.

In planning for the interviews, we considered how to structure the interview time, how to ask questions, and how to make follow-up comments. We used the abbreviated life story interview model that Brooke Bryan (Antioch College) recommended in the Oral History Institute.[10] We went from specific questions to open-ended ones and had common questions as well as questions tailored to each participant. We interviewed two college professors, four workers in the business sector, three agricultural workers, the head of a social service organization, an athlete, and youth of various ages, representing a range of experiences, cultural origins, and personal and family values. Questions reflected the interviewees' context. Based on our goals, we made a list of fifteen potential participants, made phone calls, and set up appointments. By mid-June, we were on the road. Project director and student summer scholars conducted research on and with local Latino community members during the months of June and July 2015 to produce the bulk of the materials, including archival work on the history of Latinos in Knox County, video interviews of local community members, short multigenerational narratives, and photographs of community members.

Research and Oral History Outcomes

In this section, we discuss research outcomes including demographic background of Latinos in Knox County and analysis of the oral history collected. We highlight Latinos' distinctive challenges and rewards as they conduct their daily lives in rural Ohio. We trace their journey stories, cultural values and bicultural experiences, and interpret recurring themes that emerge from our personal interactions with members of the community. From the intermingling of these voices emerges a picture that informs the interest of this immigrant community to become integrated into the broad fabric of Knox County through improved educational opportunities and the inclusion of key elements of their cultural identity into the larger community.

Demographic Background

From the available historical records of Knox County, we learned that until the mid-twentieth century, Kenyon College was the only institution to document Latinos in the county, who came to attend the college. Until the middle of the 20th century, no other local historical records documented this population. In the latter half of the 20th century, the county records show two other Latino residents living in Mount Vernon. In 2013, there were 789 Hispanic people living in Knox County, which is about 1.3% of the population. While small, that amount was double that of the preceding decade, and the growth likely will continue given that Latinos are driving a demographic transformation in Ohio.[11] Our research on poverty levels, income, and educational attainment indicates that among Latinos in Knox County, 67% are employed and 33% are actively searching for a job. In contrast, among whites, 93% are employed, while 7.4% are unemployed. Interestingly, more whites than Latinos fall under the poverty line in Knox County[12] although the median household income and per capita income in Knox County tend to be lower for Latinos compared to whites.[13] In terms of education, Latinos in Knox County are more likely than whites to finish high school but less likely to continue into higher education. In part, this may reflect that Latinos in Knox County do not have the support systems that would enable a path to higher education, such as bilingual education, affordable college preparatory courses, or bilingual workshops for parents of Latino students aspiring to a college degree.[14]

Analysis of Interviews

The research team transcribed, translated, and analyzed the interviews, searching for recurring themes, areas of concern and aspirations. From these conversations emerged key themes that help frame the experiences of Latinos in Knox County. We characterize these as: circular journeys, a sense of place and displacement, values and culture, intercultural identities, visibility/invisibility, and dreams and aspirations. Each of these themes was used to headline the individual panels of the exhibit. Highlighted below are the main findings in each of these areas.

Circular Journeys

While it might be logical to conceive of migration as a one-way occurrence, this was not the case for the Latinos we interviewed. The proximity of many Latin American countries to the United States, the strong ties that exist between extended families, and the rich cultural identities of many Latino immigrants all seem to contribute to what we called circular journeys: Latinos' physical and emotional back-and-forth between their homelands and the United States. Participants included, for example, a Venezuelan shuttled between divorced parents in different countries throughout her childhood; a Puerto Rican woman who was born in the United States but quickly left for her parents' homeland, only to return years later; and a Mexican father who brought his American-born children to Mexico for three years so that they would learn Spanish and become engaged with Mexican culture. Others spoke of emotional circular journeys—those moments of return taking place within their hearts that they cannot realize in a physical way.

Latino immigrants may choose to come to the United States for better work or study opportunities or to reunite with their families. However, few Latinos in Knox County ever seek to abandon their cultural heritage. They stay connected through visits to their countries of origin, whether yearly or once in a lifetime, for only a couple of days or for several years. Extended family networks ensure that they always have a place to stay, should they choose to return. As some of the participants explain.

> I came here when I was about maybe eight, and then went back to Mexico when I was about fifteen, sixteen, then came back. When my kids were growing up, I took them to Mexico for three years … so they got the Spanish completely, and a little bit of Mexican culture. (José Ávalos, owner of Fiesta Mexicana restaurant, Mount Vernon)

> I went to Georgetown [University] to do law, thinking that. … I wanted to be the Secretary of Education of Puerto Rico [laughs]. After finishing half my degree, I returned to Puerto Rico. I returned to the United States because of Hurricane George, which destroyed 98 percent of the electric grid on the island. It was a terrible devastation in 1998. Then my husband found work in Ohio, and we moved here in 2001. (Ivonne García, associate professor of English, Kenyon College, Gambier)

> They put everything on a big boat and we sailed to Venezuela and eventually ended up in Caracas. When my parents got divorced, I was around seven or eight, my mom, who really at that point felt very strongly that her daughters should grow up American, came back to Oklahoma, and that's where I grew up. We went back every summer during break. When my grandfather, who was the real patriarch of the family, died, we ended up moving back for a while. (Balinda Craig-Quijada, professor of dance, Kenyon College, Gambier)

> So, I decided to leave to change my life for my daughters, so they wouldn't lack anything. Thanks to God they liked it here, and it's a relief that they continue to be happy, that their smiles don't fade. But yes, for the opportunity of work,

> I have been more well off, more peaceful, yes. (Amneris Pérez-Román, Knox County Community Hospital administrative assistant, Mount Vernon)

Whatever the nature of these journeys, the decision to immigrate to the United States is not always easy, but neither is it final.

A Sense of Place and Displacement

Latinos in Knox County experience both a sense of place and a sense of displacement. They belong to the larger local community, yet belonging also involves traveling through unsettled territories, exploring what for many of them is new, and transplanting what they brought with them: family values, culture, and stories. Similar to what Gloria Anzaldúa (1999) describes in her book *Borderlands/La Frontera: The New Mestiza*, rural Ohio Latinos travel into what is new, but with their homes on their backs, metaphorically: "I am a turtle, wherever I go I carry 'home' on my back" (p. 43). Many are born on wheels and experience the hunger for belonging and stability that results from displacement. Yet, they root themselves in family, faith, and work to create a sense of place.

In Knox County, the Latinos we interviewed have diverse networks that enable a sense of belonging. For example, a Spanish Mass offered every last Sunday of the month at Mount Vernon's St. Vincent De Paul Catholic Church offers Latinos an opportunity for inward exploration, towards the core of what sustains them spiritually, and for praying in Spanish in the company of other Latinos. The harvest crew for a large local orchard is almost exclusively comprised of Latinos. The local restaurant, Fiesta Mexicana, closes to the public several times every year to celebrate with its employees and families and thus helps to foster a sense of community among local Latinos. Kenyon College supports the scholarship and teaching activities of professors from many Latin American countries, including Argentina, Cuba, Mexico, Puerto Rico, and Venezuela. Some of the participants explain their sense of place and displacement as follows.

> We [Puerto Ricans] are a migrant community that is continuous, that doesn't only cross one-way; one crosses in both directions and on multiple occasions. And that creates, to a certain extent, a life experience in which one doesn't belong to one place. If there were a country for the misfit toys, you know, that's where I would feel okay. (Ivonne García, associate professor of English, Kenyon College, Gambier)

> Here in Mount Vernon, well, we found a church, which is St. Vincent De Paul. I have become involved here because, thanks to God, they hold Mass in Spanish every month, and we participate by reading the scriptures, collecting the

> offerings, the petitions. And so, now we are a little bit more involved. (Irene Rivera, manager of Fiesta Mexicana restaurant, Mount Vernon)

> I really liked living here. Now that I'm in Columbus, I do miss it. I like it a lot because it's a small community, so all the Latinos know each other. I liked it a lot that for the holidays, businesses closed and all the families got together. I miss them a lot. We were a community. (Vanessa Ávalos, raised in Mount Vernon, now a college student at Ohio State University, Columbus)

These testimonies illustrate how Latinos have shaped and have been shaped by Knox County as individuals, families, and communities, and how they negotiate the crossing of physical and cultural borders in order to build a sense of place.

Values and Culture

Within the varied group of those who identify as Latinos in rural Ohio, family, education, faith, and food culture are defining values. Despite the distance that separates Latinos from their countries of origin, this population makes a priority of holding on to their cultural roots. As a growing community in Knox County, those interviewed shared with us the particularities that make up Latino culture. A strong sense of *familismo*—the centrality of family ties, both immediate and extended—is instilled from a young age (Smith-Morris, Morales-Campos, Alvarez, & Turner, 2013). Older family members insist that younger members be respectful and that they understand the importance of honor and hard work. *Familismo* is nurtured through the preparation of food and the experience of eating together, and *la sobremesa* (table-talk) offers social opportunities for family members to give advice and strengthen friendship (Smith-Morris, Morales-Campos, Alvarez, & Turner, 2013). In the words of several participants:

> Food was like a really important aspect growing up, and we had a lot of conversations around the table. (Gigi González-Cottrell, lieutenant for the Salvation Army, Mount Vernon)

> I think because of that connection to the extended family, there's a feeling that you will go to extreme measures to help your family. If they come to visit, they can stay as long as they want. If they want to send their kids, and my cousins and my cousins' kids to come visit, you never say no to family. (Balinda Craig-Quijada, professor of dance, Kenyon College, Gambier)

The conviction that education is a foothold to the "American dream" places certain expectations on children to do well academically. Language barriers may inhibit parents' ability to communicate effectively within the school system, but Latinos do whatever they can to ensure that their children obtain more educational opportunities. As some interviewees explain:

> Education was always important, and the expectation was that I would do well in school. And because of that expectation, a lot of the education just like fell on me, I didn't really have a lot of help from [my family] because they didn't understand a lot of the schoolwork that I was doing. (Gigi González-Cottrell, lieutenant for the Salvation Army, Mount Vernon)

Although not everyone identifies as Roman Catholic, for many Latinos living in Knox County the church greatly influences family life and community involvement, and it serves as a place of social gathering and communion.

> Another thing that my parents instilled in me was the value of our Christian beliefs that we have. We went to church every single Sunday. My parents were always at church. I was always at church. You know, we only just didn't go to church on Sundays, but we went to church probably like four days out of the week. (Gigi González-Cottrell, lieutenant for the Salvation Army, Mount Vernon)

Although on the surface Latinos may look different than the majority of Knox County residents, the collectivism of Latino culture is complementary to the ideals of hard work and effort that are fundamental to rural America.

> Just like any Latino, my family instilled in me the value of family first, the value of becoming successful, achieving my desires, and always doing my best to try to help. (Vanessa Ávalos, raised in Mount Vernon, now a college student at Ohio State University, Columbus)

In sum, defining values for Latinos in Knox County include: family or devotion to the familia, a tight knit unit that includes extended family, preserving Spanish, their native language, receiving an education as a means to a better life, traditions or celebrating through fiestas and holidays, sharing food, and *la sobremesa* or table-talk after meals.

Bicultural Identities

While acknowledging the tension between assimilation to United States culture and preservation of Latino cultural identity, those interviewed enumerated the ways in which being bicultural enriches their lives. Most participants are bilingual and plan to pass on that bilingualism to their children someday (if they haven't already). Many also voiced the desire to proudly display their biculturalism to other residents of Knox County. For some, this has a practical benefit: being bilingual opens doors to job opportunities. For others, biculturalism is a tool for engaging in daily life and understanding the world more broadly.

> Just being able to speak two languages very well, it just helps so much, especially if you're looking for a career or an occupation one day. (Mario Álvarez-León, middle school student, Mount Vernon)

> [Biculturalism] just gives you a broader picture of the world. It just helps me see the world in a better way. And it helps me to relate to other cultures that aren't necessarily of my own, at least for me more easily. (Gigi González-Cottrell, lieutenant for the Salvation Army, Mount Vernon)

Some individuals expressed unease at the prospect of identifying as bicultural in Knox County. A high school student spoke of being misunderstood, not because of a language barrier but because of negative stereotyping; another recalled a lack of school resources that would have eased the transition into the new school environment. And in identifying with a specific ethnic background, it is possible to feel somewhat distant from mainstream American culture, which historically has promulgated the notion of the cultural melting pot. As expressed by some interviewees:

> When I talk to my friends they're always interested in it [my ethnicity]. They're like, 'That's so cool.' Others don't really accept it. They didn't really understand me, not because of the language, but because of our culture. They go based on what they see on the news and the things other people say. They don't really understand that we are just people like them. They believe that we came here to get their jobs. I know one student at my school that used to bully me because of it [my ethnicity]. I really started not wanting to go to school. And I mean some students don't understand that what they say actually hurts another person. (María Esmeralda Villa, high school student, Mount Vernon)

> At the beginning, I felt alienated. I was shy. Many people just looked at me because I had just arrived and didn't know English. There were only three Latinos in my school. There was a translator at school, but he was only with me one full day, the first week of classes. After that, he used to come in the mornings because he also had to help my brother. (High school student, Mount Vernon)

Some project participants have been bicultural their entire lives, while others came to embrace this later in life. Bicultural identity is influenced not only by self-perceptions and community acceptance (or lack of it) but also by immigration status. In some cases, achieving citizenship or residency greatly affects how individuals perceive their identity. One Mexican man characterized his achieving U.S. citizenship as a milestone in cementing his bicultural identity.

> I came to this country many years ago and became a resident. And it was very difficult for me to become a citizen because I didn't speak English. But thanks to God, I was able to achieve that, and now I am an American citizen. (Lupe Rivera, cook at Fiesta Mexicana restaurant, Mount Vernon)

The following testimonies reflect the multiple ways in which Latinos' intercultural interactions shape their bicultural identities. For instance, one young woman remembered how her first American friend reached out and compassionately freed her from isolation in school. A young man mentioned a teacher who came over to his house many times to help him with homework. An agricultural female worker praised her Anglo-American boss for supporting her dual role as mother and worker. A businessman explained how he deliberately supports the local economy by using local services and goods. The testimony of moving out of Mount Vernon and returning because of nostalgia for "my little town" confirms that Latinos have strong emotional ties to the local community. To them, this is also their place; this is home.

> [Speaking about her first American friend] She would look at me and see that I was Hispanic and that I couldn't speak [English]. She took compassion in me and from there we became friends. (High school student, Mount Vernon)

> When my daughter was growing up, [my boss] would give me permission to pick up my daughter; and if my daughter was sick, she herself would inform me that she was sick. [My boss] went to pick up my daughter two times. I don't think there's another boss who would do the same for your children. (Female agricultural worker, Mount Vernon)

> People here I've met are always nice people and have only helped me and have helped my family. They've taught me new things, and I know that even after school or even summer—a teacher I know would come over and try to help me sometimes, especially when I was learning still English. So that's just something that has changed me, in a way, from this community and Knox County. (Mario Álvarez-León, middle school student, Mount Vernon)

> We try to use a lot of companies here, for instance food service companies like Lanning's Foods. So, whatever we get into the restaurant we try to buy here, too. (José Ávalos, owner of Fiesta Mexicana restaurant, Mount Vernon)

> When I arrived here, I didn't like it. In fact, I said, 'Oh God, I moved from North Carolina to Ohio.' But, I don't know, it may be that people have treated me well here. I have moved twice, but returned because I get nostalgic for my little town of Mount Vernon. (Irene Rivera, manager of Fiesta Mexicana restaurant, Mount Vernon)

> Yes, I do know people that are Mexican. I also know Americans and they are good people to me, they don't act badly, they aren't racist. (Male agricultural worker, Mount Vernon)

These testimonies reveal that Latinos experience life in Knox County as living in two cultures, yet one community. They hold on to their cultural roots while recognizing and embracing the warmth and hospitality of the local community. In spite of language barriers and cultural differences, Latinos and non-Latinos exchange values and goods freely and openly. Testimonies also reveal which virtues of Knox County are most valued by local Latinos. These include the warmth and hospitality of the community, the possibility to work and provide their children with opportunities for the future and, of course, the freedom to hold on to their bicultural identities.

(Hyper) Visibility/Invisibility

Both invisibility and (hyper)visibility characterize Latino daily experience. Latinos may feel invisible, or sense that there is a lack of representation of their culture in the community. Sometimes they attribute this to a tendency among Latinos to keep to themselves. Others feel a responsibility to stand up for the Latino community, and thus rendering themselves extremely visible and hyper-visible. For instance, a Venezuela-born professor voiced an acute awareness of how her identity can impact her working environment.

> I feel, being at a place like Kenyon, that strives to be more diverse, that I have a responsibility to be visible in that side of my identity and who I represent. (Balinda Craig-Quijada, professor of dance, Kenyon College, Gambier)

Clearly, invisibility can become a barrier to fully engaging with both Latinos and non-Latinos. Some Latinos experience both simultaneously: they are hyper-visible in appearance (clothing, occupation, status) yet invisible in the degree to which they can control their circumstances. This sense of invisibility sometimes is balanced, though, by taking pride in cultivating the land for the sustenance of the entire community. A female agricultural worker explains this simultaneous perception of self as follows:

> I am not invisible. I am always present, but no one wants to talk to me [laughs]. And you know, for me, I like to get along with all people, but well, not everyone likes me, because of my clothing or because I am always working. But thank God, we don't ask for anything, as of now. (Female agricultural worker, Mount Vernon)

The perception of both invisibility and (hyper)visibility in the lives of Latinos is an interesting tension sometimes difficult to negotiate. While (hyper)visibility may function to create a space for Latino culture in the larger context of the community, it can also become a barrier to intercultural understanding by highlighting differences in a negative way.

Dreams and Aspirations

The immigrant story is a powerful narrative founded on a hope for a better life. For those arriving, the American dream promises that hard work will result in social mobility. Yet, amidst the growing Latinization of the United States, the perception of difference can produce an outlook that establishes newcomers as a threat rather than a positive addition to the receiving community (Cohen & Chavez, 2013). While this may be commonplace in the history of immigration to the United States, the contrary seemed to be true among our participants.

Latinos' experience and reception here have been mostly positive. They do hope for stability, progress, and success in general, but they also have individualized goals. Dreams of becoming a professional soccer player or a registered nurse, and a father's simple but powerful wish that his children attend college, characterize Latinos' aspirations for the future. The children of immigrants inherit the hopes and dreams of those who have come before them, and in this sense their successes are family achievements. As writer Sandra Cisneros beautifully articulates through her character Esmeralda in *The House on Mango Street*, Latinos' dreams and aspirations are not only about individual prosperity but also about solidarity: "One day I'll own my own house, but I won't forget who I am or where I came from. Passing bums will ask, 'Can I come in?' I'll offer them the attic, ask them to stay, because I know how it is to be without a house" (1984, p. 3). In the selections provided here, we find a deeply rooted desire to witness a better world, an America that is open to difference, and an Ohio that accepts and celebrates Latinos.

> Of course, why not, like every Latino, why not go pro? But first I want to go with school. I want to find a college that I know I can do well in soccer. I'm in the nation of opportunity, so I know I should take one of those opportunities. (Mario Álvarez-León, middle school student, Mount Vernon)

> [I wish for] more acceptance of different races, ethnicities, religions, sexualities—again, that's probably one of the most important things at this current time; and more respect for mental disabilities, because when you're diagnosed with that, nobody understands other than you and your family, and you want to be accepted because it really, like, it hurts! Being misunderstood like that. So, I just wish there was a bit more respect for that in this community, and the rest of the entire world. (Kiana Reyes-Parson, middle school student, Mount Vernon)

> I want to become a nurse, a registered nurse, and that's my dream. I find [agriculture] very important; it has taught me a lot about what my parents go through, and it has made me appreciate them a lot more because it's not easy being out there in this hot weather and it's really tiring. And now I understand them completely, and I am just so thankful for everything they have done for me. (María Esmeralda Villa, high school student, Mount Vernon)

In the aggregate, a key element that emerges from these conversations is the way in which Latinos create and transform their place in society, first through crossing borders, and later through circular journeys, intercultural exchange, and hard work. Family, faith, education, and community enable their freedom to move and explore. Their views of the world are informed by biculturalism, bilingualism, and sustained contact with their countries of origin and cultural practice.

In the end, LiRA brings to light a well-known and universal reality: Latinos are an immigrant community not so different from those that preceded them. They demonstrate a commitment to advancing their lot in life through honest hard work and, in doing so, to enriching the society that gave them the opportunity. Their experiences reaffirm the key element of a democratic society: that we are all equal and have the right to pursue that equality and to reap the benefits of progress and prosperity that accompany it. What distinguishes Latinos from many other immigrant communities is their commitment to maintain their rich cultural heritage, paired with their willingness to share it with the new homeland in which they find themselves. The next section of the chapter will discuss how community-engaged learning can serve as a strategy to support public humanities. It will show how students worked across and within community contexts and structures to achieve a civic aim. Based on *LiRA* interviews, students had opportunities to translate, archive digitally, create new materials for distribution in local social service organizations and schools, and engage in social justice work through the creation and implementation of a college-preparation course for Latino youth.

CEL as a Vehicle for Civic Action

Students enrolled in Román-Odio's Introduction to Chicano/a Cultural Studies (SPAN 380, Fall 2015) worked a minimum of thirty hours on different CEL projects to support LiRA. Students chose to work on one of four projects (1) translation of interviews from Spanish to English and vice versa, (2) digital archiving of LiRA materials in Digital Kenyon, (3) the creation of primer on Latino culture, values and communication norms and (4) the creation and implementation of a college-prep course, requested by parents, to familiarize high-school and middle-school students with the college application process, research potential schools, and study for the SAT and ACT at the local Salvation Army.

Without opportunities for students to reflect upon their community work in the context of course content, the learning potential of community projects is limited. Therefore, students kept a short journal where they were asked to link their community experience to the course content and to reflect upon why community work is important. They could describe one aspect of their community work, analyze how course content related to the community experience, or comment on how the experience and course content could be applied to their personal of professional life. In addition, each group gave a formal class presentation, which contained evidence of processes and products, culminating the semester work. Students involved in the creation of the college-prep course for Latino youth described their CEL project as follows:

> This collaborative effort empowers first-generation students and their families to navigate the complicated college admissions process. As a community-engaged learning project, Kenyon students applied their academic research on education inequalities, the Latino/a civil rights movement and standardized testing strategies to develop a sustainable partnership with the Salvation Army unit in Mount Vernon. Kenyon students work weekly with 6th through 12th graders to improve their critical reading, math, vocabulary, science and test-taking skills in preparation for taking the SAT and ACT. The Kenyon students get experience towards future careers in bilingual education, nonprofit collaboration and minority rights activism. (Mary Sturgis, Alexa McElroy, Andres Herrera, & Bridget Murdoch, students, Kenyon College)[15]

This summary reflects how these students connected and extended knowledge (facts, theories) from their academic context to their community-based experience and how this experience reinforced and clarified their sense of civic identity and commitment to public action. It also captures their understanding of how the experience and course could be applied to their personal and professional life.

Students working on the primer on Latino culture, values and communication norms described their CEL experience as follows:

> Through the Latinos in Rural America (LiRA) project, students learned how Latinos in Knox County have navigated multiculturalism and how celebration of multiculturalism by the broader community can empower both Latinos and non-Latinos. The creation of a primer demonstrated the indispensable role of oral narratives in establishing collective identities, cultural norms, a recorded history, and political or social demands. This research centered on the voices of a local community showed that further support and cultural outlets enhance the well-being of the communities and imbues the academic research with purpose. (Sonia Prabhu, Jonathan Urrea-Espinoza, & Hannah Celli, students, Kenyon College)

Their academic and civic learning is highlighted here by a heightened awareness of cultural difference and how the project promoted others' engagement with diversity of communities and cultures. Students tailored communication strategies to effectively engage the local community in listening and adapting to Latino cultural and communication norms in order to establish relationships for further civic action. Such work suggests that students developed deeper understanding of course materials by having the opportunity to actively construct meaning.

The richness of student journals confirmed Chris Johnson's (2006) view that "Service learning reflection is a crucible in which academic knowledge and these kinds of big questions permeate each other. Questions like: Who am I, really, and why am I here? What does it mean to be human, and how ought I to live? What's my place in the world, how can I make a difference? … Whom do I see when I look in the mirror of experience, the mirror of the Other?" (p. 209). For instance, one student questioned the applicability of decontextualized academic knowledge and highlighted the value of linking it to community life:

> Each semester, I take classes related to social justice issues, and all too often, I find myself frustrated in how inapplicable the course material seems to be. Participating in the CBL project made me realize that community-based-learning does not mean you must compromise traditional academia. Rather, by creating the primer, I was able to learn course content and more importantly, assist a greater need in the community. (Hannah Celli, junior, Kenyon College)

Another student made sense of her college experience by embracing civic responsibility locally:

> It is one thing to read the statistics, and quite another to sit with a student as they attempt to overcome years of struggling in a system that neither supports nor celebrates their unique background. Before this course, I thought of my college career as something that would prepare me to take on the world's problems. My Spanish degree allowed me to study cultures from around the world, but it had never before challenged me to take on the problems facing Latinos/as ten minutes down the road. It is through taking on this leadership role that I have realized that college is not the time to study problems from afar, but engage with them head-on. (Mary Sturgis, senior, Kenyon College)

Yet another spoke of CEL as Johnson did, as a "crucible" in which academic knowledge and "big questions permeate one another." Such understanding resulted in a new level of social consciousness that is changed-oriented.

> The translation project immersed me in a dynamic intellectual environment, in which I wrestled with meaning and authenticity, while also grounding me in the experiences and the perspectives of people in my own community. Doing these translations drove home the sense that now that I'm reaching the end of my time of intellectual incubation, I do have a responsibility to apply what I've learned in a way that will benefit my community. (Jessica Bolter, senior, Kenyon College)

Reflecting on issues of social justice, another student highlights the value of oral history as a tool to understand systems of oppression and privilege, a lens through which we can see our pluralistic but unequal society. In this case, the analysis of the social context changed the analyst by catalyzing a rethinking of stereotypes and biases.

> I believe oral histories and narratives of marginalized groups allow people to re-think their stereotypes and biases. They are an act of affirmation and assertion of one's identity in the face of a society that does not provide avenues for non-hegemonic expressions of identity. (Maggie Stohlman, senior, Kenyon College)

Going beyond the learning goals and academic content of the course, another student discovered the purpose and value of higher education as a public good.

> In retrospect, I strongly believe that LiRA encouraged me to be critical of an education that lies solely within the confines of textbooks. I believe that my participation in this project has helped build my future in teaching because it encouraged me to question what scholarship does and what it can do for the community around me. (Patricia Mota, senior, Kenyon College)

As these journals suggest, CEL can strengthen undergraduate research while serving as a powerful strategy to develop civic engagement, and critical thinking about larger societal issues that will continue to emerge way beyond college years.

The CEL College Student Evaluation reflects the positive impact these community-based experiences had on student development into aware and active community participants. Through an anonymous survey, we asked students to indicate their level of agreement with statements relating to their CEL experience including:

1. Connection between CEL and course content
2. Increased interest or investment in the course
3. Meaningful opportunities to develop valuable knowledge, relationships, and/or skills
4. Increased knowledge of campus community or wider world, and
5. Increased involvement off-campus

We also asked open-ended questions, including: What was most valuable, meaningful, or satisfying about your community-engaged learning experience? What was least valuable, meaningful, or satisfying about your community-engaged learning experience? We also offered additional space for comments. The open-ended questions offered a view of how CEL can be an effective pedagogy to shape student learning and civic life by creating authentic opportunities to analytically engage with the social fabric of a place. In this case, such opportunities helped bridge the town-gown divide and made theoretical learning applicable to current local and national issues. Overall, in answering the question about the value of their CEL experience, students made quite positive remarks in relation to all the categories listed above. Among them:

> My academic learning was extremely enriched knowing that we were serving a real need in the community.

> My interactions as a teacher with my students has been one of the most, if not the most enriching part of my Kenyon experience.

> This project illuminated the function of oral narratives as a root of sociopolitical change. Centering the voices of local community members requiring further support, or cultural outlets, imbued academic work with purpose and (hopefully) enhanced the well-being of these communities.

> Meeting people from the community I would never have otherwise met and hearing their stories. It helped to contextualize a lot of the theoretical or statistical information from the course.

Student answers also reflect a deepening of self-understanding. Knowing the other helped shape the self in meaningful ways.

> What was most meaningful about this CEL experience was that I got to see a new perspective of my current life. I was able to look back at people's struggles and realize I saw all the opportunities I had as a given.

Students also addressed the low points of the project. For instance, they would have liked to have had either longer journals or alternative modes of reflection.

> The journals, honestly, were not a sufficient word count to adequately reflect. I would prefer having some in class discussion in groups, maybe in triplets or quartets, with people working on different projects.

Other students felt limited by the type of project in which they were involved. They would have welcomed the opportunity to participate in the various projects encompassing LiRA. They also suggested new ways of bringing Latinos together from diverse educational contexts as a mode of mutual enrichment.

> I wish we could all participate in the various projects and get a sample of what other groups were working on beyond just our presentations.

> I didn't feel like I was able to directly interact with the community partners through my project, and I wish that I had gotten to do more of that.

In spite of such limitations, the open-ended questions of the evaluation speak about CEL as an experience that can deeply and positively impact undergraduate research and learning. In their words:

> CEL has opened my world at Kenyon and provided me with opportunities for after school.
>
> Now I see teaching as a platform to community-engaged learning and how powerful that can be, bringing what you learn in the classroom and extending it out. "It's made my goodbye to Kenyon a much more powerful goodbye.

Community Response to LiRA

Reflecting on the community response to the first opening of LiRA, we found that the audience effectively embraced cultural difference, from the bilingual/bicultural content of the text, pictures, and video, to the discovery of social tensions and educational disparities. Walking around the room to engage with cultural difference provided an opportunity to be touched by talent, skill, insight and imagination. As the results of the exhibit survey indicate, people truly enjoyed learning in the company of others and being informed by diverse perspectives. This is illustrated by the citations below:

> [I] love that it is bilingual. The variety of stories told also show the multiplicity of experiences—crossing age and socio economic spectrum.
>
> [I most enjoyed] the personal part- who these people are- what they do, think, value, worry about.
>
> So diverse! So many different kinds of Latinos, journeys and stories.
>
> It was a fascinating and moving look into a part of Knox County history I was not familiar with.
>
> This was such an amazing, well-organized exhibit. Learned a lot in an aesthetically pleasing way.
>
> I really enjoyed learning about the Latinos/as in and around Kenyon College. It was insightful and inspiring to hear their stories and understand the difficulties of being a minority in rural Ohio. I was impressed with the posters and thought the pictures helped make it more relatable and engaging.

The community response to LiRA also showed that attendees made connections between local issues and national debates and questioned the world where they live. They faced disparities, social tensions, and alternative views, and this led them to reflect on their changed perceptions.

> Relevant study undertaken at the right time in the larger context of debates on immigration.

> I was kind of shocked to see the disparity in income and employment levels between Latinos and whites. I would have assumed most Latinos would have come here specifically based on a job.
>
> The locality of it. Always amazing to learn more about something that is right in front of your face!

When asked for ideas that would further increase knowledge about Latinos in the community, the audience urged us to open up more spaces that would enable cultural exchanges and social dialogue. This is illustrated by the comments below:

> Open dialogues, MORE EXHIBITS, Programs which support Latin@ children and educators who are culturally sensitive to these issues, equipped with the tools to provide support.
>
> More spaces like this, creating connections. Maybe taking the exhibits out into the community to encourage exploration and connection.
>
> More events like this! It is great to get people together to talk and create a dialogue.

These reactions speak of the promise to public humanities and CEL and of the critical role they can play in addressing important societal issues of the day.

Concluding Thoughts

An aspiration central to the conception of this work was to produce an empirical demonstration of Cantor's notion of the university as a public good. To succeed in this objective, we aimed to achieve two primary goals through LiRA: first, to enable the creation of a safe space where social introspection, informed by difference, may emerge; second, to enrich student learning in the classroom via the addition of a CEL component to the syllabus. The evidence gathered to date from the outcomes of this project, while qualitative in nature, demonstrates that our initial aspiration was successfully achieved.

Through an oral history framework, we documented the experiences of Latinos and Latinas in Knox County, Ohio. The collected stories gave visibility to this community and offered them the opportunity to voice their challenges and aspirations. We learned how a family grew a restaurant from scratch, what Latino children dream for their future, and how Latino women, so often agents of social change in their communities, altered their behavior because of their rural surroundings. The first two openings of the exhibit brought together approximately 225 members of the local community from diverse economic, ethnic, and social backgrounds. This exchange of peoples and ideas, in the public sphere, helped promote cross-cultural interactions and created points of contact and affinity between two coexisting communities. In this sense, public humanities served as a vehicle for intercultural development and the potential for further social justice work.

The testimonials offered by students in their reflections about the CEL projects of the course, as cited earlier, amply support the pedagogical benefits achieved. Students highlighted the value of a direct connection with the Latino/a community to ground and inform meaning and authenticity in textual translation. They remarked on the importance of oral histories and narratives to bring perspective to the plights of marginalized groups and their oppression by cultural stereotypes and biases. The CEL project helped still other students to recognize the necessity of thinking about, and committing to, applying what is learned in academia to what is needed in society through civic engagement efforts. Still others recognized that there can be, in fact, an underlying and direct connection between what an individual learns and how he/she will be able to implement it to effect social change. From these insights emerge at least two high-impact contributions of the CEL project to the overall learning outcomes of the course: (1) the recognition of the civic responsibility associated with the privilege of higher education, and (2) knowledge of the Other as a means to shape the Self in meaningful ways.

In turn, the reflections offered by attendees at the exhibit support the achievement of the second aspiration of the project, namely, to enable the creation of a safe space where societal introspection can take place to address and shed light on the notion and the value of difference. To reaffirm this point, we return to Cantor's insight that we understand the most when we can let down barriers, acknowledge each other genuinely, and feel at ease expressing discomfort and ignorance. As LiRA has shown, sidestepping the silencing that comes with power and status is critical to allow those who are least heard a place at the table. We believe that this opening of new spaces for social dialogue constitutes one of the greatest promises of public humanities and community-engaged learning.

Notes

1. Community engaging pedagogies encompass a diverse terminology that includes: service learning, community-engaged learning, community-based research, community development, among others. To explore differences in terminology and approaches see Bandy (2017); Howard (2001); Minkler and Wallerstein (2008); Philips and Pittman (2014); Strand, Marullo, Cutforth, Stoecker, and Donahue (2003).
2. It takes a great deal of collaboration and friendship to make a project like this happen. We extend special thanks to all of the community members who so warmly welcomed

us into their homes and workplaces. Our deepest appreciation to the Latino families who generously shared their journey stories with us as residents of Knox County. Additional thanks to various offices of Kenyon College, including the Center for Innovative Pedagogy, the Rural Life Center, the Office of Public Affairs, and Kenyon Library and Information Services for their strong support and endorsement. We gratefully acknowledge those individuals whose perspectives and commitment to community-based projects have guided our efforts. Thanks especially to Rob Colby, Meg Galipault, Howard Sacks, Ric Sheffield, and Peter Rutkoff for their guidance throughout the creation of this project. We also extend our deep appreciation to the following individuals: Sarah Murnen and Nikole Hotchkiss of Kenyon College for their contribution to the creation of the reflection survey; Emily Klesner for her historical research on Latinos in Knox County; Quentin Karpilow (Kenyon alumnus, class of 2012) for his outstanding demographic data analysis contribution; Jim Gibson of the Knox County History Society for supporting this research; Rose Shilling of Kenyon College Public Affairs for her help in publicizing the project; Jenna Nolt for technical and archival assistance; Joe Murphy of Kenyon College for his support with the media and pedagogical aspects of the project; Lucy Adams for her outstanding video editing contributions; Justin Bryant for his beautiful design; and Deacon Tim Birie and Irene Rivera for enabling the first gathering of the local Latino community. We owe gratitude to those who provided the venues for this exhibit: Amy Badertscher (Kenyon College), John Chidester (Mount Vernon Public Library), Yolanda Zepeda (The Ohio State University), and Jacqueline Rioja Velarde and Anna Klosowska (Miami University).

3. This project was made possible in part by the Ohio Humanities, a state affiliate of the National Endowment for the Humanities. Any views, finding conclusions, or recommendations expressed in this exhibition do not necessarily those of the National Endowment for the Humanities.
4. Román-Odio, the faculty leader of Kenyon's community-engaged learning initiative, working with the new Office for Community Partnerships (http://www.kenyon.edu/directories/offices-services/community-partnerships/), wanted to chronicle the lives of Latinos who have been recorded as residing in Knox County since the beginning of the last century.
5. After the showing at Kenyon, the display was moved to the Mount Vernon Library in January, Ohio State University in February, and Miami University in southwest Ohio in March.
6. We want to acknowledge the work and dedication of students enrolled in Román-Odio's (SPAN 380) course, who fully engaged with translation of interviews, the development of a college-preparation curriculum for Latino/a youth (still on-going), and the research and creation of the primer.
7. Kenyon's Office of Admissions is also contributing to this program with college-prep workshops for students and parents enrolled.
8. *LiRA* exhibit materials, including original and translated interviews, video with captions, photographs, exhibit panels as well as student CEL projects are permanently archived in Digital Kenyon at http://digital.kenyon.edu/lkca/
9. Four venues hosted the exhibit: Kenyon College, Olin Library (December 1–18, 2015), The Mount Vernon Public Library (January 13–27, 2016), the Global Gallery in Hagerty Hall, at the Ohio State University (February 9–23, 2016), and the Mc Millan Hall Gallery, Miami University, Oxford, Ohio (March 30–April 12, 2016).

Other three institutions in Ohio also expressed interest in hosting LiRA during 2016–2017.

10. Brooke Bryan (2013) suggests that interviewers divide their questions into six domains: (1) introductory lead, (2) early life context, (3) purposeful turn toward the theme, (4) depth questions, (5) reflective turn towards generalized meaning, and (6) wrap-up.
11. Latinos have helped shape the United States over the last five centuries and constitute the country's largest minority group today, with more than 50 million people. There are 357,000+ Latinos in Ohio. Nearly every county across the state has seen their numbers rise in the last decade. Latino Ohioans are reshaping our classrooms and churches, expanding the offerings on our grocery store shelves, and strengthening the state economy where 9,700 Latino-owned businesses generate $2.3 billion in annual sales. Many might be surprised to learn that the overwhelming majority of Latino Ohioans (78%) were born in the U.S., and three-quarters speak English only or very well. Additionally, Latinos in Ohio trace their ancestry to some two-dozen countries across the Americas. For more information see https://public.tableau.com/profile/laverdad.marketing.media#!/vizhome/OhioHispanicDashboard/LaVERDADHispanicDashboard
12. U.S. Census Bureau, Social Explorer Tables: ACS 2013 (5-Year Estimates) http://www.socialexplorer.com/tables/ACS2013_5yr/R10988008
13. U.S. Census Bureau, Social Explorer Tables: ACS 2013 (5-Year Estimates) http://www.socialexplorer.com/tables/ACS2013_5yr/R10988008
14. Difficulty speaking English may inhibit success in schools, businesses, and agencies. Students from Spanish-speaking households may face difficulty pursuing higher education due to a lack of bilingual SAT and ACT materials, and Eurocentric curricula. For more information see http://towncharts.com/Ohio/Education/Knox-County-OH-Education-data.html
15. The college preparatory curriculum that these students created for their CEL course project continues to support the college prep program that began three years ago. The curriculum and workshops can be downloaded for free from the Kenyon Digital Archives at: http://digital.kenyon.edu/lkca_pub/1/

References

Adler-Kassner, L., Crooks, R., & Watters, A. (1997). Service learning and composition at the crossroads. In L. Adler-Kassner, R. Crooks, & A. Watters (Eds.), *Writing the community: Concepts and models for service learning in composition* (pp. 1–17). Washington, DC: American Association for Higher Education.

Anzaldúa. Gloria. (1999). *Borderlands/ La Frontera*. Introduction by Sonia Sladívar-Hull. 2nd ed. San Francisco: Aunt Luke Books.

Bandy, J. (2017). *What is service learning or community engagement?* Retrieved from https://cft.vanderbilt.edu/guides-sub-pages/teaching-through-community-engagement/

Boss, J. (1994). The effect of community service work on the moral development of college students. *Journal of Moral Education, 23*(2), 183–197.

Bryan, B. (2013). A closer look at community partnerships. *Oral History Review, 40*(1), 75–82.

Cantor, N. (2004). Civic engagement: The university as a public good. *Liberal Education, 90*(2), 18–25.

Castañeda, M. (2008). Transformative learning through community engagement. *Latino Studies, 6*, 319–326.

Cohen, J., & Kinsey, D. (1994). "Doing good" and scholarship: A service learning study. *Journalism Educator, 48*(4), 4–14.

Cohen, J. H., & Chavez, N. M. (2013). Latino immigrants, discrimination and reception in Columbus, Ohio. *International Migration, 51*(2), 24–31.

Cushman, E. (1999). The public intellectual, service learning and activist research. *College English, 61*, 328–336.

Danielson, S., & Fallon, A. M. (2007). *Community-based learning and the works of literature*. Bolton, MA: Anker Publishing.

Howard, J. (Ed.). (2001). *Michigan journal of community service-learning course design workbook*. Ann Arbor, MI: University of Minnesota OCSL Press.

Johnson, C. (2006). Deep learning and the big questions: Reflection in service learning. In B. T. Johnson & C. O'Grady (Eds.), *The spirit of service: Exploring faith, service, and social justice in higher education* (pp. 209–230). Boston, MA: Anker Publishing.

Mathieu, P. (2005). *Tactics of hope: The public turn in English composition*. Portsmouth, NH: Boynton.

Minkler, M., & Wallerstein, N. (2008). *Community-based participatory research: From process to outcomes*. San Francisco, CA: Jossey-Bass.

Nieto, S. (2000). Foreword. In C. R. O'Grady (Ed.), *Integrating service learning and multicultural education in colleges and universities* (pp. ix–xi). Mahwah, NJ: Erlbaum.

Phillips, R., & Pittman, R. (2014). *An introduction to community development*. New York, NY: Routledge.

Smith-Morris, C., Morales-Campos, D., Alvarez, E. A. C., & Turner, M. (2013). An anthropology of Familismo: On narratives and description of Mexican/immigrants. *Hispanic Journal of Behavioral Sciences, 35*(1), 35–60.

Strand, K., Marullo, S., Cutforth, N., Stoecker, R., & Donohue, P. (2003). *Community-based research and higher education: Principles and practice*. New York, NY: Jossey-Bass.

Warren, K. (1998). Educating students for social justice in service learning. *Journal of Experiential Education, 21*(3), 134–139.

Weah, W., Simmons, V. C., & Hall, M. (2000). Service-learning and multicultural/multiethnic perspectives: From diversity to equity. *Phi Delta Kappan, 81*, 673–675.

Wu, J. Y. (2007). Race matters in civic engagement work. In S. A. Ostrander & K. E. Portney (Eds.), *Acting civically: From urban neighborhoods to higher education* (pp. 158–182). Medford, MA: Tufts University Press.

Section II

Community Voices and the Politics of Place

6. *Community as a Campus: From "Problems" to Possibilities in Latinx Communities*

JONATHAN ROSA

The language practices of U.S. Latinxs[1] are frequently viewed as educational impediments, particularly in light of this population's rapid demographic rise in recent decades.[2] In Milltown,[3] a small, urban New England city in which Latinxs constitute nearly 80% of K-12 students, popular discourses often link educational underachievement to cultural and linguistic diversity. For example, a recent local news story touting improving graduation rates throughout the region includes the following discussion of ongoing educational difficulties in Milltown:

> Milltown again was among the lowest in the state despite a high school graduation rate that improved slightly, to 53.8 % from the previous year's 52.8%. The city of 40,000 is roughly half Hispanic. Among challenges, officials have said, is that English is not the first language for more than 70% of public school students.

Perspectives such the one voiced in this media portrayal present language differences, specifically those associated with "Hispanic" students for whom English is not their "first language,"[4] as problems to be overcome rather than legitimate forms of communication. This vantage point involves language ideologies that presume upon English language "proficiency"[5] as a readymade pathway toward educational success. Yet this is not the case for millions of U.S. Latinxs, as well members of other minoritized[6] populations, who identify as native English speakers and still face profound experiences of educational inequity. In Milltown, Latinx language use is positioned as an impediment and scapegoated as the cause of educational underachievement, despite the fact that from the perspective of normative linguistic logics many Latinx residents' bilingual linguistic repertoires could be viewed as more expansive than those of the monolingual teachers, administrators, and policy makers who seek to fix them. As one Milltown-based Latinx poet put it, "This city is allergic to Spanish." This linguistic stigmatization naturalizes prevailing conceptions of educational underachievement as well as broader forms of societal exclusion across a range of mainstream institutional settings. Efforts toward denaturalizing these ideas must redirect attention from modifying the practices of marginalized populations to contesting the structures of power through which their communities are systematically stigmatized.

In this chapter, I point to the exciting possibilities that emerge when we shift from viewing marginalized communities as static objects of academic analysis to dynamic sites of collaborative knowledge production. In order to do so, I describe the development of a collaborative civic engagement project that brought together my students in an undergraduate Latinx Studies course with a teacher and students in a predominantly Latinx high school. In this project, titled VOCES (Voicing Our Community in English and Spanish), the high school teacher and I worked collaboratively as co-instructors and the university students and high school students worked collaboratively as co-learners. The goal of the project was to learn ethnographic research skills to document, analyze, and contest the stigmatization of language practices in a predominantly Latinx community where linguistic diversity is often viewed as a problem from mainstream perspectives. By approaching this community as a campus, the students and teachers were able to work together to present an alternative view of a stigmatized community that challenged the institutional reproduction of disparities, while also demonstrating the resilience and ingenuity of its residents.

Conceptualizing and Approaching Communities as Campuses

In this section I document how the VOCES project in Milltown was informed by previous work in other predominantly Latinx communities and educational settings. Specifically, I describe the Chicago-based development of the Community as a Campus model, as well as my efforts to synthesize it with inside-out and culturally sustaining pedagogies, Community-Based Participatory Research and Youth Participatory Action Research approaches, and a commitment to sociolinguistic justice. This combination of theories, pedagogies, methodologies, and ethical commitments provided a robust toolkit for the VOCES project. The Community as a Campus model was developed by Chicago's Puerto Rican Cultural Center.[7] The guiding ethos of Community as a Campus is a social ecological perspective that views communities not as passive objects of inquiry but rather as dynamic contexts in which residents are constantly producing, circulating, and redefining knowledge.

While teaching a civics course in Chicago's Dr. Pedro Albizu Campos High School, which was founded by the Puerto Rican Cultural Center more than forty years ago, I experienced firsthand the power of Community as a Campus. Rather than structuring the school as an atomized institution that is isolated from the rest of the community, the entire curriculum is framed around culturally sustaining pedagogies[8] that draw from, respond to, and engage with everyday life in the surrounding community. Classrooms are situated in the school's main building as well as in storefronts, so that students walk throughout the community as they move from class to class. Coursework in traditional subjects is reimagined in relation to the mathematics of spatially designing and budgeting for community events; the science of greening the community's rooftops and understanding a local diabetes epidemic; the social studies of gentrification, food deserts, and colonialism; and the arts and literature of hip hop, community members' oral histories, and vernacular expressive practices. This curricular approach integrates not only disparate academic subjects, but also differing community institutions and residents. By enacting this Community as a Campus model, communities that are often highly stigmatized come to be experienced as powerful sites of knowledge production. Rather than embracing a vision of educational success in which escaping marginalized communities is the goal, Community as a Campus involves reimagining and recreating these communities.

The Community as a Campus model corresponds to Community-Based Participatory Research (CBPR) and Youth Participatory Action Research (YPAR) approaches, which center on partnerships with community members—specifically youth—in all stages of the research process, from the development of research questions, to data collection, analysis, and the dissemination of findings. Importantly, these approaches have an "explicitly political and action focus" that distinguishes them from other research that might be situated within communities but not explicitly grounded within communities' efforts toward addressing the inequities they face (Atalay, 2012, p. 50). Within the discipline of anthropology, CBPR has been presented as an attempt to "combine Indigenous systems of knowledge and traditional ways of understanding with those of Western science … to work cooperatively—to use the diverse knowledge of all to build strength on the path to mutual success and peace" (Atalay, 2012, p. x). Thus, CBPR centers mutuality and justice in questions about "what knowledge is produced, by whom, for whose interest, and toward what ends" (Atalay, 2012, p. 59). Relatedly, education scholars and other youth-focused researchers have formulated YPAR as an approach that "provides young people with opportunities to study social problems affecting their lives and then determine actions to rectify these problems" (Cammarota & Fine, 2008, p. 2). Thus, CBPR and YPAR provide frameworks for revolutionizing the production, circulation, and reception of knowledge.

When I became a faculty member at an institution near Milltown, I began adapting these various approaches in my community-based teaching and research. A central component of this effort involved familiarizing myself with the educational and cultural terrain within Milltown's predominantly Puerto Rican community. I served as an apprentice under the guidance of a senior colleague with extensive community-based teaching and learning experience in Milltown. This colleague introduced me to a model of teaching and learning based on the Inside-Out Prison Exchange Program, in which university students and incarcerated populations study together as co-learners (Allred, 2009; Pompa, 2005). Bringing together people in differing social circumstances as co-teachers and co-learners, this transformative approach challenges traditional community-based learning models that position university students as knowledge holders or service providers and community members as recipients of their assistance. By positioning university students and community members as co-learners, they become collaborators in the production of knowledge.

In this particular instance, my colleague and mentor was working with an Adult Basic Education program in Milltown. I attended this colleague's class weekly in order to learn how they collaborated with one of this program's instructors as a co-teacher and how their students collaborated as co-learners. By challenging traditional hierarchies associated with teaching and learning, this class became a transformative experience for all of the participants. Similar to the Community as a Campus model and CBPR/YPAR approaches, university students and faculty were not simply extracting information from a marginalized community to bring back to the academy, but rather collaborating with community members as co-learners and co-researchers to understand and address the inequities they face.

This work inspired me to adapt one of my courses, Languages and Latinxs, into a community-based research practicum. In this language-oriented practicum, I sought to synthesize the aforementioned approaches with a commitment to "sociolinguistic justice," which has been defined as "self-determination for linguistically subordinated individuals and groups in sociopolitical struggles over language" (Bucholtz et al., 2014, p. 145; Fishman, 2010; Wolfram, 2001). Scholarly efforts in support of sociolinguistic justice combine longstanding theoretical deconstructions of deficit-based perspectives on linguistic diversity, with reciprocal methodologies that seek to avoid the pitfalls associated with speaking on behalf of research participants rather than empowering them to advocate for themselves (Cameron, Frazer, Harvey, Rampton, & Richardson, 1992; Labov, 1969; Wolfram, Adger, & Christian, 2007; Zentella, 1997, 2005). In the context of a collaboration with linguistically marginalized youth, teaching informed by sociolinguistic justice exemplifies what education scholars have described as culturally sustaining pedagogies, whose practitioners ask, "what if, indeed, the goal of teaching and learning with youth of color was not ultimately to see how closely students could perform White middle-class norms, but to explore, honor, extend, and, at times, problematize their heritage and community practices?" (Paris & Alim, 2014, p. 86). This question was at the center of the community-based VOCES project, which I describe in the following section.

The VOCES Project: Voicing Our Community in English and Spanish

After obtaining funding for a collaborative university-community research practicum to train undergraduate students and high school students as linguistic ethnographers, I began meeting with potential participating teachers and students. I selected six undergraduate students with bilingual English-Spanish skills and extensive community-based learning experience. I also identified a Spanish teacher at the high school with whom to partner, and delivered presentations in several of her classes in an effort to recruit high school student participants. High school students filled out applications and obtained parental consent to participate in the project. The teacher and I reviewed the applications and selected fifteen high school students. My undergraduate students and I met one day a week to discuss readings and plan for our meetings in Milltown, and one day a week in Milltown for two and a half hours to conduct the practicum with the high school students and teacher. The goal was to develop skills not only for documenting and analyzing linguistic practices and identities, but also to identify linguistic inequities and propose interventions.

During our initial meetings, we discussed the history of Milltown, particularly the political and economic dynamics that have produced stark structural inequities through which Latinxs are marginalized across a range of societal domains, including public schools, employment, housing, and city governance. We analyzed the ways that the Puerto Rican migration to Milltown during the mid to late 20th century coincided with the decline of industry, namely paper manufacturing, which had allowed previous (im)migrant groups, such as Irish, German, Polish, and French Canadians, to experience upward socioeconomic mobility and societal inclusion across generations. We examined "culture of poverty" (Lewis, 1966) narratives that obscure these political and economic histories by attributing Puerto Rican marginalization to cultural pathology rather than structural inequity. We also considered the ways that, unlike previous (im)migrant groups, Puerto Rico's colonial history vis-à-vis the United States racialized Puerto Rican migrants as non-White second-class citizens. We connected these dialogues to language by discussing how, in the post-Civil Rights era, race and racism have been remapped from biology onto language and culture (Urciuoli, 2001). Through this remapping, racism is less frequently articulated in relation to presumed biological inferiority, as it was in previous historical moments. Instead, purported linguistic and cultural pathologies have become prime targets for the expression of racial animosity. Thus, language practices and ideologies can provide important vantage points from which to understand how racial inequity is (re)produced and experienced.

Based on these preliminary discussions, we developed a set of research questions about language practices and ideologies in Milltown: (1) How are the English and Spanish languages positioned in relation to one another in different settings? (2) How does language use become a symbol of identity? (3) What stereotypes are associated with the English and Spanish languages? (4) What are the different varieties of English and Spanish that people use and with whom do they use which variety? (5) How is language related to inequity and social justice? Based on these interests and questions, we named our research project "Voicing our Community in English and Spanish" (VOCES). Each university student partnered with two or three high school students and decided to focus on a particular research topic/methodology: (a) linguistic landscape; (b) ethnography of language; (c) oral history; (d) language policy; (e) slang; and (f) social media.

The linguistic landscape group focused on documenting and analyzing the range of visual displays of language use in public, such as signs, advertisements, and graffiti, with which they came into contact in their everyday lives (Shohamy & Gorter, 2009). Students in this group drew on Photovoice research methodologies, which involved using cameras to document the linguistic landscape and then conducting follow-up interviews and recording sessions in which they commented on the significance of visual data that they collected (Gubrium & Harper, 2013). This group discovered that while neutral informational signs, such as directions to the school's main office, were displayed in standardized English and Spanish, posters and signs with important information about college were displayed exclusively in standardized

English. Meanwhile, punitive signs warning students about the prohibition of particular behaviors, such as signs posted in front the school that state *NO HANGEO* (a nonstandardized way of writing "no loitering"),[9] were displayed exclusively in nonstandardized Spanish. In community settings, such as the public library, students found signs that were bilingual in English and Spanish, yet the Spanish translations were often nonstandardized or appeared in a smaller font below the much larger, standardized English characters. In the predominantly Puerto Rican downtown area, there were many signs exclusively in Spanish. Thus, this group concluded that Milltown's linguistic landscape reflects the marginalization of the Spanish language and its users, while also noting that exclusively English or Spanish signage in different areas indexed segregation throughout Milltown.

The ethnography of communication group analyzed language use in particular community contexts (e.g., corner stores, barbershop/beauty shops, churches, malls, etc.). They documented the linguistic and cultural symbols and practices associated with these contexts from both in-group and out-group perspectives, and also analyzed the relationship between language ideologies and linguistic practices associated with these contexts. The group decided to focus specifically on language use within different retail settings in Milltown. They found stark contrasts between language use within the Milltown Mall, a mainstream commercial setting, and downtown Milltown, where Puerto Ricans predominate. They conducted an experiment in which they entered stores, waited to be greeted by an employee, and then respond to English language greetings in Spanish or Spanish language greetings in English. In the Milltown Mall, they were greeted in English in every store. Roughly half of the employees ignored them when they responded in Spanish; they classified approximately 20% of their interactions as successfully bilingual.

This group discovered that while the clientele of Milltown Mall is racially and linguistically diverse and there is some bilingual signage throughout the mall, the vast majority of employees are white, monolingual English speakers. In contrast, in downtown Milltown, they were greeted in Spanish in the majority of stores they entered, and every employee who greeted them in Spanish switched to English when the students responded in English. They concluded that while Spanish might be the default language in downtown Milltown, there is widespread bilingualism not only in signage, but also among employees and patrons. By observing and comparing linguistic dynamics in these two ethnographic settings, the students were able to document the inequitable ways in which English monolingualism becomes privileged within particular settings, as well as the ways in which bilingualism and Spanish language use are devalued or stigmatized.

The oral history group analyzed interviews that all of the program participants conducted with their immediate and extended families in order to learn about their linguistic heritage and identify local language ideologies. Interviews were conducted in English, Spanish, or a combination thereof. After conducting the interviews, students in this group compared their findings with one another to identify similarities and differences in linguistic heritage and language ideologies. One fascinating pattern that emerged within the interviews was that the majority of them were asymmetrically bilingual, with the student interviewers speaking English and the family respondents speaking Spanish. This is demonstrated in the following excerpt from an interview between Daniel, a Puerto Rican sophomore, and his mother (brackets signal overlapping speech and equal signs signal interruption):

D: Um, what's your primary language?
M: Mi lenguaje primario es inglés, [pero
(My primary language is English, [but)
D: [Can, oh
D: Can you elaborate on that, like=
M: =Es que, yo hablo inglés porque en la escuela yo (It's that, I speak English because in school I
hablo inglés [y con mis amigos yo hablo
speak English [and with my friends I speak)
D: [Oh, when you were younger
M: Sí, y con mis amigos yo hablo inglés, pero con familia yo hablo en español.
(Yes, and with my friends I speak English, but with family I speak in Spanish.)
D: That's good, mom.

Interestingly, when Daniel asks his mother in English what her primary language is, she responds in Spanish by telling him that her primary language is English. In their analysis of these data, the oral history group concluded that complex linguistic repertoires within Milltown challenge assumptions about relationships between language and identity. They also found that despite the linguistic and racial stigmatization that interviewees reported experiencing in Milltown, they continue to be proud both of their Milltown and Latinx identities, as well as their English-Spanish bilingualism.

The language policy group analyzed policies at the local, state, and national levels. These included policies associated with bilingual education, voting rights, courts, citizenship, and medical contexts. They researched the views of advocates or opponents of these policies and identified the language ideologies associated with each of these positions. The group focused specifically on a 2002 English-only ballot initiative in Massachusetts. The initiative replaced Transitional Bilingual Education with Sheltered or Structured English Immersion, effectively making English the sole language of instruction for all K-12 students. They found that while 68% of voters approved this eradication of Transitional Bilingual Education, 92% of Latinxs voted against this initiative. They also found that this initiative was overwhelmingly rejected within Milltown's predominantly Latinx precincts. After discovering the ways that language policies often marginalize languages other than English and their users, the students worked together to draft language policies that reflect a more inclusive view of language in society. Specifically, they advocated for a dual-language curriculum in Milltown's K-12 schools, and the requirement of Spanish-English bilingualism for all district teachers and administrators.

The slang group studied peer language use, with a focus on what students understand as examples of slang. Each time they identified a slang usage, they documented specific examples of these usages and followed up with linguistic elicitations in which they asked peers to define these usages and to provide different examples of how they are used. They compiled these usages into a slang dictionary. One of the most compelling examples of Milltown-based vernacular language use that they discovered was the term "lingy" (singular)/ "lingys" (plural). This term is used pejoratively by students who identify as monolingual English users or English dominant to refer to students they view as monolingual Spanish users or Spanish dominant. Ironically, while lingy/ lingys is local shorthand for bilingual, many of the Latinx students who use this term might be more conventionally categorized as bilingual than the Spanish dominant students they use the term to deride. The slang group used this and other examples to analyze social networks and hierarchies within the school, and to consider how certain language use comes to be viewed as more or less correct and legitimate.

The social media group documented and analyzed the particular ways that digital communicative platforms are used throughout Milltown, as well as the ways in which Milltown is represented in these platforms. They investigated the vernacular cultures and communicative logics involved in the use of social media platforms such as Facebook, Twitter, YouTube, Instagram, Snapchat, Yelp, and Vine (Coleman, 2010). One recurring theme in social media was the notion that Milltown is "little Puerto Rico." Many social media users joked that the bridge into Milltown is "the longest bridge in the world—from America to Puerto Rico." Others referenced language issues, such as one person who wrote: "Just told a rude ass lady who didn't speak a lick of English to go fuck herself in Spanish. Thank you, Milltown high lingys." This example demonstrates the ways that themes overlapped across the different student research groups. For example, when the slang group discovered the term lingy, the social media group was able to help them find examples. The group used these examples in order to analyze the ways that social media platforms become sites for performances of identity that might not be viewed as legitimate in offline settings. They concluded that such digital presentations of self play a key role in circulating ideas about language and identity in Milltown.

Each group of students wrote a final report and presented their findings to one another. Their reports and presentations were shared with the superintendent of schools, as well as with a group of teachers who were working to develop more culturally responsive curricula. Collectively, the students acquired a range of skills through their participation in this project, including methods for collecting, analyzing, presenting, and applying social science research data. More importantly, they developed new perspectives on their own linguistic identities and ideologies. The university students were able to enhance and apply the knowledge they acquired throughout their undergraduate careers by teaching and learning with high school students. The high school students were provided with access to college-level curricula, developed academic relationships with undergraduate college students, and discovered that their lived experiences constituted important forms of knowledge. The high school teacher had the opportunity to develop and co-teach a college course and I, as the university instructor, learned new pedagogical strategies for working with hybrid university-community educational settings. Thus, the VOCES project truly demonstrated the potential for the Community as a Campus model to create transformative academic experiences for everyone involved.

Conclusion

By approaching Latinx communities not simply as test sites for academic study but rather as important intellectual collaborators, we dramatically enhance our capacity to create scholarship that identifies, analyzes, and contributes to the eradication of contemporary inequities. Community as a Campus is a powerful model for doing so. This model involves reimagining the places where learning happens, the participants in learning processes, the pedagogies that facilitate learning, the practices associated with learning, and the paradigms that structure ideas about learning. It reimagines places where learning happens by viewing communities as contexts in which legitimate knowledge is cultivated and created. It reimagines the participants in learning processes by positioning community members as legitimate teachers and researchers. It reimagines the pedagogies through which learning takes place by rooting educational experiences in culturally responsive curricula. It reimagines the practices associated with learning by not simply passively observing existing realities but seeking to understand, analyze, and transform those realities. Lastly, it reimagines the paradigms that structure ideas about learning by drawing on and synthesizing skills from across academic disciplines that are too often separated. The VOCES project described in this chapter is just one example of an effort to implement the Community as a Campus model. It is exciting to envision the educational possibilities that might arise from other such efforts.

Notes

1. Throughout this chapter I use the term Latinx as a gender non-binary alternative to Latina, Latino, and Latin@, in reference to U.S.-based persons of Latin American descent. I also use the alternative term Hispanic when referencing direct quotations.
2. Rodríguez-Muñiz (2015) cautions against viewing demographic predictions as straightforward reflections of empirical population shifts. Instead, he argues that we must attend to the performativity of statistics and the ways that they structure both popular anxieties and Latinx political organizing.
3. Pseudonyms are used for the city and school to protect anonymity.
4. It is crucial to reconsider the ways that categories such as first language and native speaker reproduce troublesome ideas about linguistic boundaries and proficiencies. Bonfiglio (2010), García and Torres-Guevara (2010), Makoni and Pennycook (2007), and others have critiqued these language ideologies at length.
5. Like the phrase "native language," it is important to understand "proficiency" as a situated ideological and institutional perception rather than an objective linguistic assessment (Rosa & Flores, 2017).
6. I use the term "minoritized" rather than "minority" to emphasize processes of marginalization instead of demographic calculations. This distinction draws attention to the ways that many populations and practices actually predominate within a given context yet are still characterized as "minority."
7. For a more in-depth description of the development and implementation of the Community as a Campus model in Chicago, see http://www.humboldtparkportal.org/news/2613 and https://greatcities.uic.edu/uic-neighborhoods-initiative/humboldt-park-initiative/.
8. Paris (2012) and Paris and Alim (2014) argue that we must build from asset-based pedagogies that view minoritized students' practices as useful starting points to enact culturally sustaining pedagogies that seek to disrupt racial and cultural hegemonies within mainstream schools. Rosa and Flores (2017) analyze the ways that these culturally sustaining approaches are particularly relevant in relation to Latinx students and their linguistic practices.

9. *NO HANGEO* is an iteration of the slang verb *janguear* (to hang out) but in standardized written Spanish it would be spelled with a "j" instead of an "h," a "u" between "g" and "e," and presented in the infinitival form *No Janguear* or the negative command form *No Janguee.*

References

Allred, S. L. (2009). The Inside-out prison exchange program: The impact of structure, content, and readings. *Journal of Correctional Education, 60*(3), 240–258.

Atalay, S. (2012). *Community-based archaeology: Research with, by, and for indigenous and local communities.* Berkeley, CA: University of California Press.

Bonfiglio, T. P. (2010). *Mother tongues and nations: The invention of the native speaker.* New York, NY: Mouton de Gruyter.

Bucholtz, M., Lopez, A., Mojarro, A., Skapoulli, E., VanderStouwe, C., & Warner-Garcia, S. (2014). Sociolingusitic justice in the schools: Student researchers as linguistic experts. *Language and Linguistics Compass, 8*(4), 144–157.

Cameron, D., Frazer, E., Harvey, P., Rampton, B., & Richardson, K. (1992). *Researching language: Issues of power and method.* London: Routledge.

Cammarota, J., & Fine, M. (2008). Youth participatory action research: A pedagogy for transformational resistance. In J. Cammarota & M. Fine (Eds.), *Revolutionizing education: Youth participatory action research in motion* (pp. 1–11). New York, NY: Routledge.

Coleman, E. G. (2010). Ethnographic approaches to digital media. *Annual Review of Anthropology, 39,* 487–505.

Fishman, J. A. (2010). *European vernacular literacy: A sociolinguistic and historical introduction.* Bristol: Multilingual Matters.

García, O., & Torres-Guevara, R. (2010). Monoglossic ideologies and language policies in the education of U.S. Latinas/os. In E. G. Murillo, Jr., S. A. Villenas, R. T. Galván, J. S. Muñoz, C. Martínez, & M. M. Casas (Eds.), *Handbook of Latinos and education: Theory, research, and practices* (pp. 182–193). New York, NY: Routledge.

Gubrium, A., & Harper, K. (2013). *Participatory visual and digital methods.* Walnut Creek, CA: Left Coast Press.

Labov, W. (1969*). The study of non-standard English.* Washington, DC: National Council of Teachers of English.

Lewis, O. (1966). *La vida: A Puerto Rican family in the culture of poverty—San Juan and New York.* New York, NY: Random House.

Makoni, S., & Pennycook, A. (Eds.). (2007). *Disinventing and reconstituting languages.* Clevedon: Multilingual Matters.

Paris, D. (2012). Culturally sustaining pedagogy: A needed change in stance, terminology, and practice. *Educational Researcher, 41*(3), 93–97.

Paris, D., & Alim, H. S. (2014). What are we seeking to sustain through culturally sustaining pedagogy? A loving critique forward. *Harvard Educational Review, 84*(1), 85–100.

Pompa, L. (2005). Service-learning as crucible: Reflections on immersion, context, power, and transformation. In D. W. Butin (Ed.), *Service-learning in higher education* (pp. 173–192). New York, NY: Palgrave Macmillan.

Rodríguez-Muñiz, M. (2015). *Temporal politics of the future: National Latino civil rights advocacy, demographic knowledge, and the "browning" of America* (Unpublished doctoral dissertation). Brown University.

Rosa, J., & Flores, N. (2017). Do you hear what I hear? Raciolinguistic ideologies and culturally sustaining pedagogies. In D. Paris & H. S. Alim (Eds.), *Culturally sustaining pedagogies: Teaching and learning for educational justice in a changing world* (pp. 175–190). New York, NY: Teachers College Press.

Shohamy, E., & Gorter, D. (Eds.). (2009). *Linguistic landscape: Expanding the scenery.* New York, NY: Routledge.

Urciuoli, B. (2001). The complex diversity of languages in the U.S. In I. Susser & T. Carl (Eds.), *Cultural diversity in the United States: A critical reader* (pp. 190–205). Newcastle upon Tyne: Cambridge Scholars Publishing.

Wolfram, W. (2001). From definition to policy: The ideological struggle of African-American English. In J. E. Alatis & A.-H. Tan (Eds.), *Language in our time: Georgetown roundtable on languages and linguistics* (pp. 292–312). Washington, DC: Georgetown University Press.

Wolfram, W., Adger, C. T., & Christian, D. (2007). *Dialects in schools and communities.* New York, NY: Routledge.

Zentella, A. C. (1997). *Growing up bilingual: Puerto Rican children in New York*, NY. Malden, MA: Blackwell.

Zentella, A. C. (Ed.). (2005). *Building on strength: Language and literacy in Latino families and communities.* New York, NY: Teachers College Press.

7. *Motherists' Pedagogies of Cultural Citizenship: Claiming Rights and Space in a Xenophobic Era*

JUDITH FLORES CARMONA

With one of the fastest growing populations in the country, Latinas/os' presence has been viewed mostly in negative ways—especially in areas where their existence had been unprecedented. The primary focus of this critical ethnographic study was to find out how Latina mothers engage and enact pedagogies of the home and their responsibility to fight for basic social needs and the various forms of activism that take place through their participation in their children's education and *educación* in their community, school, and homes. This study took place in the largest city in a state in the Intermountain West. Leo Chávez (2008) writes about Latinos in the United States and how they get constructed as a threat through the media, during legislative sessions across the country, in promulgated discourses, and anti-immigrant groups' blatant messages conveyed via counter protests and policies. Latinas/os are seen as a problem or a threat rather than as contributing members of society who possess cultural assets and who participate in schools and in other social spaces (Chávez, 2008). Leo Chávez (2008) explains how the Latino threat narrative gets promulgated and the impact it has on this population as well as its basic premises.

> Latinas/os[1] are a reproductive threat, altering the demographic makeup of the nation; Latinas/os are unable or unwilling to learn English; Latinas/os are unable or unwilling to integrate into the larger society; they live apart from the larger society, not integrating socially. (Chávez, 2008, p. 51)

The "Latina reproductive threat or out-of-control fertility" promotes an exaggerated image and discourse of promiscuous women who bear children to then rip off the system as welfare beneficiaries (Chávez, 2008, p. 23). Villenas'

(2001), work focuses on Latinas' experiences in the United States and she asserts that "at the discursive level, racial ideologies serve to construct Latinas/os as an invisible, visible 'Other'—invisible as 'ghost' workers, yet highly visible as families needing education and health care" or other social services (p. 5).

Most alarming is how Latina mothers continue to be portrayed as incompetent (at best) to educate their children, to enhance their learning, or are blamed for contributing to the educational achievement gap (Fuller, Bein, Kim, & Rabe-Hesketh, 2015). Fuller et al. (2015) assert that they "found little evidence that foreign-born mothers exercised stronger home practices that advanced toddlers' early cognitive growth as posited by immigrant-advantage theory" (p. 2). Deficit-framed scholarship continues to portray Latina mothers as lacking knowledge, having no voice or agency, and as contributors to the lack of "cognitive growth" of their children. Negative portrayals of Latinas are linked directly to how their bodies come to represent or encompass certain stereotypes that bring forth their visibility but only as lacking the capability to succeed in society and whose experienced discrimination therefore becomes de-facto.

Findings from this study illustrate concrete ways in which Latina mothers' wisdom is defined and imparted in culturally-specific ways, juxtaposing traditional parental engagement scholarship. Though Latina mothers face the impact of negative stereotypes imparted on them, they are also constantly fighting to make their visibility as holders of knowledge acknowledged in their homes, in schools, and in their communities. In this chapter, I first build on the work of Chicana scholar Dolores Delgado Bernal (2001) and her coined concept of pedagogies of the home situated within cultural citizenship and Chicana/Latina feminisms. I then provide the experiences of Latina mothers as *testimonios de educación*, and lastly conclude by providing specific ways in which Latinas civically engage but more importantly, claim space and rights in the form of pedagogies of cultural citizenship.

Pedagogies of the Home

> The communication, practices and learning that occur in the home and community, what I call pedagogies of the home, often serve as a cultural knowledge base that helps … negotiate the daily experiences of sexist, racist, and classist microaggressions. … The pedagogies of the home extend the existing discourse on critical pedagogies by putting cultural knowledge and language at the forefront … because power and politics are at the center of all teaching and learning, the application of household knowledge to situations outside of the home becomes a creative process that interrupts the transmission of "official knowledge" and "dominant ideologies." (Delgado Bernal, 2001, p. 624)

Pedagogies of the home was named out of the necessity to include the epistemologies, pedagogies, and knowledge of Latina/o homes that usually does not make it into school settings, especially in a standards-based curriculum era (Delgado Bernal, 2001; Sleeter, 2005, 2008). Pedagogies of the home extend critical pedagogies by placing cultural-familial-communal knowledge at the forefront. These everyday lessons and rituals that take place in the homes of Latina mothers include teachings through oral histories, storytelling, "legends, *corridos,* and behavior" that are therefore passed on from generation to generation through mother-child interactions that are both overt and covert (Delgado Bernal, 2001, p. 624). Pedagogies of the home also situate everyday practices, contradictions, and teachings through *consejos* (wisdom passed on through advice), *respeto* (respect for elders and their knowledge), and *educación* (education based on lived experience that instills values, morals, and cultural and familial teaching) at the center of the informal education in everyday life (Elenes, Gonzalez, Delgado Bernal, & Villenas, 2001).

For example, children and youth have heard from their parent[s] about the migration stories of how their family ended up in *El Norte* and these are imbued with lessons of resistance and of making sacrifices to seek a better life and opportunities (Flores Carmona, 2010, 2011, 2014). By listening and gathering stories that will not be taught in school, pedagogies of the home provide students and their mothers with strategies of resistance that center Latina mothers as the holders and producers of knowledge (Delgado Bernal, 2002, 2008; Delgado Bernal, Elenes, Godinez & Villenas, 2006; Villenas & Moreno, 2001). The home is imbued with cultural-familial teachings and pedagogies from which teachers can draw the outside the classroom knowledge—to dispel deficit ideologies held of Latina/o parents and students (Sleeter, 2005). Delgado Bernal's (2001) work on defining pedagogies of the home is related to research done by Gonzalez et al. (1995) that draws from the knowledge that is produced within the home and defines it as funds of knowledge. Funds of knowledge revolved around conversations between scholars and primary school teachers that asserted community knowledge was essential in addressing literacy instruction for "language minority students" (Moll, Veléz-Ibáñez, & Rivera, 1990, p. iv). A shift in how schools viewed language minority children as coming from so-called cultures of poverty was necessary in order to begin to incorporate pedagogies that are relevant to Latina/o students' experiences and needs.

Indeed, Latina mothers practice more holistic forms of education (*educación*) to their children by enacting cultural signifiers or everyday teachings through their quotidian doings. Latina mothers' stories and lessons are taught to their children and arise from interactions entre *mujeres* (among women), and in sharing their own *testimonios*. Brown women theorize from their body, from the pain, from suffering, from desire, from yearning to belong, from experiences that inform their epistemologies and pedagogies for their children (Cruz, 2006). Indeed, Latina mothers' *testimonios*, are passed on to their children as a way of life or the ways of teaching and learning that they grew up with and that are expected to be learned by their children (Villenas, 2006). González, Plata, Garcia, Torres, and Urrieta (2003) argue that gathering *testimonios de inmigrantes* can better prepare future teachers to address the needs of this growing population. Delineating and further understanding Latina mothers' pedagogical moments of the home, places Latina mothers' cultural citizenship practices as fundamental in the education of their children.

Cultural Citizenship and Chicana/Latina Feminisms

Latina/o cultural citizenship (LCC) and Chicana/Latina feminist theory (CLFT) are the critical-theoretical paradigms that guided this study. LCC offers a helpful construct to understand how citizenship practices are informed by culture, how claims to citizenship are reinforced or subverted by cultural assumptions, and how one negotiates and compromises a sense of belonging and membership in different contexts (Rosaldo, 1997). A key element of cultural citizenship is the process of "'affirmation,' as the community itself defines its interests, its binding solidarities, its boundaries, its own space, and its membership" (Flores & Benmayor, 1997, p. 13). Cultural citizenship includes a broad range of activities of everyday life, similarly to everyday home practices or pedagogies of the home, through which Latinas can claim a space in society and eventually claim rights in educational settings (Flores & Benmayor, 1997). For the Latina mothers in this study, the issue of documentation/legality or citizenship is a constant struggle as they are caught up not only in a tenuous immigration status but also in a patriarchal system that may continue inhibiting their recognition as holders of knowledge who participate fully in the home, at schools, and in their community.

Cherrie Moraga (2002) explains that Chicana/Latina feminist theory does not only value *mujeres'* lived experience, but that we embody theory. Indeed, Chicana/Latina feminist scholars have written about pedagogies of Latina/o homes and communities and how these pedagogical practices can be utilized in educational settings. Claiming a space in the classroom using cultural-familial pedagogies of the home, allows for the lived experiences of Latina/o families to bridge the school-community gap while foregrounding their home knowledge and enacting cultural citizenship. A pressing issue for many Latina/o parents has been and continues to be the highly-contested immigration reform debate, navigating anti-immigrant spaces and the constant straddling of cultures or borderlands. Villenas (2006) defines the physical (territorial border between Mexico and the United States) and mental borderlands that Latina mothers inhibit as the "cultural sensibilities and ethnicities, between citizen and 'alien,' between generations, between diverse mothering practices, and between meanings of 'womanhood'. ... These borderlands where Latina mothers and daughters teach and learn through body and words are pedagogical spaces" (p. 147). The mothers' experiences come to represent the constant straddling between sites, *entre sitios y lenguas* and borderlands (Anzaldúa, 1999; Pérez, 1999).

The Gender and Cultural Citizenship Working Group (Caldwell, Coll, Fisher, & Ramirez, 2009) assert that since women of color embody multiple and intersecting identities, they are bound to occupy, experience, and engage in "social relationships infused with power and exclusionary potential" (p. 5). Therefore, they suggest a "gendered" approach to exploring and analyzing citizenship issues among women of color in order to denaturalize "the masculine [and] to disrupt the assumed dichotomy between the public and private in male lives and citizenship practices" (p. 8). Paying attention to women of color's "'vernacular' citizenship allows us to broaden our notions of what constitutes an empowered 'political actor' and how she understands and experiences her citizenship on the ground in everyday life" (Caldwell et al., p. 11). It is important to understand how Latina mothers are political actors in the public and private spheres, acknowledging their gendered citizenship practices and valorizing their activism in their quotidian lives.

Merging LCC and CLFT allows me then to continue expanding on the work of Delgado Bernal, Alemán, and Flores Carmona (2008) and to further define pedagogies of cultural citizenship.

> Cultural signifiers such as, *educación* (holistic, cultural, and moral education), *consejos* (wisdom and advice from lived experience), [and] *testimonios* ... all inform the methodology and the way we make sense of the teaching and learning of cultural citizenship across generations of Latinas/os in transnational spaces ... we understand these conceptual terms as pedagogies of cultural citizenship that facilitate the learning and sharing of life's lessons in relation to an individual's or a community's educational rights, sense of belonging, and cultural identities. (p. 32)

Throughout this chapter, I connect the cultural signifiers and practices the mothers have shared throughout and offer concrete examples of how Latina mothers instill this knowledge[s] to their children. Through their *consejos,* transgenerational *educación*, their silence and their doing, the mothers have in fact displayed manifestations of a gendered cultural citizenship—demonstrating that their "pedagogies of mothering go far beyond help with homework and volunteering in classrooms" (Gonzalez, 2001, p. 213). Pedagogies of cultural citizenship are grounded in everyday cultural practices that contribute to the teaching and learning of citizenship formation beyond the classroom. Even though the Latina mothers in this study hold vulnerable immigration statuses, in the next section I share how they are indeed "political subjects who contribute to society and claim rights for themselves, their children, and their community" (Delgado Bernal, Alemán, & Flores Carmona, 2008, p. 32).

Latina Mothers' Testimonios *and Pedagogies of Cultural Citizenship*

Collectivity and solidarity among undocumented Latina mothers is at the heart of the teaching and learning that takes place in their home and in their communities. Six Latina mothers and their son or daughter participated in this study: Angela and Karen; Monserrat and Rubén: Viviana and Maria: Lourdes and Aurora: Patty and Gustavo: and Maite and Maria Fernanda.[2] Five of the mothers are from different regions of Mexico and one is from Guatemala—all are undocumented. The participants live in a state in the Intermountain West, in its largest city. Primary data for this critical ethnographic study included observations, informal *platicas*, two interviews, their self-authored *testimonios*, documents and artifacts, a focus group, and activities in their homes, at the school or in the community. I gave the Latina mothers a 75-page notebook and a Spanish copy of chapter one from the *testimonio*, *Me Llamo Rigoberta Menchú y Así Me Nació la Conciencia/ I, Rigoberta Menchu: An Indian Woman in Guatemala* (Burgos-Debray, 1985). The mothers took the notebooks home, they called me when they needed clarification, and then they invited me over to their home when their written *testimonio* was ready. Their *testimonios* were of particular interest because the mothers were able to name their realities and lived experiences—they were authors of their own history and were able to denounce oppressive situations they had experienced. Since their pieces were written in Spanish I translated them to English (Flores Carmona, 2014). The following paragraphs demonstrate how their *testimonios* were one of their pedagogical tools.

En Sus Propias Palabras*: Motherists' Testimonios*

Undocumented Latina mothers' overt acts of activism, such as marching and demanding rights for themselves and their communities, may be "forbidden by gendered norms and standards of citizenship to use their status as mothers for anything other than the 'proper' rearing of their children" (Bejarano, 2002, p. 126). However, examples of overt acts of activism are exhibited by mothers whose sons and daughters disappeared in Ciudad Juarez, Mexico, El Salvador, and in Argentina where "mothers demanded to know what had happened to their children … and transformed prior gendered notions of citizenship into the evolution of maternal citizenship" (Bejarano, 2002, p. 130). The mothers in Bejarano's research became known as *las súper madres de Latinoamérica,* for their courage to fight against the government demanding to know what happened to their children—their maternal love action turned these mothers into motherists[3] (Bejarano, 2002). Negrón-Gonzales (2013) reminds us that, "this process of navigation for undocumented [people] can often catalyze meaning-making processes and political action … to challenge dominant societal norms and beliefs is both personal and political, and it is a fundamental component of social movements" (p. 1286). *Las súper madres de Latinoamérica*[4] redefined the "good mother" to include their demonstrated love and care for their children at home and taking their struggles to the public. Indeed, the love and care for their children guided and strengthened their battles (Bejarano, 2002).

Good mothers may be deemed as bad women when they move their motherly practices and love outside the private to the public and utilize their strength and resiliency to demonstrate that their love exceeds the four walls of their home to defy the state. Motherists are women activists who come together, in solidarity, to claim rights and space in communities where their presence has historically been minimal or nonexistent. Latinas are contributing members of society whose practices enhance and strengthen the economic and cultural wealth of the country even if they have a vulnerable immigration status (Flores & Benmayor, 1997). Lourdes, Aurora's mother, can be described as a motherist.

Early in spring 2009, when I began collecting data for this study, Lourdes shared her aspiration to be more involved in the community. She also saw a clear connection between her desire to make Aurora's school experience better and the need to make changes within the school so that all kids benefitted. I had already witnessed Lourdes' leadership skills when we both participated in a community advocacy program in 2007. She said:

> *Quiero involucrarme más en las escuelas, una porque soy madre pero una ve las necesidades que hay en tu comunidad a tu alrededor … a veces la gente no sabe la información de actividades que hay en la comunidad* (I want to be more involved in schools, first because I am a mother and because I see all the needs in my surrounding communities … sometimes people don't have information on activities taking place in our community).

Mothers, like Lourdes, have large personal networks, perhaps because they are usually most involved in school-related activities and events and they are able to form circles of kinship with other mothers. The mothers' "kinkeeper role for children's social relationships" is integral for the child to also develop his/her own relationships and networks in school and in their community (Oliveri & Reiss, 1987, p. 733). Lourdes is strategic in forming alliances because she is aware that organizing and having strong networks is foundational when doing community work.

Lourdes also recognized that she needed to feel supported by other Latina mothers and work closer with the Latina principal using their knowledge of Spanish as their primary commonality. She believed that the participation of more parents would strengthen the cause; parents would become visible in educational settings and probably produce change faster. Lourdes recognized, as Ward (1995) has as well, that in community work, "a collective identity to know that one is not alone, and one is inextricably connected to others and embedded in a network of interdependent relationships" (p. 183). Indeed, it is imperative and fundamental to bring about change in schools and in society. Lourdes also notes:

> *Y yo también he visto que en el PTA hay puros americanos [en el 2009], no hay hispanos. Es triste. Debería de haber una junta en español para saber qué es lo que está pasando en la escuela y qué hacer. Y necesitaríamos que la directora se reuniera una vez al mes con nosotros, pero que fuera en español porque a mí a veces, me desespero porque todas las cosas son en ingles, ingles, ingles. Para estar 100 por ciento con los Latinos hay que hacer juntas también en español y la directora tiene que poner de su parte* (I have seen only White Americans, there are no Hispanos [sic] in the PTA meetings. There ought to be a meeting in Spanish to learn what is going on at the school and to know what to do about it. We would need the principal to hold a meeting with us once a month and in Spanish; I lose hope because everything is in English, English, English. To be 100% with the Latino parents, the principal should cooperate and lead meetings in Spanish).

Lourdes, who is bilingual, points out how a language barrier is usually what keeps Spanish-speaking parents from showing up to English-only PTA meetings. If meetings are only held in English, then only English-speaking parents will show up. Her strong conviction and push to have equitable parent representation in PTA gatherings helped in her election as the very first Spanish-speaking president of the association. In Fall 2009, Lourdes started in her new leadership role and quickly recruited other Latina/o parents. The PTA meetings were run bilingually, with the majority of the attendees being Latina mothers, including three of the participants in this study, thus merging "*un sitio y una lengua*" (Pérez, 1999, p. 47). As Pérez (1999) states,

> I wish to point out that our works emerge from *un sitio y una lengua* (a space and language) that rejects colonial ideology and the by-products of colonialism. ... The space and language is rooted in both the words and silence of Third-World-Identified-Third-World-Women who create a place apart from white men and women and from men of color ... where we create for each other. (pp. 47–48)

This school space was not only claimed but it became transformed through language and the Latina/o presence in the PTA meetings. Indeed, mothers inspired each other to act and together they transformed *sitios* (spaces) by using their *lengua* (language) to make their concerns and needs heard as well as redefine practices of civic engagement. Before each PTA meeting, Lourdes called and rallied Latina mothers to join her, especially when she needed support and representation in numbers. Latina mothers were active agents forging change utilizing their familial-cultural-communal practices while supporting their children's education and as a result, their actions became pedagogies of cultural citizenship.

The community in which the mothers lived made them feel somewhat safe to embrace their identities and to practice their cultural traditions. However, for the six Latina mothers, their immigration status is what kept them from fighting against the structural system more overtly, especially to get involved at the political level. When mothering takes place in an anti-immigrant environment, it involves the "psychological work of teaching cultural dignity and integrity in the midst of cultural assault" (Villenas & Moreno, 2001, p. 672). A couple of the mothers mentioned to me that they felt at ease in their neighborhood because it catered to their religious, cultural, and linguistic needs, but once they left these comforts, it was a different experience. The dominance of conservative perspectives and anti-immigrant legislation along with the strong fundamentalist religious beliefs limited their freedom. Lourdes commented:

> *Soy libre porque puedo interactuar con las personas pero nomas por no tener papeles, no tener el seguro, pues se me pone una barrera, pero espiritualmente y personalmente yo pienso que soy libre.* (I am free because I can interact with different people, but since I do not have legal documentation and do not have a social security number, that's a barrier, but spiritually and personally I think I am free).

Spiritual and personal freedom is in many ways what contributed to the affirmation of the mothers' identities. Their cultural identifiers and performances allowed them to claim rights remaining grounded in their gender, class, race, and ethnic and linguistic subjectivities. The thing that held the mothers' back was their tenuous immigration status. As another mother, Montserrat asserted:

> *La verdad yo lo veo difícil [una reforma migratoria] … pues como que entra más miedo, andar manejando sin papeles y tener que ir a trabajar con ese miedo ahí adentro. Temor a que lo paren a uno. Trato de no pensar, manejo al límite, no tengo licencia, manejo con cuidado para no tener problemas con la policía, pero siempre ando con miedo* (To be honest, I think it'll be difficult [to pass immigration reform] … I have more fear driving without papers and we have to go to work with that fear inside of us. Fear of being pulled over. I try not to think about it, I drive at the speed limit, I don't have a driver's license, I drive carefully to avoid problems with the police, I have constant fear).

Both Lourdes and Montserrat described themselves as having liminal citizenship rights or not fully belonging as community members due to their undocumented status. They both live in constant fear and have therefore become model citizens in many ways: not committing any infractions, being fully involved in community and school efforts, and abiding by the law all the time. While Lourdes and other Latina mothers were able to (re)create the school space, by being (re)presented in the PTA, they continued to live in the shadows in other spaces. Pérez (1999) argues,

> the oppressed as colonial other becomes the liminal identity, partially seen yet unspoken, vibrant and in motion, overshadowed by the construction of coloniality, where decolonial imaginary moves and lives. One is not simply oppressed or victimized; nor is one only oppressor or victimizer. Rather, one negotiates within the imaginary to a decolonizing otherness where all identities are at work in oneway or another. (p. 7)

Lourdes was able to visualize, to imagine the PTA as a space of possibility where the decolonial imaginary would bring about some change for her community.

Spaces of contradictions and possibility allow Latina mothers to work from the margins or out of the shadows with resiliency. Their actions in the process are imbued with pedagogies of cultural citizenship that they instill in their children via their practices. Maite, another mother participant, noted:

> *Si estuve ahí [en las marchas para una reforma migratoria] yo creo que es para que nos den una oportunidad de trabajar mas que nada* (Yes I was there [at the marches for immigration reform]. I think it was for them, to ask them to give us an opportunity to work, more than anything).

Maite's daughter, Maria Fernanda, was born in the United States, but Maite came as an undocumented person. Maite explained to her daughter why she had to attend marches or other events: "*Yo le explico de donde venimos para que se sienta orgullosa de su identidad* (I explain to her where we came from so she can feel proud of her identity"). Maite teaches Maria Fernanda about her Mexican ancestry and about the importance of being involved in events for immigration reform. Maria Fernanda identifies as Mexicana and often asks her mother to tell her stories about Mexico. Maite's vulnerable immigration status does not limit her community involvement in pro-immigration reform efforts and she and her daughter maintain their cultural pride and dignity in the process. Ángela also supported the various causes and saw the value of people coming together toward a common goal:

> *Uno debe de apoyar todo eso para que vean que, hora que yo también tengo esa frase de que 'la unión hace la fuerza' ... entonces pues si, si uno se une para luchar, para conseguir lo que uno quiere, pues beneficia a todos* (One should support all of those events so that they see, I have this saying, 'strength in numbers/unity makes us stronger' ... so yes, if one joins others in the struggle, to fight for what we want, it will benefit everyone).

The mothers' pedagogies of the home and their public activism work in tandem—pro-immigration reform activities exemplified the possibilities of decolonial imaginary where public spaces were "transformed into locations of resistance and the mothers' voices filled these spaces as they used every means possible to draw attention to their cause" (Bejarano, 2002, p. 136).

These *testimonios* detail the various ways in which the mothers' race, ethnicity, immigration status, language, and gender "intersect with the structural, political, and representational systems of subordination" as they try to carve out spaces of belonging in a large city in the Intermountain West (Gonzalez, 1998, p. 95). However, there was contrast between the mothers' overt street politics and their more subtle forms of activism. While Maite's participation in the marches was very political, so was the other five mothers' engagement in pedagogies of cultural citizenship in more subtle forms of activism. For example, Lourdes, Viviana, and Patty participated in the PTA meetings and Ángela and Montserrat were fully aware of the anti-immigrant climate and laws because they informed themselves via the news and local agencies. All six of the Latina mothers practiced what Bejarano (2002) calls "maternal citizenship," meaning that Latina mothers draw from their maternal instinct, their motherwork, and their pedagogies of the home to teach their children about being proud of their Latina/o identities as well as informed about the oppressive situation of undocumented people in the U.S. Maite consoled her daughter whenever they watched the news regarding immigration issues:

> *Vemos las noticias y nos ponemos a platicar y todo eso. Y a veces me dice, 'mami, ¿si un día nos separan a nosotras?' Le digo, ¡ay mi vida! Pues yo a veces le tengo que decir que eso solo pasa en la televisión, que no se preocupe. Pero, pues es que es la realidad ... Y no, no sabemos. Pero si, hablamos de todo esto, siempre con las noticias* (We watch the news together and then we talk about all that. Sometimes she says to me, "mommy, what if they separate us one day?" I say, "Oh my dear"

> Sometimes I have to tell her that that only happens on television shows and that she shouldn't worry. But that's a reality … and we just don't know. But yes, we talk about all of those issues from the news).

Indeed, staying informed and discussing topics that affect families of mixed immigration status is also a type of motherist practice and pedagogy of cultural citizenship. While some mothers took to the streets to demand rights, being active in the private sphere was and is also of high importance.

Silence was not an option for the six Latina mothers when expressing their *sobrevivencia* (survival) and *supervivencia* (traumatic, near death survival) experiences to their children. Telling their *testimonios* allowed the mothers to not only convey their border-crossing experiences, but to connect them to the sociopolitical realm and to the information on laws that affect undocumented people. The Latina mothers were engaged in various ways, discursively and performatively, in claiming rights and in teaching their children to remain proud of their Latina/o identity in the midst of anti-immigrant xenophobic times. They understood the urgency and importance of instilling in their children knowledge and tools to know how to defend themselves. Lourdes firmly stated:

> *A veces nada más por el color lo maltratan a uno aunque no tengan ni idea de dónde venimos. La discriminación comienza por el color de piel y por eso yo les digo a mis hijas que siempre va haber racismo. Yo las educo, les enseño que tenemos que tener buenas relaciones con gente de diferentes razas, les digo que el color no debería de importar, pero si* (Sometimes they want to mistreat us just based on our skin color and they have no idea where we come from.
> Discrimination begins based on skin color and so I tell my daughters that there will always be racism. I educate them, I teach them to have good relationships with people from different races and I tell them color shouldn't matter, but it does).

Developing good relationships with people of a different race or ethnicity is a strategy Lourdes taught her daughter. Knowing that racism prevails in the U.S. and that as undocumented people, coalescing, and relationship building is of extreme value and importance, demonstrated Lourdes' political motherwork and maternal citizenship.

The mothers' pedagogies of cultural citizenship were demonstrated through their collectivity and engagement to and with other subordinated groups—a necessary strategy to bring about collective social change. These pedagogies required the mothers to use their *consejos*, their *testimonios*, and their community activism as they exerted resiliency through their organized motherist practices. Ángela, Maite, Lourdes, Patty, Montserrat, and Viviana, as mothers of Latina/o children who are citizens and non-U.S. legal residents, were nonetheless expected to enact their roles as wives and as mothers, raising respectable future contributing members and citizens. The Latina mothers used their cultural-familial everyday practices to claim space and rights. Their motherist practices or pedagogies of cultural citizenship against oppression are tools of resistance for their children to utilize now, in their future, and across generations.

Conclusion

Patricia Hill Collins (1994, 2000) asserts that women of color's subjective experiences of mothering/motherhood are inextricably linked to sociocultural concerns and issues and when their children are under attack, their motherwork pushes them to take action against authority. Indeed, Mohanty (1991) affirms that women are subjects in historically and culturally specific ways—but they are also active agents of change in their communities. They are "agents of resistance in their own self-empowerment" but also agents of change for the betterment of their children's lives and their communities (Morales & Bejarano, 2009, p. 421). The Latina mothers' pedagogical moments enacted by them cannot be easily conveyed as specific "positive lessons" (i.e., hard work, emotional strength, cultural traditions), but rather, their childrearing beliefs that they valued were purposefully set out to teach me [us] through their actions. The lessons occurred in the improvised and contextual moments, when a story or a *testimonio* was told for a purpose.

Reflexivity on how these teachings can be applied sheds light on the possibilities these concepts offer us for further understanding Latina mothers. We need to be able to understand how these concepts can also be incorporated into our classrooms and how these pedagogical practices can make a clear connection between the home, the community and the school. There are possibilities in conceptualizing mother-child epistemologies and pedagogies necessary for *sobrevivencia* in the borderlands as they allow us to see how Latina mothers enact their civic engagement (Villenas, 2006). Their teachings to survive and thrive in anti-immigrant, xenophobic, nativist spaces situate Latino children moving passed "cognitive growth" (Fuller et al., 2015) to assert their cultural-familial-communal knowledges as imperative, essential, and not measurable by tests or biased curricula.

Lessons Learned

Villenas, Godinez, Delgado Bernal, and Elenes, (2006) ask an important question: "How might we view children differently when we understand their mothers' living pedagogies?" (p. 5). As educators, theorists, and practitioners, being able to understand Latina/o children and their mothers' mujer-oriented pedagogies of cultural citizenship is of integral importance to know how to merge their *educación* of the home with the education children receive at school. *Educación, consejos*, and lessons imparted by mothers, form the foundation for being and becoming citizens in the nation-state. These intersecting realities of Latina mothers, "shape and reshape a homeplace for children" as they learn to resist assimilation, to embrace their Latina/o identities, and develop "cultural integrity" (Gonzalez, 1998, p. 88).

These pedagogies of cultural citizenship are skill sets, tools of how to network, tools of resistance, and understandings necessary for survival in the U.S. The mothers' "gendered citizenship" and motherist practices are manifestations of pedagogies of the home to claim space and rights in their everyday lives. Pedagogies of cultural citizenship redefine teachings about what it means for Latina mothers and their children to participate in schools, to be involved as cultural citizens in public spaces and to claim rights via the incorporation of pedagogies of the home. Pedagogies of cultural citizenship offers possibilities for understanding how "A liminal space where women of the Americas ... learn to *sobrevivir* (to survive) sexism, class oppression, and discrimination while laying their mark on the world," and become teachings that help their children navigate xenophobic, nativist spaces (Villenas, 2006, p. 152).

Notes

1. Chávez (2008) only used the Latino category when referring to this group; I included Latinas/os to include women specifically and also to broaden the definition and to include single mothers/parents from Mexico and Central America.
2. All pseudonyms were chosen by the participants to protect their identities and for purposes of anonymity. At the time, the kids/students were ten or eleven years old.
3. Motherist is a term coined by Cynthia Bejarano to define the motherwork, activism performed by mothers.
4. The super mothers of Latin America.

References

Anzaldúa, G. (1999). *Borderlands/La frontera: The new mestiza* (2nd ed.). San Francisco, CA: Aunt Lute Books.

Bejarano, C. L. (2002). *Las super madres de Latino America*: Transforming motherhood by challenging violence in Mexico, Argentina, and El Salvador. *Frontiers: A Journal of Women's Studies, 23*(1), 126–150.

Burgos-Debray, E. (1985). *Me llamo Rigoberta Menchú y así me nació la conciencia* (Vol. 3). México Districto Federal, México: Siglo XXI Editores.

Caldwell, K. L., Coll, K., Fisher, T., & Ramirez, R. K. (2009). *Gendered citizenships: Transnational perspectives on knowledge production, political activism, and culture.* New York, NY: Palgrave Macmillan.

Chávez, L. R. (2008). *The Latino threat: Constructing immigrants, citizens, and the nation.* Stanford, CA: Stanford University Press.

Collins, P. H. (1994). Shifting the center: Race, class, and feminist theorizing about motherhood. In E. Nakano Glenn, G. Chang, & L. R. Forcey (Eds.), *Mothering: Ideology, experience, and agency* (pp. 45–65). New York, NY: Routledge.

Collins, P. H. (2000). *Black feminist thought: Knowledge, consciousness, and the politics of empowerment* (2nd ed.). New York, NY: Routledge.

Cruz, C. (2006). Toward an epistemology of a Brown body. In D. Delgado Bernal, C. A. Elenes, F. E. Godinez, & S. Villenas (Eds.), *Chicana/Latina education in everyday life: Feminista perspectives on pedagogy and epistemology* (pp. 59–75). New York, NY: SUNY Press.

Delgado Bernal, D. (2001). Learning and living pedagogies of the home: The mestizo consciousness of Chicana students. *Qualitative Studies in Education, 14*(5), 623–639.

Delgado Bernal, D. (2002). Critical race theory, Latino critical theory, and critical raced gendered epistemologies: Recognizing students of color as holders and creators of knowledge. *Qualitative Inquiry, 8*(1), 105–124.

Delgado Bernal, D., Alemán, E., & Flores Carmona, J. (2008). Transnational and transgenerational Latina/o cultural citizenship among kindergarteners, their parents, and university students in Utah. *Social Justice: A Journal of Crime, Conflict, & World Order, 35*(1), 28–49.

Delgado Bernal, D., Elenes, C. A., Godinez, F. E., & Villenas, S. (Eds.). (2006). *Chicana/ Latina education in everyday life: Feminista perspectives on pedagogy and epistemology.* Albany, NY: State University of New York Press.

Elenes, C. A., Gonzalez, F. E., Delgado Bernal, D., & Villenas, S. (2001). Introduction: Chicana/Mexicana feminist pedagogies: Consejos, respeto, y educación in everyday life. *Qualitative Studies in Education, 14*(5), 595–602.

Flores Carmona, J. (2010). *Transgenerational educación: Latina mothers' everyday pedagogies of cultural citizenship in Salt Lake City, Utah* (Unpublished doctoral dissertation). University of Utah. Salt Lake City, Utah.

Flores Carmona, J. (2011). Veracruz to Amherst: Undocumented student to postdoctoral fellow. *Chicana/Latina Studies: The Journal of MALCS, 10*(2), 32–39.

Flores Carmona, J. (2014). Cutting out their tongues: Mujeres' testimonios and the malintzin researcher. *Journal of Latino/Latin American Studies (JOLLAS) Special Issue: (Re)envisioning Chicana/Latina Feminist Methodologies, 6*(2), 113–124.

Flores, W. V., & Benmayor, R. (Eds). (1997). *Latino cultural citizenship: Claiming identity, space, and rights.* Boston, MA: Beacon Press.

Fuller, B., Bein, E., Kim, Y., & Rabe-Hesketh, S. (2015). Differing cognitive trajectories of Mexican American toddlers: The role of class, nativity, and maternal practices. *Hispanic Journal of Behavioral Sciences, 37*(2), 139–169.

Gonzalez, F. E. (1998). Formations of Mexicananess: Trenzas de identidades multiples: Growing up Mexicana: Braids of multiple identities. *International Journal of Qualitative Studies in Education, 2*(1), 81–102.

González, N. (2001). *I am my language: Discourses of women and children in the borderlands.* Tucson, AZ: The University of Arizona Press.

Gonzalez, N., Moll, L. C., Tenery, M. F., Rivera, A., Rendon, P., Gonzales, R., & Amanti, C. (1995). Funds of knowledge for teaching in Latino households. *Urban Education, 29*(4), 443–470.

González, S. M., Plata, O., Garcia, E., Torres, M., & Urrieta, L. (2003). Essays and interviews: Testimonios de inmigrantes: Students educating future teachers. *Journal of Latinos and Education, 2*(4), 233–243.

Mohanty, C. T. (1991). Under Western eyes: Feminist scholarship and colonial discourse. In C. T. Mohanty & L. Torres (Eds.), *Third-world women and the politics of feminism* (pp. 51–80). Bloomington, IN: Indiana University Press.

Moll, L. C., Veléz-Ibáñez, C., & Rivera, C. (1990). *Community knowledge and classroom practice: Combining resources for literacy instruction.* Washington, DC: The United States Department of Education.

Moraga, C. (2002). Theory in the flesh. In C. Moraga & G. E. Anzaldúa (Eds.), *This bridge called my back: Writings by radical women of color* (p. 21). San Francisco, CA: Aunt Lute Press.

Morales, M. C., & Bejarano, C. (2009). Transnational sexual and gendered violence: An application of border sexual conquest at a Mexico-U.S. border. *Global Networks, 9*(3), 420–439.

Negrón-Gonzales, G. (2013). Navigating "illegality": Undocumented youth & oppositional consciousness. *Children and Youth Services Review, 35*, 1284–1290.

Oliveri, M. E., & Reiss, D. (1987). Social networks of family members: Distinctive roles of mothers and fathers. *Sex Roles, 17*(11–12), 719–736.

Pérez, E. (1999). *The decolonial imaginary, writing Chicanas into history.* Bloomington, MD: Indiana University Press.

Rosaldo, R. (1997). Cultural citizenship, inequality, and multiculturalism. In W. V. Flores & R. Benmayor (Eds.), *Latino cultural citizenship: Claiming identity, space, and rights* (pp. 27–38). Boston, MA: Beacon Press.

Sleeter, C. E. (2005). *Un-standardizing curriculum: Multicultural teaching in the standards based classroom.* New York, NY: Teachers College Press.

Sleeter, C. E. (2008). Critical family history, identity, and historical memory. *Educational Studies, 43*, 114–124.

Villenas, S. A. (2001). Latina mothers and small-town racisms: Creating narratives of dignity and moral education in North Carolina. *Anthropology & Education Quarterly, 32*(1), 3–28.

Villenas, S. A. (2006). Pedagogical moments in the borderland: Latina mothers teaching and learning. In D. Delgado Bernal, C. A. Elenes, F. E. Godinez, & S. Villenas (Eds.), *Chicana/Latina education in everyday life: Feminista perspectives on pedagogy and epistemology* (pp. 147–159). Albany, NY: State University of New York Press.

Villenas, S. A., Godinez, F. E., Delgado Bernal, D., & Elenes, C. A. (2006). Chicanas/Latinas building bridges: An introduction. In D. Delgado Bernal, C. A. Elenes, F. E. Godinez, & S. Villenas (Eds.), *Chicana/Latina education in everyday life: Feminista perspectives on pedagogy and epistemology* (pp. 1–9). New York, NY: SUNY Press.

Villenas, S. A., & Moreno, M. (2001). To *valerse por si misma* between race, capitalism, and patriarchy: Latina mother-daughter pedagogies in North Carolina. *Qualitative Studies in Education, 14*(5), 671–687.

Ward, J. (1995). Cultivating a morality of care in African American adolescents: A culture-based model of violence prevention. *Harvard Educational Review, 65*(2), 175–189.

8. *Responsibility, Reciprocity, and Respect: Storytelling as a Means of University-Community Engagement*

J. Estrella Torrez

I was raised in a family of chaos. Chaos is the ideal concept to characterize a family that is incredibly large as mine. On my father's side of the family, I have approximately eighty-five first cousins and twenty-seven *tías y tíos* (aunt and uncles including their spouses). We lived in loud, loving, chaos. During the summer months, it was not uncommon to have a family cookout meant for five to easily swell to include over thirty people. In the winter months, my family would reserve the local VFW hall to accommodate our annual Christmas party complete with dozens of roasters filled with *frijoles, arroz, carne asada, tortillas,* and *enchilada* casserole (a staple in the Midwest). However, when my immediate family was away from family gatherings, our home was silent save for the consistent humming of the television. From time to time the quiet was disrupted by visits from relatives, who sought my father's counsel on automotive troubles, issues with rebellious teenagers, or a blessing of sorts before deployment to a land unbelievably different from our little farming town.

As the eldest daughter, it was my responsibility to offer coffee or pop (again, a Midwest staple) to anyone walking in the door, regardless of the hour. The opportunity to listen in on these conversations, offset the 6:30 am Saturday visits that required me to get out of bed to put on a fresh pot of coffee. Oftentimes, I listened intently to conversations that detailed the telltale signs of one's transmission on the verge of going out, the escape routes of my older male cousins despite their parents attempts to thwart late night excursions, or my *tía's* plans on moving her family of six (yet again) from Michigan to Florida with her abusive husband. I observed as my father sat and listened, sipping coffee, lit cigarette calmly in hand, only commenting with an occasional "eh?" At the end of the story, my father would begin his response with, "*mira* …" In his counsel, he would chide the storyteller for allowing their vehicle to get to a point of disrepair or in my *tía's* case, ask her to really think about what is awaiting her if she leaves the state with her *familia*. Unfortunately, I was not allowed to linger in the room when my father (a two tour Vietnam Veteran) spoke with his nephews who enlisted in a military branch. I have a suspicion that my cousins assumed my father would glow with pride of their choice to serve the US military, however his message was much different. Based on their sagging shoulders, overturned shot glasses, and bottle of tequila less two drinks, my father's solemn words were rooted in a place of grief that yet another young Latinx may be physically and emotionally lost.

I'd like to say that it was in these moments where I learned to become more of a listener than a storyteller. I learned to listen to both the said and unsaid, I learned to listen to the silence, and I learned to listen for the unsaid meanings of my father's advice or the missing details from the stories shared. My listening skills were refined from these years of pouring coffee, refilling glasses with Coke, or keeping my young cousins occupied while our parents visited. It wasn't until years later that I recognized two important things: I absolutely detest coffee; and storytelling is a practice of love rooted in responsibility, reciprocity, and respect.

The message I took away from my years spent listening was responsibility—the responsibility that one gave what they could to the people they love. Reciprocity was also imparted through the years of listening. Reciprocity was often the practice of exchanging one form of love for another. Oftentimes, it came in the form of hours of car repair, small amounts of money, a place to sleep for a few days, or, in my case, hours of caring for children. A third lesson that I have extrapolated from this time in my life is the importance of respect. This came by way of offering an attentive ear, and the genuine consideration of suspending judgment.

My male cousins would arrive at our doorstep with fresh venison or fish, while my aunts would arrive with steaming pots of menudo or freshly baked German chocolate cake. On a rare occasion, a *tío* would knock on our door right around the time bars would close with a random gift—a bunny, an air hockey table, a television, a bicycle. My parents never inquired as to how these gifts were acquired, instead we accepted the gifts graciously, offered a cup of strong black coffee and made up a bed on our couch. Years later I have seen the relevance of all of this gifting. One gave what they could and it was all accepted. For my father, time was the greatest gift of all, and it would come in the form of listening.

Danish scholar, Johanna Kuyvenhoven (2009), would argue that my years serving coffee to the stream of family members seated in our tiny living room, was in fact preparing me to become a storyteller. For her, storytelling was a complicated relationship in which all those involved were to take risks, be personal and, ultimately, make themselves vulnerable. Storytelling is inherently reciprocal, it is "an activity of identity-making, healing, and counseling" (Kuyvenhoven, 2009, p. 18). Storytelling is, as my undergraduate students have noted, communal, evolutionary, dialogue, and intrapersonal.

The practice of listening creates a relationship stemming from the mutual agreement of respect. The impact of listening can have a deep impact on both student and community, in some cases, an effect that will forever shift their perspective. In some cases, these listening opportunities excavate harmful thoughts influencing how students view experiences dissimilar from their own, as well as a community's perceptions of the university. The latter is especially significant given the distance the university historically maintains from the local community.

It has always fascinated me that, as sites of knowledge production, universities have historically failed to recognize the immense knowledge base produced by those within a few short miles of its campus. The university imagines itself to be the only space in which valuable knowledge is produced, a perspective consistently challenged as the face of the academy shifts to reflect a changing and diversifying student body (Montoya, 1994). Recent university trends, such as the emergence of campus centers and institutes of service-learning and community engagement, seem to support faculty community engagement efforts; which is creating a different context than in the past. In 2015, the Carnegie Foundation classified 240 US colleges and universities with its Community Engagement Classification (Saltmarsh & Driscoll, 2015). This current state of the academy has surrounding community members in fact finding themselves invited into the gates of the ivory tower as invaluable collaborators. It is in this space, the shifting of academia and community climate, where I intentionally situate my scholarly efforts and encourage others to consider doing the same.

As a member of the communities in which I serve, I have directly faced poverty, lack of educational opportunities, restricted access to health care, and an inadequate food system. Despite such challenges, my family (and those struggling against similar systems of inequity) drew from their ingenuity to develop strategies to persist and thrive. It is this often-unrecognized knowledge-base that I believe the academy can draw from as its growing body of faculty grapple with pervasive and globalized systems of oppression. The university, as one site of knowledge production, has the potential to bring together collaboratively-generated and sustained knowledge from historically marginalized communities.

In this chapter, I clarify my use of responsibility, reciprocity, and respect as a community engaged-scholarship framework situated within feminist Indigenous ideologies dedicated to working with urban Indigenous communities. The coproduction, reclamation, and resurgence for Indigenous and Latinx communities in the Great Lakes region is one avenue in which I committed my work as an engaged-scholar. It is my hope that these experiences may assist emerging scholars committed to the intersection of engaged-scholarship as they develop their own ways of situating community-based work within the academy. The chapter will then offer a brief introduction to how responsibility, reciprocity, and respect are interwoven threads in community-engaged scholarship. Ultimately, I demonstrate the need for university-community collaborations to be firmly rooted in equitable partnerships, as well as the role storytelling plays in establishing such relationships.

Civic Engagement in the University: Responsibility

Civic engagement, community engagement and service learning, oftentimes, are used on university and college campuses interchangeably. The Carnegie Foundation, an entity that annually identifies U.S. colleges and universities as falling within particular community engagement classifications, identifies community engagement as collaboration between institutions of higher education and larger communities for the mutually beneficial exchange of knowledge and resources in context of partnership and reciprocity (Driscoll, 2008). Unfortunately, it is the case that these engagements lean more towards benefitting the university, particularly in enhancing the student experience, and less toward sustainable systemic change for the surrounding community.

The use of a critically oriented community engagement requires that faculty (or other higher education representatives) commit to power-sharing with community partners. The principles of this democratic research process, requires that all those participating (not just the faculty) to be involved in every stage of research. Such a research processes enables disenfranchised communities to actively participate in the examination of structural injustices. Normally, civic engagement is linked to a student's engagement with educational activities that support either the general population or the political system. (Almond & Verba, 1963) In reorienting the institutional value of civic engagement from a student-centered experience to a commitment to community development, Critical Service Learning (CSL) scholars like John Saltmarsh and Matthew Hartley (2011) suggest that "the answer lies in reorienting the work from a vague emphasis on community involvement toward an agenda that seeks significant societal change." (p. 4) For those dedicated to pursuing a social justice approach to community engaged-scholarship, it is important to differentiate between service-learning and critical service-learning. While a universal definition of service-learning has yet to be established (Furco, 2002; Furco & Billig, 2001; Stelljes, 2008), there is general agreement with its use as a pedagogical tool that incorporates community service into classroom learning as a way to expand students' understanding of course materials (Mitchell, 2008; Rimmerman, 2009).

Service-learning (SL) may also be used to empower students to solve issues within communities in which they may or may not be members (Farber, 2011). Typically, SL advocates abide by what is often referred to as the four "R's": respect, reciprocity, relevance and reflection. (Butin, 2010; Michigan Journal of Community Service Learning, 2001) However, the usage of reciprocity tends to have undertones of an inequitable scholar/partner power dynamic. Alternatively, Cree scholar Verna Kirkness (1991) offers a differing perspective of the four R's: respect, reciprocity, relevance and responsibility. As a First Nations scholar, Kirkness who has worked for decades to change the existing educational landscape that has disadvantaged First Nations' children, the use of responsibility is crucial in community work. Responsibility underscores the significance of individuals assuming responsibility over their own lives (Kirkness, 1991).

Inversely, SL course objectives focus on university students, whereas faculty research objectives are on the implications of SL experiences on university students. Although service-learning is not overtly political, critical service-learning is purposefully infused with social justice components (Mitchell, 2008; Porfilio & Hickman, 2011; Rhoads, 1998). Essentially, critical service-learning operationalizes as a political project moving toward a socially just society. Critical service-learning (CSL) diverges from service-learning in that by using critical pedagogy "students develop the critical awareness in relation to what gives rise to the dark social realities of the present as well as gain the desire to remake the social world for the lives of all people (Porfilio & Hickman, 2011, p. xi)." Unlike normative service-learning efforts, CSL projects often interrogate systems of oppression, and in turn, work to dismantle social inequities while forging authentic relationships between higher education institutions and their community partners.

In my years in the academy, I have co-developed culturally responsive models for working with and for Latinx and Indigenous communities. These models are situated within what Dan Butin (2010) calls a cultural perspective, integrating critical growth at both the micro-level and macro-level. For

Butin, the macro-level is concerned with developing an individual's sense of democratic renewal and active participation for the public good. (Butin, 2010; Lisman, 1998) The cultural perspective's micro-level fosters an individual's awareness of diversity and willingness to engage in service-learning. (Butin, 2010; Coles, 1993) Butin (2010) writes: "a cultural perspective-at both the micro/individual and macro/societal level-is thus concerned with normative questions of acculturation, understanding, and appropriation of innovation." (p. 9)

One crucial element to the process of co-development of CSL models with community partners is to intentionally center the process of co-generating transformative moments through the examination of social inequities with and for historically disenfranchised communities in addition to including student experiences. Involving community partners in all aspects of community programming is not a nicety—it is essential to authentic and meaningful community engagement. The co-development of CSL models begins with community involvement in identifying issues, generating ideas to address those concerns, organizing activities, evaluating the programming, and finally community participation is integral in revising implementation on a frequent basis. It is never enough to create a linear plan for community engagement. The most transformative moments arise when challenges emerge causing the plan to be drastically revised. I find that in these moments of revision, hidden strengths emerge that are then woven into the new framework. It is in these moments, that the academy's responsibility to give attention, time and a genuine interest in collaboratively addressing those issues impacting surrounding communities is salient.

Storytelling Is Our Medicine: Reciprocity

Reciprocity is often forgotten in the research process or is reduced to something along these lines: I (the researcher) have given you (the community) resources (materials, funds, volunteers, etc.) and in return I have gained information to complete my research goals. The long history of this type of engagement has left historically marginalized communities distrustful of the academy (Smith, 1999). This is not to say that there are not instances where this giving and receiving are responsive to the community's needs, and therefore completely appropriate for that particular context. In this instance, reciprocity is reduced to the practice of give and take. Given this model used across disciplines in universities nationwide, it is no wonder students have a difficult time understanding the meaning of reciprocity which can take other forms which are mutually beneficial or stem from a desire to build community.

The confusion can lead to students conflating community-building engagement with service-learning experiences, where the objective prioritizes student academic needs over those of the community. SL primarily focuses on a value-added learning experience for university students; whereas, CSL is fundamentally based on reciprocal benefits. The result of decades of SL approach to engaging with communities is that historically exploited communities have become wary of inviting representatives of outside agencies into their lives.

In my community, storytelling is oftentimes the preferred practice to invite individuals into one's life, as well as a formidable practice to pass along important lessons. Because of its ability to draw people together, I have selected storytelling as the forum to situate my work as a community-engaged scholar. Storytelling, as often used in my family, reminds younger generations of both the struggles and triumphs of life as Midwestern Latinxs. Older family members modeled the reciprocal nature of storytelling by sharing stories of their younger years, and then listening to my grandparents impart stories of generations long since gone. In those moments, I learned history. Elders shared stories of picking cotton alongside Polish immigrants, settling in a town whose residents were mostly white, and of racism in states alongside the migrant trail. Kuyvenhoven (2009) would say that in these moments of storytelling "involves a particular language and set of relationships; it's body of knowledge and abilities that are activated only within it's happening. Its learning and teachings are loosed when people share stories with each other, from memory for memory" (p. 4). The memory of my family is long, detailed, and peppered with both stories of joy, anger, and heartbreak. It was in these moments where storytelling represented a powerful tool from bringing people together, and a practice focused on collective healing. Translating this community-building tool into the classroom setting proved to be useful in learning about one another and ourselves (Nelson, 2009; Phillips, 2013).

bell hooks convincingly discusses the powerful role of storytelling in building community in classrooms.

> Students listen to one another's stories with an intensity that is not always present during a lecture or class discussion. One of the ways we become a learning community is by sharing and receiving one another's stories; it is a ritual of communion that opens our minds and hearts. Sharing in ways that help us connect, we come to know one another better. (hooks, 2010, p. 51)

The leading step in the storytelling-process is to establish mutual trust through the intentional process of listening.

In fact, I oftentimes begin my first day of class meeting by asking students to consider the difference between listening and hearing. While the question may seem a bit reductive, it becomes telling of how we are trained to interact with one another. Oftentimes, students cannot clearly delineate the difference between the two. In turn, I model listening as the active participation of individuals present in the moment. The key is *presence*, in those moments one must listen to what is being said, intimated, and omitted. Listening goes beyond serving as a tool of communication. It transpires through a mutual respect that one another is committed to being present in a shared moment.

In my own community-engaged projects, I use storytelling to establish trusting and sustained relationships through the "multidirectional flow of knowledge" (Saltmarsh & Hartley, 2011). This time spent with my partners doing everyday activities and engaged in ordinary conversations, time that many university bureaucracies may not acknowledge, emerges from my willingness to listen, reflect, and act when called upon. Cree sociologist Michael Anthony Hart (2010) calls this deep listening. Importantly, these acts of deep listening demonstrate that my interest in working with community partners is not driven by a research agenda, rather my research agenda is reflective of my own dedication to uplifting stories challenging the detrimental narrative often told about Indigenous and Latinx communities.

I encourage students to listen, suspend judgments, and to be diligent in critical self-reflection. In storytelling, the responsibility for sharing one's story falls reciprocally on both the storyteller and the audience. As such, storytelling becomes an intimate relationship that one willfully enters, what we can call, the storying space. Literacy scholars Valerie Kinloch and Timothy San Pedro (2012), use the concept of storying in their argument for what they call Projects in Humanization. Rooted in the Bahktinian notion of dialogism (Bahktin & Emerson, 1981), Projects in Humanization privilege the co-construction of knowledge, human agency and voice, diverse perspectives, moments of vulnerability, and acts of listening. Kinloch and San Pedro (2012) use the dialogic spiral in their project as it develops trust between speakers or, as they have labeled it, the space between. They explain the space in between as "allowing room for conflict, complications, silences, and pauses to exist between and among people as they learn to listen to each other in the space in between language and silence, language and action" (p. 29). The foundation of my community-engaged pedagogy and hope for those I work alongside is founded in the collective trust to build a reciprocal and thus intimate relationship. It is possible when all those involved are expected to enter the storytelling relationship (i.e., the storying space) through the revelation of emotions, memories, and vulnerabilities.

Reciprocity in this type of relationship is based in traditional and Indigenous relationships to place and to one another. Algonquin-Cree scholar Lynn Lavallée (2009) writes that "within an Indigenous research framework the principle of reciprocity, or giving back, is essential ... Reciprocity extends beyond the immediate research participants" (p. 36). For Lavallée, and within my own work, the research is secondary to the greater goal: collaboration to address social inequities. Frameworks such as CSL have served tremendously in my work with the local community, specifically, when engaging multiple K-12 schools to address low retention-rates among Latinx and Indigenous students. This collaboration on retention began in dialogue with elders, community leaders, youth, and parents. Through these dialogues students and families noted a general sense of disconnection and instability, neither of these issues were addressed within the schools at the time. As in all of my collaborative works, I intentionally began in dialogue with the community to understand their experience and listen for what I may be able to offer. Rather than following the dominant model of service-learning in which researchers independently define learning outcomes, research questions, strategies, and methodologies, CSL methodologies is wholeheartedly collaborative—from its inception to its planning to data collection and analysis and onto program delivery—and firmly grounded in a dedication to reciprocity.

Referring to the initiative addressing low retention rates for local Latinx and Indigenous students, dialogues with the youth revealed that the issue did not stem from lack of motivation, disconnect with course content, or lack of resources. Elders, families, and youth intimated that students were less likely to graduate from high school due to a sense of disconnection. Indigenous students were struggling to situate themselves in an Indigenous community that was consistently marginalized from any local community conversations. Meanwhile, Latinx students spoke of a constant concern of familial financial stability. Latinx students could not connect with their peers because of external pressures partly due to their need to secure economic stability. Currently, I am working alongside Latinx families, students, and school officials to develop programming addressing the identified concerns. The students' concerns, and the resulting programming, would not have emerged had an earnest dialogue not been at the core. The school community may not have the same level of investment in enriching their existing situation had they not believed there to be a commitment to a collaborative resolution. Furthermore, it was a paradigm shift in the way in which power was distributed throughout this process. Students led the dialogues, school officials assisted in the organization of the dialogues, and the parents are crucial in the programming development. It is clear had students and family not been involved in the beginning stages of the research, the project may not have the same level of involvement or demonstration of sincere interest in community-building from the school district.

It has been my experience, that the authentic engagement needed for community-engagement takes time to develop, needs room for critical reflection, and the space for patience and revision. Often times, in their rush to begin working with community partners, university students commonly forget that establishing trusting and equitable relationships is fundamental to sustainable community-work. As bell hooks (2003) writes, "[c]ollege education is so often geared toward the future, the perceived rewards that the future, the perceived rewards that the imagined future will bring that is difficult to teach students that the present is the place of meaning" (p. 165). I would add that by fixating on rewards, university students and faculty completely miss the most significant lesson: understanding how to forge reciprocal relationships.

Understanding My Place: Respect

In my years engaged in this work, I have observed students eager to begin the work without putting the time in to be respectful of the process of community-building. Specifically, students, enthusiastic to get in community forget the time necessary for building community. I find myself, recounting to these students the innumerable hours building rapport through quotidian activities, such as sharing coffee with elders, preparing for rummage sales, wrapping tobacco ties, or doing beadwork with youth. Although outside the parameters of the traditional faculty responsibilities of teaching-scholarship-service, I have cooked and cleaned alongside community members in preparation for celebrations, ceremonies, or feasts. It is in these moments that have learned how to establish respectful community-relationships. Serving as a member of the community responsible for organizing, cleaning, preparing, cleaning, visiting, and more cleaning (the most tender moments take place when cleaning), I have observed that all roles are not only needed, but respected.

In other circumstances, I am called into dialogue with teens regarding difficult school situations or with administrators desperate to assist in reaching out to families distrustful of the school system. In these instances, the nature of relationship shifts from one in which I am community member to an expert availed with resources connected to the university. The tension of this role is delicate, and one that must be navigated consciously. Despite my best efforts during my first years as faculty to not be looked to by either families or the school district as the *expert*, I learned to take this role on respectfully. My change of heart was precipitated by a gently chiding from an elder, who (in the most lovingly scolding possible) said, "We will look to you, Dr. Torrez. Take that name. We know it wasn't easy for you to get that title. We need our children to see that it isn't only about getting there, but about coming home and helping the community." As someone with access to resources, and the knowledge of navigating an educational system historically disconnected from communities of color, I have learned to put on the expert role with respect for those that I represent. An expert is invited to school district meetings, or adds institutional credit to a request for grant funding, or is able to intervene on behalf of the family when Child Protective Services is threatening to remove children.

When I am asked to meet with school officials, I am reminded of Myles Horton's story of a community of Black parents in Tennessee who struggled to have schools integrate their children, beyond the symbolic gesture enforced by federal policy. Horton working alongside the parents offered to arrange a meeting bringing together the parents with a lawyer versed in civil rights cases. Prior to making the formal introductions, Horton advised the lawyer to "tell them [the parents] the facts and let them decide what to do" (Horton, Freire, Bell, & Gaventa, 1990, p. 129). It is among these critical conversations that the reciprocity of relationships is dependent upon trust, patience, commitment, and humility. Horton et al. (1990) reminds us that "there's a big difference in giving information and telling people what to do with it" (p. 129). Parents trust I will have the utmost respect for their families and act accordingly. Families trust that I will work alongside them in advocating for their children, rather than speak for the families. I have access to information, it is my responsibility to share the information, and stand aside while the families discuss the next steps. If requested by the family, I will not step back, my presence is needed as part of (not central to) the dialogue.

The use of CSL, influenced by an Indigenous feminist framework, provides meaningful structure to work with disenfranchised communities to understand and investigate the macro-systems of oppression impacting their lives. One cannot strive to create an equitable society if the voices heard only represent the dominant society, thereby perpetuating a misinformed meta-narrative situating marginalized communities within a deficit framework. It is therefore vital to not allow university students participating in these projects to merely become spectators of marginalized communities lived realities, but it's imperative they also move out of their comfort zone and enter meaningful dialogue with these communities. For those dedicated to such social justice work, it is imperative to be active in interrogating systems of injustice, particularly on a local level (Reinharz, 1992). It is further crucial for those with university resources to leverage accessible to support communal efforts.

In my position as insider-outsider (Brayboy & Deyhle, 2010), I am able to gain an intimate perspective on community issues while relying on specialized knowledge accrued through my advanced academic training in the academy. Feminist scholar, Shulamit Reinharz (1997) argues that researchers "both bring the self to the field and create the self in the field" (p. 3). Indeed, the community has played a significant role in creating my own self in the field. Bridging these two distinct knowledge systems affords me the opportunity to collaborate with communities in unique ways, such as understanding the urgency of the issues targeted and developing models that are culturally appropriate alongside community members. Moreover, my position enables me to create learning situations in which university students enter into dialogue with community partners in a space where respect is central. This is a role, laden with responsibility to both the university and community partners. In these spaces, I challenge each side to engage in a respectful relationship. That is, students must migrate from passive spectator to active community member. In this migration from one place to the next, I remind students to not forget their place in the existing power dynamic. It is also crucial that I recognize the existing tension of my place as stemming from both the academy and the community.

It is a place where university students can easily shift from collaborator to expert, or becoming dependent upon the community as expert based solely on their experiences (Harrison, MacGibbon, & Morton, 2001). The problem than becomes that, as Myles Horton points to in his conversation with Paulo Freire, "there's a time when people's experience runs out" (Horton et al., 1990, p. 128) If each depends upon the other to serve as expert, both students and community members become unable to extend their individual knowledge to a place of collective knowledge building. Each member of the community engagement, either from the community or the university, must respect the experiences of the other. Similarly, there must be a mutual trust that each will leverage resources at their disposal.

Conclusion

As a recently tenured faculty in the nation's first land-grant university, I respond to an increased interest in engaged-scholarship by engaging with the Midwest's Latinx and Indigenous populations, the very communities in which I live, work, and raise my children. As an engaged-scholar, my teaching-scholarship-service revolves around the co-production of community-based knowledge, as well as its recovery and resurgence. It is from this position, one based in my own experiences as a former migrant farmworker of Indigenous descent raised in Michigan, that I situate my commitment to community-engaged teaching-scholarship-service.

Systemic change must transpire, and reshape the prevailing narrative of Latinxs and Indigenous communities that is not only erroneous, but at times destructive. My studies in education, critical pedagogy, language, culture and literacy have afforded an academic well in which I may draw upon. It is also because of my membership within these communities that I am able to argue that existing structures must be reshaped by Michigan's Latinx and Indigenous peoples. I have found that existing structures are detrimental to youth identities, self-confidence, academic success, and general sense of community, all aspects of a vibrant and diverse democracy. All of which points me toward linking my Indigenous feminist knowledge with that of my community knowledge to co-create projects, programs, and research agendas focused on storytelling as an instrument of critical pedagogy, developing school-home connection models for urban Latinx and Indigenous families, and re-envisioning existing ways in which the university interacts with the surrounding community.

The practice of storytelling, the commitment to listening, and the dedication to maintaining reciprocal relationships has proven to be invaluable tools in this work. Learning from those gracious to share their experiences, memories, and knowledge is in direct conflict with the traditional ways in which scholars are trained to engage in research. For me, a Midwestern Chicana, engaging in storytelling was a natural method of inquiry. It was never question of how I would put the multiple years of pouring coffee to use. Adding to this practice, I have learned to emulate the Anishinnabeg tradition of gifting tobacco to demonstrate respect for the knowledge shared, and enter the space in a respectful way (Lavallée, 2009). Integrating the practices, I learned in my home with the new knowledge learned from my Indigenous community, I have found a path to community-engagement that is reflective of my expanding community. Folding my university students into these experiences has transformed the way in which the university is engaging with the local Latinx and Indigenous community.

Years ago, while embarking on my dissertation project, a project focused on examining the linguistic practices of one agricultural laborer community, I first met with one of the area's longest serving migrant service directors. Sitting in the director's office, amongst stacks of yellowing papers, carefully organized binders dating to the early 1960s, the eighty-year-old woman offered the following advice, "Never start off with a question. Always go hungry. And, just listen." Listening and accepting the plates of lovingly prepared food proved to set the backdrop for storytelling. Families appreciated the time I spent listening, actively interested in their concerns with the local health clinic displayed when migrants sought assistance, or the concerns that local school districts were unable to matriculate students appropriately (oftentimes students found themselves retaking courses or in classes that did not fulfill graduation requirements in their home states). One mother requested that

I share the families' stories; stories about the difficulty in requesting medical services specific to young women or wanting a culturally responsive summer literacy program, with the director of the migrant clinic, as well as with the director of the summer migrant program. The directors greatly appreciated the information and creatively revised their services in response to the families' requests. The most significant moment in my time with the families, was that I found myself (un)intentionally creating the practices of my childhood: I listened, respected the words shared, and carried the responsibility of sharing what I learned with others.

Jo-Ann Archibald (2008) says it best: stories "have the power to make us think, feel, and be good human beings" (p. 139). Stories open the possibility of healing, of connecting, understanding, finding comfort, exploring and risk-taking. Stories offer an opportunity to heal individually and as a community. However, if we as an academic community underestimate the most basic principles of responsibility, reciprocity, and respect we are perpetuating a sordid practice of exploiting, especially Indigenous and Communities of Color that continue to suffer the consequences of our inactions. It does not take much to change this, just *un regalito del tiempo*.

References

Almond, G., & Verba, S. (1963). *The civic culture: Political attitudes in five democracies.* Princeton, NJ: Princeton University Press.

Archibald, J. (2008). *Indigenous storywork: Educating the heart, mind, body and spirit.* Vancouver, Canada: University of British Canada Press.

Bahktin, M., & Emerson, C. (1981). *The dialogic imagination: Four essays.* Austin, TX: University of Texas Press.

Brayboy, B., & Deyhle, D. (2010). Insider-outsider: Researchers in American Indian communities. *Theory into Practice, 39*(3), 163–169.

Butin, D. (2010). *Service-learning in theory and practice.* New York, NY: Palgrave Macmillan.

Coles, R. (1993). *A call to service.* Cambridge, MA: Harvard University Press.

Driscoll, A. (2008). Carnegie's community-engagement classification, intentions and insights. *Change, 40*(1), 37–41.

Farber, K. (2011). *Change the world with service learning.* Lanham, MD: Rowman and Littlefield Publishers.

Furco, A. (2002). Institutionalizing service-learning in higher education. *The Journal of Public Affairs, 7*(1), 39–68.

Furco, A., & Billig, S. (2001). *Service-learning: The essence of the pedagogy.* Charlotte, NC: Information Age Publishing.

Harrison, J., MacGibbon, L., & Morton, M. (2001). Regimes of trustworthiness in qualitative research: The rigors of reciprocity. *Qualitative Inquiry, 7*(3), 323–245.

Hart, M. (2010). Indigenous worldviews, knowledge, and research: The development of an Indigenous research paradigm. *Journal of Indigenous Voices in Social Work, 1*(1), 1–16.

hooks, b. (2003). *Teaching community: A pedagogy of hope.* New York, NY: Routledge.

hooks, b. (2010). *Teaching critical thinking: Practical wisdom.* New York, NY: Routledge.

Horton, M., Freire, P., Bell, B., & Gaventa, J. (1990). *We make the road by walking: Conversations on education and social change.* Philadelphia, PA: Temple University Press.

Kinloch, V., & San Pedro, T. (2012). The space between: Listening and story-ing as foundations for Projects in Humanization. In D. Paris & M. Winn (Eds.) *Humanizing research* (pp. 63–80). Thousand Oaks, CA: Sage Publications.

Kirkness, V. (1991). *Creating space: My life and work in Indigenous education.* Winnepeg, Canada: University of Manitoba Press.

Kuyvenhoven, J. (2009). *In the presence of each other: A pedagogy of storytelling.* Toronto, Canada: University of Toronto Press.

Lavallée, L. (2009). Practical application of Indigenous research framework and two qualitative Indigenous research methods: Sharing circles and Anishnaabe symbol-based reflection. *International Journal of Qualitative Methods, 8*(1), 21–40.

Lisman, C. (1998). *Toward a civil society: Civic literacy and service learning.* Westport, CT: Bergin and Garvey.

Michigan Journal of Community Service Learning. (2001). *Service-learning course design workbook.* Ann Arbor, MI: Office of Community Service Learning Press.

Mitchell, T. (2008). Traditional vs. critical service-learning: Engaging the literature to differentiate two models. *Michigan Journal of Community Service Learning, 14*(2), 50–65.

Montoya, M. (1994). Mascaras, trenzas, y greñas: Un/masking the self while un/braiding Latina stories and legal discourse. *Chicana/o-Latina/o Law Review, 15*, 185–220.

Nelson, A. (2009). Storytelling and transformation learning. *Counterpoints, 341*, 207–221.

Phillips, L. (2013). Storytelling as pedagogy. *Literacy Learning: The Middle Years, 21*(2), ii–iv.

Porfilio, B., & Hickman, H. (Eds.). (2011). *Critical service-learning as revolutionary pedagogy: A project of student agency in action.* Charlotte, NC: Information Age Publishing.

Reinharz, S. (1992). *Feminist methods in social research.* New York, NY: Oxford University Press.

Reinharz, S. (1997). Who am I? The need for a variety of selves in the field. In R. Hertz (Ed.), *Reflexivity and voice* (pp. 3–20). Thousand Oaks, CA: Sage.

Rhoads, R. A. (1998). Student protest and multicultural reform: Making sense of campus unrest in the 1990s. *Journal of Higher Education, 69*, 621–646.

Rimmerman, C. (2009). *Service-learning and the liberal arts.* Lanham, MD: Lexington Books.

Saltmarsh, J., & Driscoll, A. (2015). *Carnegie selects colleges and universities for 2015 community engagement classification.* Retrieved from http://www.carnegiefoundation.org/newsroom/news-releases/carnegie-selects-colleges-universities-2015-community-engagement-classification/

Saltmarsh, J., & Hartley, M. (2011). *To serve a larger purpose: Engagement for democracy and the transformation of higher education.* Philadelphia, PA: Temple University Press.

Smith, L. (1999). *Decolonizing methodologies: Research and Indigenous peoples.* London: Zed Books.

Stelljes, A. (2008). *Service-learning and community engagement.* Amherst, MA: Cambria Press.

9. *Arizona-Sonora 360: Examining and Teaching Contested Moral Geographies Along the U.S.-Mexico Borderlands*

CELESTE GONZÁLEZ DE BUSTAMANTE

In 2010, Arizona Governor Jan Brewer signed Senate Bill 1070 into law. The "show me your papers" law requires local police to check the immigration status of anyone who they reasonably suspect to be in the country without authorization. Prior to the signing, Governor Brewer on several occasions fomented a sentiment of fear and attempted to justify the legislation by stating that it was needed because of growing, so-called, spill-over violence from Mexico into Arizona, and that apparently "decapitated heads" were being found in the Arizona-Sonora desert. The statement, was never substantiated, but it became symbolic of the political discourse that conservative politicians employed to gain support for SB 1070, and other pieces of anti-immigration legislation (Santa Ana & González de Bustamante, 2012).

At the same time, groups of scholars in the borderlands convened in response to growing challenges to teaching and research (O'Leary, Deeds, & Whiteford, 2013). One group produced a book on the ethical methods of conducting research in the region, which included a personal code of ethics. Another group of journalism educators formed the Border Journalism Network, "to create deeper public understanding of the U.S.-Mexico borderlands in all its diversity and complexity. Towards that end, the network functions as a hub through which professionals, educators and their students can gather, develop and share knowledge to improve the quality of border journalism" (Border Journalism Network, n.d.).

The two conflicting currents outlined above transpired on contested terrain—one upon which students and faculty endeavored to (de)construct a moral geography of the U.S.-Mexico borderlands. As this essay explains, when coupled with a critical borderlands pedagogy, the concepts of moral geography and counter-cartographies can be useful tools for both unearthing past media transgressions as well as for skill building of a new generation of journalists about how to improve media coverage of the Arizona-Sonora borderlands; while simultaneously strengthening community-based relationships among borderlanders, which ideally enhances the possibilities for social change in these communities.

Following definitions of moral geography, counter-cartographies, and critical borderlands pedagogy, the chapter describes two community-based journalism projects that I helped to design and organize, which employed these frameworks and pedagogical approaches. The final part of the chapter reflects upon some of the challenges that exist with respect to community-based learning (CBL) in the Arizona-Sonora borderlands. Ultimately, the chapter suggests that effective CBL and civic engagement with communities in this particular geographic location necessitate pedagogical paths that are rooted in social justice, and which prioritize the historical and contemporary realities of the marginalized border and its peoples. Further, historical and contemporary contingencies help to explain why the border has taken on its current form, and why the construction of the geopolitical landscape is not without contestation.

Situating Arizona's Political Landscape

After a five-year hiatus from highly publicized attacks on communities of color in Arizona, which mainly targeted undocumented immigrants and Latinos,[1] the conservative dominated Arizona State Legislature reignited its efforts in 2016. Lawmakers introduced at least six pieces of anti-immigrant legislation during the 2016 session, including one bill (HB 2451) that Republican Governor Doug Ducey signed, which forces undocumented prisoners to serve 85% of their sentences before being released to the U.S. Immigration and Customs Enforcement Service. Prior to the law, undocumented immigrant prisoners could be released after serving half of their sentences (Van Velzer, 2016). In addition to the legislature's measures, Governor Ducey, at the time of the writing of this chapter, was working to create another layer of law enforcement to "secure the border" through a multi-agency border strike force (Blust, 2016).

At the same time, the nation's 2016 presidential campaign brought tensions to the surface in communities throughout the state. In Tucson, the state's second largest city, at a rally for Republican presidential candidate Donald Trump, one of the candidate's supporters attacked a protestor inside the event (Steller, 2016). At another Trump event, outside of Phoenix, activists from Puente Arizona blocked the road to a rally that was being planned for the candidate, and where Maricopa County Sheriff Joe Arpaio waited for the candidate to arrive so that he could introduce him. Arpaio vowed that the rally would go on and that Trump would be allowed to express his First Amendment rights. At least three protestors were arrested (Bartels, 2016).

The recent wave of anti-immigrant bills should not be viewed as an isolated effort, but instead must be understood as part of a protracted and historical strategy by a white hegemony to exclude communities of color (González de Bustamante, 2012). The history of exclusion, by and large, has been supported by news media that rarely questioned the status quo, and more often participated in the reaffirmation of the prevailing powers and attitudes of the time (González de Bustamante, 2012). In other words, the news media helped to shape the dominant moral geography of the region; one that deemed that a white hegemony should determine what was right and good for the state and its peoples.

More recent efforts to construct what is right and good for the state have been manifested through a buildup of infrastructure and agents along the Arizona-Sonora border. Militarization of the line between the neighboring states increased dramatically over the 1990s, through efforts such as Operation Hold-the-Line in El Paso, Texas, and Operation Gatekeeper in San Diego, and later Operation Safeguard in the more than 350-mile border between Arizona and Sonora. Militarization included a dramatic increase in the number of agents, a 20-foot-high fence along most of the line, and surveillance tools such as stadium lighting, cameras and drones (Isacson, Meyer, & Davis, 2013). As a result of the militarization, migrants have been crossing in more desolate areas, increasing their chances of being assaulted and dying of exposure to the elements. According to the human rights group Humane Borders, 2,471 people perished in the Arizona-Sonora desert between 1999 and 2013 (Isacson et al., 2013). It is in within this context that Arizona scholars are attempting to intervene and educate through their research, teaching, and outreach efforts. The interventions are buttressed by key conceptual frameworks that fit with the social justice goals of community-based and community service learning.

Conceptual Frameworks for Community-Based and Community Service Learning at the U.S.-Mexico Border

The challenges of teaching in the U.S.-Mexico borderlands require a specific set of pedagogical tools. The confluence of critical borderlands pedagogy alongside the conceptual frameworks of moral geography and counter-cartographies combined provide a powerful foundation with potential for transformative learning as well as opportunities for societal change. First, though, what are the challenges that all faculty face, and in particular, faculty of color in this region?

Faculty of Color

Teaching students about the history of racism and discrimination from an anti-racist perspective in Arizona, and the media's role and connections to historical realities, while certainly necessary, is not always welcomed inside and outside of the classroom. In predominately white classrooms, women faculty of color must walk along a cultural tightrope—one on which they might wish to engage students about issues of inequality, race and ethnicity, but they do so with the risk of becoming labeled as "that professor" (Hassouneh, 2006). Faculty of color, and in particular, women faculty of color must deal with various micro-aggressions in the classroom and outside through the ubiquitous process of student evaluations, which allow students to anonymously write comments that are intended to assess teaching effectiveness, but frequently become sources of anxiety for professors because students sometimes comment about matters unrelated to teaching, including having one's own intelligence being judged (Sharp-Grier, 2015). In addition, the typical feelings of isolation present among faculty of color in predominantly white institutions are compounded in Arizona, where an openly hostile environment toward migrants and dark-skinned people exists in online media content and on the streets (Ross & Edwards, 2016). Despite these challenges, Arizona scholars continue to examine critical pedagogies, including analysis of Mexican American studies programs in the state, and teaching about whiteness in a predominately white institution (Cabrera, 2014a, 2014b; Ochoa O'Leary, Romero, Cabrera, & Rascón, 2012). Aside from some of the factors mentioned above, faculty of color are confronted with additional struggles of most faculty who work in public institutions.

Community Engagement and the Contradictions of Academic Capitalism

In the 21st century, educators increasingly see the value of student engagement in communities as essential for learning (Shelton, 2016), and these efforts are perhaps especially noteworthy in an era of renewed and overt animosity toward people of color (Castañeda, 2008). Community service learning (CSL) and community based-learning (CBL) can offer advantages beyond what happens in the classroom to promote "transformative learning, and, at times, even individual and social transformation" (Castañeda, 2008, p. 320). It is here that Castañeda's approach can be appreciated, in that it suggests going beyond having students merely engage with the community, and argues that the engagement should also include goals for social justice and social change.

While these efforts should be acknowledged, and are commendable, they also can be costly in terms of university resources. The implementation of community engagement pedagogy requires both additional resources and commitments of faculty, students and of the academic institution beyond the traditional classroom setting such as a means to transport students to the border, making a commitment beyond the normal class hours for a three-unit class, and the recognition that CBL courses function best when designed for small groups of students (e.g. less than 20). All of these factors, however, run against the force of academic capitalism that has taken root in so many public institutions across the country (Slaughter & Rhoades, 2004). So that, what emerges is a tension between calls from administrators to engage students beyond the classroom, while at the same time they want faculty to teach more students and produce more research. In spite of the increase in academic capitalism, community-based learning in concert with critical borderlands pedagogy has been possible.

Critical Borderlands Pedagogy and the Media

Stereotypes of destitute immigrants coming across the border to "take our jobs" have been repeated time and time again for more than a century through the uncontested statements of politicians in mainstream news media and entertainment (González de Bustamante, 2012; Martinez, 2001). It is no wonder, then, that for most students and many Arizona residents, Mexico is seen as a "threat rather than a partner" (González de Bustamante, 2012; Heyman, 2008). The challenge and goal for journalism professors should be to move beyond these stereotypes in teaching about the history of the news media as well as instruction on how to better cover the region (González de Bustamante, 2015).

Critical borderlands pedagogy represents a valuable tool that is useful as part of a long-term strategy to improve news coverage and student understanding. The approach emerged from Chicanas/os studies scholarship, and in opposition to viewing the region merely as the border. As Elenes (1997) states, this transnational region between the United States and Mexico should be known as the borderlands, should be seen as being "constructed from the condition of living in the margins of U.S. society and culture" (p. 363). While this perspective often is used to refer to the inhabitants on the U.S. side, the same could be argued for those borderlanders who reside in northern Mexico along the *frontera*. They, too, reside on the political and social margins of the center.

In Arizona, critical pedagogy of the borderlands coupled with Community service learning (CSL) and Community based-learning (CBL) opportunities further enhances and increases transformative learning for students. Further, borderlands theory takes into account difference and the multiple subjectivities of the peoples who live in the region (Elenes, 1997). In journalism courses that involve stakeholders along the border, critical pedagogy of borderlands in conjunction with CBL forces students to move beyond the frequent reaffirmation of the geo-political and economic hegemonies that are in place. Through CSL and CBL courses along the *frontera*, students become border crossers "in order to understand otherness in its own terms" (Giroux, 1992, p. 28), thereby increasing pathways for personal and intellectual transformation. Further, focusing on this multiculturalism of the borderlands enhances the experience service learning (Rosner-Salazar, 2003). Through their experiences, students are more likely to engage and interrogate power relations that are in place along and across the U.S.-Mexico borderlands, which are defined by the dominant moral geography that historically has been in place.

Moral Geography

The making and remaking (mapping) of the Arizona-Sonora borderlands began long before the arrival of European settlers in the 16th century (Truett, 2004). However, the process became more complex after the delineation of nation-state boundaries in 1848 (Treaty of Guadalupe Hidalgo) and the 1854 ratification of the Gadsden Purchase (Truett, 2004). As national boundaries solidified, geopolitical lines that were tied to racial and ethnic concepts of superiority began to take hold (González de Bustamante, 2012). Notions about who should or should not be allowed into the United States fit into and helped to forge a dominant moral geography (Opie, 1998; Taylor, 2007). Moral geographies can be viewed as a "political process" and can be defined as "an ethical choice made about a particular people and place, and it is also an internal logic that belong to the particular people and place" (Opie, 1998, p. 242). In Arizona, since the turn of the 20th century, a white hegemony has driven attitudes and legislation about geographical and political spaces. Like other political stakeholders such as elected officials and law enforcement authorities, the media hold power and authority to create and construct dominant viewpoints, which result in the shaping of moral geographies (González de Bustamante, 2012).

Creating Counter Cartographies

Despite the reaffirming role of mainstream media in shaping a dominant moral geography in the United States, and in particular its borderlands, this essay argues that contested moral geographies can exist in tandem. These contested ways of defining the borderlands can be thought of as counter cartographies or counter maps of the region (Counter-Cartographies Collective, n.d.). Indeed, the emergence of new media and digital technologies have assisted in the ability of marginalized and underrepresented groups to be able to counter dominant viewpoints. Through a counter cartography approach in journalism education and media production, contrasting viewpoints to the mainstream media's focus on narco-tunnels and the negative impacts of undocumented migration, students can reach out to community members and contribute to a deeper and broader understanding of the region. As Mitchell and Elwood (2015) state, "although maps are often hegemonic in their orientation, they can nevertheless be produced in alternative ways for counter-hegemonic purposes as well" (p. 2). With new digital technologies, journalists can sometimes function as cartographers, essentially re-mapping contemporary circumstances. And, that is what occurred with the two specific projects that are explained below.

Critical Borderlands Pedagogy and Community Action

During my tenure as a faculty member at the University of Arizona in the School of Journalism and as an affiliated faculty of the Center for Latin American Studies, I have been involved in numerous community-based projects that attempt to bring together ideas of moral geography and critical pedagogy of the borderlands in Latina/o communities such as in Ambos Nogales (Nogales, Arizona, and Nogales, Sonora), where populations on both sides are more than 95% Latina/o (U.S. Census Bureau, 2014). Two examples stand out as pedagogical alternatives to the general coursework in journalism schools, and whose goals include: deepening understanding about journalism about the region; improving news coverage on the Arizona-Sonora borderlands; and enhancing the potential for social justice and transformation.

Though not all aspects of the two projects can be described as counter-maps in the strict sense of the word, the storytelling and projects that have been created have resulted in unseating historical and contemporary hegemonic portrayals of the people and places frequently published and viewed in mainstream media. In following section, the two projects; Arizona Migrahack, a community-wide open event, and a co-convened undergraduate/graduate course titled Reporting in the U.S.-Mexico Borderlands, signal the remapping/reshaping our understanding of the region. Combined with other counter-mapping activities, they help to construct an alternative moral geography that contrasts that which has been in place for the past century.

Migrahack, March 22–25, 2015

Developed by journalist, Claudia Nuñez, Migrahacks aim to connect three seemingly disparate groups: journalists, community non-profits/activists, and web developers. The goals of Migrahacks are twofold (1) to improve understanding about the phenomenon of migration using open data and journalism and (2) to train student and professional journalists about data visualization and data journalism. By "hacking" open source data related to migration, the discourse can potentially move beyond politically charged and sometimes racist rhetoric to shed light on migration issues. The first event in 2012 was held in Los Angeles, California, at the offices of *La Opinión*, the largest Spanish-language daily newspaper in the United States.

Unlike most hackathons, which tend to draw white programmers and participants, and whose goals do not necessarily focus on social justice, Migrahacks seek to bring together ethnically diverse groups of participants into one room for three days. Over the course of the free event, participants split up into teams and devise a plan to create an online project that the group decides to produce.[2] Another distinct feature of the Institute for Justice and Journalism's (IJJ) Migrahacks is one day of free data visualization training. In other words, in contrast to most hackathons that are geared toward the creation of applications that will result in monetary gain, Migrahacks focus on connecting community partners to increase knowledge about migration. In Spring 2015, the IJJ collaborated with the Center for Border and Global Journalism (based at University of Arizona School of Journalism) to hold Arizona Migrahack in Tucson, Arizona. Organizers argued because April 2015 would be the five-year anniversaries of former Governor Brewer's signing of both SB 1070 ("show me your papers law") and HB 2281, which led to the dismantling of Mexican American Studies at Tucson's largest school district, that Tucson would be an ideal location for a Migrahack.

Almost 100 community members attended Arizona Migrahack, including strong participation from students and professional journalists who work for Spanish-language news media outlets. Reflecting on the large turnout of Spanish language journalists, Claudia Nuñez, Migrahack director stated,

> the Latino demographic is growing and its education level along with it. Quality information is now a requirement and Hispanic journalists know this; that's why

> they seek opportunities to improve their journalism by learning new tools that technology and data offer. (Institute for Justice and Journalism, 2015b)

By the end of three days, eleven distinct online projects had been created. UA journalism student Amanda Martinez was on the "No Timely Response" team, which won the $2,000 Grand Prize. The team used local traffic stop data gathered by reporters from the *Arizona Daily Star* to create an interactive game (see http://notr.s3-us-west-2.amazonaws.com/index.html) that puts the user in the shoes of local law enforcement, giving them a chance to see how local police deal with issues of immigration status during traffic stops.

Martinez, who was the president of the National Association of Hispanic Journalists student chapter at the School of Journalism, noted,

> I'm really proud of the work that we all did. It was really great because everyone on the team I worked on came in with a different skill set and a different level of knowledge, but we really pulled together to make a project that was really cohesive and really relevant to Tucson. (Institute for Justice and Journalism, 2015a)

Other online project topics ranged from comparing "Arizona Dreamers" with other college students, to analyzing open source data to find out how many undocumented children receive legal assistance as their cases move through the courts. Students involved in the event came from throughout Arizona, and California, specifically Cal State University-Northridge. Some of the Pima Community College students were involved in activist organizations such as Scholarships A-Z, whose purpose is to raise money for undocumented students in Arizona.[3] Several community activist groups also attended the event, including the Colibri Center, a non-profit organization that focuses on re-connecting families and the remains of migrants who have died in the Arizona-Sonora desert.

By connecting activists, journalists and developers, Arizona Migrahack increased the potential for social justice and transformation in three distinct ways. First, the event strengthened the possibilities for awareness and change by providing free all-day training for activists, journalists members of the community. In other words, activists could use the skills acquired in the Migrahack to tell their own stories and contribute to the media landscape. One tangible example was a video produced by members of the Colibri group. The video discussed the economic and structural reasons for migration and the importance of connecting family members with the remains of migrants who have perished in the Arizona-Sonora desert. Examples like this point to the reciprocal aspect of community-based learning whose foundational goals include social justice. Second, the event provided a networking opportunity for community members, faculty and students. The event gave students a chance to work with veteran reporters, and helped to inspire one student to increase her coverage of Latino/a communities and enroll in the UA graduate program in journalism. Third, the online content created through Arizona Migrahack increased awareness about migration and the U.S.-Mexico borderlands among members of the wider community. The multimedia projects that were produced moved beyond traditional ways of storytelling, thereby possibly leading to increased interest among news readers and viewers, and ideally, improved overall understanding about the complexities of migration and the region.

Security 360: Mapping Militarization of Ambos Nogales

In fall 2015, another community based learning project with social justice goals occurred, which involved taking students to the U.S.-Mexico border cities of Ambos Nogales to report on security and militarization in Latino/a communities. The course titled, Reporting in the U.S.-Mexico Borderlands, included numerous visits with community organizations on both sides of the Arizona-Sonora line, and was offered in conjunction with an anthropology of the border class. Through these courses, we drove students to Ambos Nogales (Nogales, Arizona, Nogales, Sonora) every Wednesday and spent the entire day there. Throughout the semester, students visited with community members and learned about a wide variety of community groups, from the Kino Border Initiative, which operates migrant shelters in Nogales, Sonora, to the Pimería Alta historical museum on the Arizona side, which was directed by Teresa Leal, a local activist, who lived on the Sonoran side, but who worked on the north side. Students were highly encouraged to take both courses. In fall 2015, 17 students enrolled in the journalism course, and 19 students enrolled in the anthropology class, with 15 of the 19 students taking both courses.

This suite of classes received a $12,000 grant from the University of Arizona 100% Engagement Initiative, whose primary goal is to assure that all UA students have the opportunity to build on what they are learning in their classrooms through a variety of core applies experiences on and off campus, such as:

1. original and collaborative advanced lab and field research;
2. creative events, performances, and activities developed and lead by students;
3. internships and externships;
4. practicums and preceptorships;
5. study abroad experiences
6. service learning projects that ask students to apply course content to community-based activities to address needs;

7. student-centered co-curricular activities that build on students' educational experience.

Selecting from the grant criteria, our classes focused on developing global and intercultural comprehension and this was to be achieved through intercultural exploration.

The demographic make-up of the class was distinct from most classes in the School of Journalism and the UA, which, at the time of this writing, is not yet a Hispanic serving institution. Of the 17 students, seven (41%) self-identified as Latina/o. The rest of the students were white (non-Latina/o). Three students were men (18%), and 14 were women (82%). The class was co-convened with eleven undergraduates (65%) and six graduate students (35%). Most students had some working knowledge of Spanish, which helped them make connections and work with people in Nogales, Arizona, and Nogales, Sonora. Also, somewhat distinct from the typical upper-division and graduate course experience was a diverse intellectual representation of students who came from various academic disciplines including: journalism, anthropology, Latin American Studies, Mexican American Studies, and history.

Throughout the semester students collected data and reported on security and militarization on in Ambos Nogales. They took photographs of and documented the presence of security (e.g. U.S. border patrol vehicles, agents, and infrastructure such as stadium lights) in a one-square mile area of the border with the main point of entry as ground zero of the map, so that they could eventually map security on both sides. The project titled, Security 360: Mapping Militarization in Ambos Nogales, grew to include much more than a map. In the end, students produced a series of published reports, including a cover story that was printed in the alternative newspaper, *The Tucson Weekly* (2015), and a mobile app of the project was created (Security 360, 2016) including a 360 VR video of the area in which 16-year-old José Antonio Elena Rodriguez was killed in 2012. In short, as the front page of the online project states,[4]

> What began as a simple endeavor to visualize security in one-square mile of Ambos Nogales, ended up expanding to quite literally a 360° view of the issue. From the history of militarization and the voices and responses to security, to the social and economic costs to the future of security in the region, this multimedia effort aims to improve public understanding about militarization and what it means to the people who live on both sides of this small stretch of the Arizona-Sonora line. (Security 360, 2016)

At the end of the semester, students presented their research at an open forum to members of the Nogales community at the UA satellite campus in Nogales, Arizona. About 50 people showed up for the event, including more than 20 students from a local Catholic high school. Staff from the Nogales Community Development Center (NDC) also attended. The NDC office provided classroom space for both classes during the semester, and the event gave the students and faculty an opportunity to thank the organization publicly. The work that the students produced along with the public presentations enabled students to give something tangible back to the community. The CBL model followed for the reporting the borderlands course also allowed students to reflect on what they had learned, one of the principles of good practice for combining service and learning (Honnet & Poulsen, 1989).

Student Experiences and Learning Outcomes

The combined undergraduate and graduate course provided additional learning opportunities and allowed students with various levels of expertise to share existing knowledge. For example, journalism undergraduates helped graduate students in other disciplines such as history and Mexican American studies develop multimedia skills, while graduate students assisted undergraduates by helping them better understand the concept of moral geography. Additionally, over the course of the semester, a mutually supportive cohort had formed. Developing a supportive cohort among undergraduates and graduate students was necessary for implementing engaged learning activities. Without a basic level of respect among a group of 17 students, serious problems might have emerged, especially when meeting and working with various community groups.[5] Undergraduate and graduate students' comments from the end of course evaluations provide some insights into the potential transformative elements of the class.[6]

Undergraduates: Overall Experiences

> I loved being exposed to two different cultures that are only feet from each other. You gave us the opportunity to see more than what is in a regular class, so thank you.

> It was such a different class experience, from very impactful field trips, especially going to the garbage dump and hearing about that community's lives and the battle to continue there. As well as using two different lenses to view a topic we have always been immersed in by living so close the border. I also like having such a mix of [disciplinary] backgrounds, which created very interesting conversations.

> I had come into the class knowing quite a lot of what is going on in the borderlands, especially coming from a migrant family. However, this course taught me more about the everyday life of people living in Ambos Nogales. Experiencing the borderlands taught me more about what it means to navigate between two different identities and *culturas*. The sights, the smells, the sounds, the art—I have embraced many more aspects of this city.

> I definitely feel more comfortable conducting research in an international setting because this class forced me—in a good way—to step out of that comfort zone. I learned to communicate with other people and learned different rules and policies surrounding the U.S.-Mexico border that helped me move forward in my research.

The undergraduates' comments suggest that the course deepened their knowledge and understanding of Ambos Nogales and its peoples; even for some students who had previous experience in the area. In addition, having the opportunity to conduct research in the borderlands helped students gain confidence. It is clear from the comments that the experiential activities were crucial for developing and strengthening their knowledge and understanding. The experience and knowledge gained will ideally be long lasting, and will help those students who end up working in and with Latina/o communities.

Graduate Students: Overall Experiences

> I absolutely loved learning more about Nogales. Reporting there between classes was my favorite part. I had been to Nogales many times in the past, but I got to know Nogales in a much more intimate way because of this class.

> I think my knowledge has greatly improved when it comes to the ethics of journalism at the border. I feel like I better understand the ways in which the media can subtly dehumanize migrants and I think that sensitivity (while probably intuitive before the class) now has a concrete outline of structural violence and how the media can (even inadvertently) feed into that.

> This course challenged me and made me think outside of the box. I would never have considered the project that we ended up putting together, and there were times when I doubted that it would work. I feel like I learned not only about putting things together, but that it is important to challenge yourself and to trust your group members. People are capable of more than I sometimes give them credit for.

> I really learned a lot about people's perspectives of the border wall and security. In viewing the final presentations, I feel like I really learned a great deal … I really enjoyed the trips to Nogales, Sonora and Nogales, Arizona very much. The fieldtrips were very interesting and contributed significantly to my knowledge of the area.

> I feel very comfortable conducting research in the border region, especially after this class. I have much more experience crossing and finding my way around in Nogales, which makes me more comfortable if I were to go to other areas as well.

Like their undergraduate counterparts, graduate students enjoyed the very experiential aspects of the course. Their comments suggest that the class took them to intellectual and physical places that they had never been to, and helped them think "outside of the box." The graduate students' comments connote a slightly deeper reflection on their experiences, which was to be expected. Several graduate students who were in the class have plans to work among Latino/a communities, and therefore it is hoped that their experience and knowledge gained will help make them be effective in the future.

It was clear that by the end of the course, undergraduates as well as graduate students—though they felt emotionally drained – were, in some ways, changed by this community-based learning experience. Going back and forth between Nogales, Arizona, and Nogales, Sonora, almost every week throughout the semester, students and the faculty did indeed become border crossers (Giroux, 1992). Through both the anthropology and journalism courses they began to literally put themselves into the shoes of the residents of the borderlands. As the next section explains, there is value in creating these educational paths for students, irrespective of some of the obstacles.

Opportunities, Challenges, and Limitations

Despite some of the challenges associated with implementing community-based learning projects, critical pedagogies have proven to be successful in their learning outcomes. At the same time, CBL and CSL seem to contradict some of the current financial goals and models for universities around the country, including The University of Arizona.

Critical Borderlands Pedagogy and Moral Geography

A critical pedagogy of the borderlands approach coupled with the conceptual framework of moral geography proved valuable for the participants and the final projects that were produced in the Migrahack and the Reporting the U.S. Mexico Borderlands course. By the end of the three-day Migrahack, more than eleven projects were created, and all sought to increase knowledge among the public about the complex and transnational issue of migration. With the Reporting the Borderlands course, undergraduate and graduate students not only grew in terms of their understanding of the region, the students helped to create alternative perspectives about the region through the Security 360 project. In a broad sense, through both the Migrahack and the reporting course, students, professional journalists, and activists created counter-cartographies of migration and the region. These alternative perspectives offered a counter-weight to what, historically, in the news media has been a white hegemonic lens through which the public hears and learns about the borderlands.

The best learning outcomes seemed to occur when the students self-select for these types of experiences. While, the Reporting the Borderlands class is open to all students, a high percentage of students (41%) who enroll are Latina/o, which is much higher than the percentage of Latino/a students among the general UA student body. Further, because the reporting course is offered as an elective, students must choose to take the class. Numerous students who have taken the course remarked that they have family in Sonora, Mexico, and for that reason they wanted to learn more about the region. The fact that a high number of Latina/o students enrolled suggests that the class appeared to be fulfilling a need for engaged and diversity experiences with a particular emphasis on issues relevant to Latina/o students. This is critical in a state such as Arizona, where, historically these educational opportunities have not existed. At the same time, the current state of academia presents some challenges to developing these kinds of community-engaged experiences for students.

Community Engagement in the Age of Academic Capitalism

The ability to organize a Migrahack depended on broad support from both the UA campus community and beyond. As has been noted, more than a dozen university and outside foundations and companies contributed financially to the event. Garnering support took time and commitment from the organizers and faculty at the School of Journalism. While worthwhile, the academy does not necessarily value these endeavors with equal weight as research and published scholarship (Fairweather, 2005). As a result, given the time and resource commitment, and the lack of emphasis that the wider academy places on what it considers to be teaching or service related efforts, research professors are less inclined to pursue these types of activities, especially if they know that they will be financially rewarded more for research rather than teaching efforts (Fairweather, 2005).

The Reporting in the U.S.-Mexico Borderlands course too requires additional support that is not necessary in most undergraduate and graduate courses. Faculty in the journalism and anthropology courses, for example, dedicate their entire days (12 hours) to the class and trips, including driving students in vans to and from the border on class days. Despite the additional time commitment, the course counts as three units of teaching, which translates to about three-hours/week in a typical three-unit course. Additional support for this course includes funding for student transportation to and from the university and the border.

At the same time, because of national accreditation standards, enrollment in the class is capped at 20 students, but the university's economic model, Responsibility Centered Management (RCM) does not view this as being very productive. In the RCM model, departments that have an increase in student credit hours are rewarded financially. If enrollment declines, so do budgets (Carlson, 2015). In short, the trend and philosophy of academic capitalism seem to be in conflict with universities' desires and calls for 100% student engagement. Having 20 students in a class, where students are visiting sensitive areas along the borderlands is challenging, but if that number were to be increased, it would be costlier, as well as logistically untenable for one or two professors. University economic models aside, the need is greater than ever for courses like Reporting in the U.S.-Mexico borderlands and community-based activities such as Arizona Migrahack.

Conclusion

More than five years have passed since the signing of SB 1070, and the State of Arizona remains a less than welcoming environment for immigrants as well as students and faculty of color (Jaquette, 2016). The on the ground realities inform faculty and student decisions in the classroom and beyond. The university's economic situation and the state's political climate might be enough to dissuade some professors from taking on the challenge of engaging with communities. Yet, it is clear that despite the academic and social environments, courses such as Reporting in the U.S.-Mexico Borderlands and activities such as the Migrahack can be valuable and truly transformative. Shortly after the Migrahack, a graduate student and a local journalist who both participated in the March 2015 event organized two separate data-focused hackathons. Some students who have taken the borderlands reporting course have commented that they see the region in a different way, and that they now "feel very comfortable conducting research in the border region, especially after this class," which demonstrates that they have been transformed on an individual level.

Collective transformation, though, might prove to be more elusive and difficult to evaluate. Community and cultural change are inherently more daunting and difficult than individual level change. Notwithstanding of some of academic challenges, and because of the political realities, and given the success of community-based learning experiences, in the future, more resources (not less) should be devoted to CBL for Latina/o students and in Latina/o communities, especially in places such as Arizona where there is still much knowledge and understanding to be mapped and shared. Using critical borderlands pedagogy along with the conceptual framework of moral geography and the creation of counter-cartographies, new and significant ways of the learning and knowing about the borderlands are being constructed and disseminated through multimedia. This is not to say that the CBL experiences discussed in this chapter have severely altered or undermined the power relations that are in existence in the borderlands. Nevertheless, upon evaluation and reflection of results from Arizona Migrahack and the reporting the borderlands course, it is evident that more than one perspective about the borderlands can exist alongside and even resist the dominant viewpoints of the region. Along the long road to social transformation, critical borderlands pedagogy and counter-cartographies have moved us a few steps forward.

Notes

1. In Arizona, 90% of the Latino/a population is of Mexican origin.
2. Support from community organizations was an essential element for the success of Migrahack. The event was funded with grants from the Ethics & Excellence in Journalism Foundation, Unbound Philanthropy, the University of Arizona School of Journalism, UA College of Social and Behavioral Sciences, UA Office of Student Engagement. Partners included Microsoft, InterWorks, Hoy Los Angeles and the Arizona Press Club. Other UA collaborators included UA Libraries, Center for Latin American Studies, Department of Mexican American Studies, Southwest Center, National Institute for Civil Discourse, and the Graduate Program in Rhetoric, Composition and the Teaching of English
3. In May 2015, the Arizona Board of Regents, which governs the state's three public universities, voted to allow DACA (Deferred Action for Childhood Arrivals) students to pay in-state tuition. Up until then, voter approved Proposition 300 banned in-state tuition for all undocumented students (Jung 2015).
4. At the writing of this chapter, students continue to produce reports related to the Fall 2015 class online and in the *Tucson Weekly*.
5. It should be noted that not all interactions between undergraduates and graduate students were positive. At times, undergraduates felt intimidated by graduate students. On other occasion, graduate students perceived undergraduates as less serious about the course. This became a concern during the group project as some students in the class felt that they had done much more work than others.
6. The examples provided here do not include comments from all students in the class, but they are, in general, representative of the types of comments that students wrote.

References

Bartels, J. (2016). *Three protestors arrested at Donald Trump Fountain Hills rally: ABC15.com.* Retrieved from http://www.abc15.com/news/region-northeast-valley/fountain-hills/three-protesters-arrested-at-donald-trump-fountain-hills-rally

Blust, K. (2016). Security 360: Mapping security in Ambos Nogales. *Tucson Weekly.* Retrieved from http://www.tucsonweekly.com/tucson/mapping-security-in-ambos-nogales/Content?oid=6051732

Border Journalism Network. (n.d.). *Homepage.* Retrieved from https://borderjnetwork.com/

Cabrera, N. L. (2014a). Exposing whiteness in higher education: White male college students minimizing racism, claiming victimization, and recreating white supremacy. *Race, Ethnicity, and Education, 17*(1), 30–55.

Cabrera, N. L. (2014b). But we're not laughing: White male college students' racial joking and what this says about "post-racial" discourse. *Journal of College Student Development, 55*(1), 1–15.

Carlson, S. (2015). Colleges "unleash" the deans with decentralized budgets. *The Chronicle of Higher Education.* Retrieved from http://www.chronicle.com/article/Colleges-Unleash-the-Deans/151711/

Castañeda, M. (2008). Transformative learning through community engagement. *Latino Studies, 6*, 319–326.

Counter-Cartographies Collective. (n.d.). Retrieved from http://www.countercartographies.org/

Elenes, C. A. (1997). Reclaiming the borderlands: Chicana/o identity, difference and critical pedagogy. *Educational Theory, 47*(3), 359–375.

Fairweather, J. S. (2005). Beyond the rhetoric: Trends in the relative value of teaching and research in faculty salaries. *The Journal of Higher Education, 76*(4), 401–422.

Giroux, H. A. (1992). *Border crossings: Cultural workers and the politics of education.* New York, NY: Routledge.

González de Bustamante, C. (2012). Arizona and the state of exclusion, 1912–2012. In O. Santa Ana & C. González de Bustamante (Eds.), *Arizona firestorm: Global immigration realities, national media and provincial politics* (pp. 19–40). New York, NY: Rowman and Littlefield.

González de Bustamante, C. (2015). Beyond narco tunnels and border security. *IRE Journal, Spring, 1*, 27–29.

Hassouneh, D. (2006). Anti-racist pedagogy: Challenges faced by faculty of color in predominantly white schools of nursing. *Journal of Nursing Education, 45*(7), 255–261.

Heyman, J. (2008). Constructing a virtual wall: Race and citizenship in U.S.-Mexico border policing. *Journal of the Southwest, 50*(3), 305–333.

Honnet, E. P., & Poulsen, S. J. (1989). *Principles of good practice for combining service and learning.* Racine, WI: Johnson Foundation.

Institute for Justice and Journalism. (2015a). *Press release.* Retrieved from http://ij.org/press-release/ij-asks-supreme-court-to-protect-grassroots-speech/

Institute for Justice and Journalism. (2015b). *Arizona migrahack overcoming division.* Retrieved from http://justicejournalism.org/whiteboard/arizona-migrahack-overcoming-division/

Isacson, A., Meyer, M., & Davis, A. (2013). *Border security and migration: A report from Arizona.* Retrieved from http://www.wola.org/publications/border_security_and_migration#remains

Jaquette, M. (2016). Protestors make demands for marginalized students. *The Daily Wildcat.* Retrieved from http://www.wildcat.arizona.edu/article/2016/03/protesters-make-demands-for-marginalized-students

Jung, C. (2015). Arizona Board of Regents Grants In-State Tuition to Certain Immigrants. *Associated Press.* Retrieved from http://kjzz.org/content/136510/arizona-board-regents-grants-state-tuition-certain-immigrants

Martinez, O. (2001). *Mexican-origin people in the United States: A topical history.* Tucson, AZ: University of Arizona Press.

Mitchell, K., & Elwood, S. (2015). Counter-mapping for social justice. In K. P. Kallio, S. Mills, & T. Skelton (Eds.), *Politics, citizenship and rights.* New York, NY: Springer.

O'Leary, A. O., Deeds, C., & Whiteford, S. (2013). *Uncharted terrains: New directions in border research and methodology, ethics and practice.* Tucson, AZ: University of Arizona Press.

O'Leary, A. O., Romero, A., Cabrera, N. L., & Rascón, M. (2012). Assault on ethnic studies. In O. Santa Ana & C. González de Bustamante (Eds.), *Arizona firestorm: Global immigration realities, national media and provincial politics* (pp. 91–120). New York, NY: Rowman and Littlefield.

Opie, J. (1998). Moral geography in high plains history. *Geographical Review, 88*(2), 241–258.

Rosner-Salazar, T. A. (2003). Multicultural service-learning and community-based research as a model approach to promote social justice. *Social Justice, 30*(4), 64–76.

Ross, H. H., & Edwards, W. J. (2016). African American faculty expressing concerns: Breaking the silence at predominantly white research oriented universities. *Race, Ethnicity and Education, 19*(3), 461–479.

Security 360: Mapping militarization in Ambos Nogales. (n.d.). Retrieved from http://jourviz.com/security-360/

Sharp-Grier, M. L. (2015). "She was more intelligent than I thought she'd be!": Status, stigma, and microaggressions in the academy. In J. L. Martin (Ed.), *Racial battle fatigue: Insights from the front lines of social justice advocacy* (pp. 29–44). Santa Barbara, CA: Praeger.

Shelton, A. J. (2016). Implementing community engagement in classrooms. *Journal of Higher Education Theory and Practice, 16*(1), 61–67.

Slaughter, S., & Rhoades, G. (2004). *Academic capitalism and the new economy: Markets, state and higher education.* Baltimore, MD: Johns Hopkins University.

Steller, T. (2016, March 24). Trump ignites free speech debate in Tucson. *Arizona Daily Star*. Retrieved from http://tucson.com/news/local/columnists/steller/steller-trump-ignites-free-speech-debate-in-tucson/article_a172ec0f-39ed-50e1-86ee-7aee4fbb4c3e.html

Taylor, L. J. (2007). Centre and edge: Pilgrimage and the moral geography of the US/Mexico border. *Mobilities, 2*(3), 383–393.

Truett, S. (2004). The ghost of the frontiers past: Making and unmaking of space in the borderlands. *Journal of the Southwest, 46*(2), 309–350.

U.S. Census Bureau. (2014). *Quick facts: Nogales city, Arizona*. Retrieved from http://www.census.gov/quickfacts/table/RHI805210/0449640

Van Velzer, R. (2016, March 31). Arizona Gov. Doug Ducey signs first immigration bill. *Arizona Capitol Times*. Retrieved from http://azcapitoltimes.com/news/author/ryanvanvelzerap/

10. Saber es Poder: *Teaching and Learning About Social Inequality in a New England Latin@ Community*

GINETTA E. B. CANDELARIO

This chapter will recount the history and theory of a community-based learning (CBL) course I developed, Sociology of Hispanic Caribbean Communities in the United States, which addresses Cuban, Dominican and Puerto Rican incorporation into mainland United States with a substantial component of the course devoted to understanding the local Puerto Rican population of Holyoke, MA as a case study of Puerto Rican experiences in the U.S. In addition to introducing students to sociological approaches to the causes and consequences of emigration from Cuba, the Dominican Republic and Puerto Rico to the U.S. mainland for both sending and receiving societies, the course also introduces students to qualitative research methods such as participant observation, feminist sociological methods such as institutional ethnography, and ethical Community-Based Learning practices. I offer students a combination of rigorous conventional pedagogy such as introduction to multi-disciplinary and interdisciplinary literatures as well as cultural production by and about the subject populations. I also include structured written assignments of various sorts, secondary census data research and analysis, and in class presentations. Lastly is the application of critical pedagogy which includes time-intensive reciprocity-based internships with non-profit, community-based organizations (CBOs) coupled with weekly ethnographic field exercises. Although this is in keeping with several academic traditions, including engaged sociology/sociology in the public interest, and with Women's Studies roots in the consciousness raising methods of the women's liberation movement in the 1970s, it best exemplifies Latin@ Studies founding principle of knowledge in the service of community empowerment as is alluded in this chapter's title.

At the most basic level, *saber es poder* translates as knowledge is power. This meaning derives largely from a sense that, know how, is empowering; that is, that having certain skills enables action, because in order to move from desire or will to action, one must have the capacity, the means, the power to do so. However, *saber es poder* can also allude to how being in the know produces advantages for those are over those who are not in the know. *Saber es poder* can also signal how particular epistemic frameworks—ways of knowing or *saberes*—have the power to constitute some things as inherently worth knowing, studying, learning about, and others as not. Finally, although not synonymous with *conocer*—which is knowledge in the sense of acquaintance or familiarity with—*saber* can be deployed as analogous to *conocer* when used to refer to knowledge of tapping into useful social networks, as in *saber quien es quien* (knowing who is who).

Thus, this chapter is organized in four sections, and each takes up how each of these significations of *saber es poder* is manifested in the course, Sociology of Hispanic Caribbean Communities in the United States (SOC 214). The sociological task is discerning patterns and similarities, and also the connections between this particular community and the larger communities and society it is part of. A core intellectual, ethical and political concern addressed by the CBL aspect of the course is what and how one comes to know a community. What do we think we know some communities before we even enter them? How did we come to know those things? How do we enter a community in order to know it better? Could we learn not only about it but also from it? How do you begin to try to know what the lived experience of this community is? What do you then gain in the way of knowledge about the larger society—and your place in it—through learning about this community? These and many other questions drive the course.

When and Where I Enter

It is not coincidental that it was a black woman sociologist, activist and educator, Anna Julia Cooper, whose famous treatise in 1892 on the profound all-encompassing violence that other black women experienced and navigated with particularly high stakes in the Jim Crowe South, asserted "when and where I enter, in the quiet, undisputed dignity of my womanhood, without violence and without suing or special patronage, then and there the whole … race enters with me." Cooper articulated how race, class and gender structured particular biographies, and how memberships in social groups both reflect and reproduce social structure and its inequities to the advantage of some and the great disadvantage of many. That is, by considering society from perspectives offered by the lives and circumstances of the society's most disadvantaged by race, class and gender—entering society with them from when and where they are—we come to know power and how it operates upon its objects.

In now canonical work on research methods, German sociologist Max Weber called for the application of *verstehen*, an empathetic understanding of the social world of the people and place the sociologist is studying. By empathetic understanding, Weber meant developing the capacity to view social reality and social problems from the perspective of those who are living them. Building on Weber's insight, U.S. sociologist, C. W. Mills, developed the theory and method of the sociological imagination. As Mills puts it, the "sociological imagination enables us to grasp history and biography and the relation between the two within society. … Perhaps the most fruitful distinction with which the sociological imagination works is between 'the personal troubles of milieu' and 'the public issues of social structure'" (Mills, 2004, pp. 3–4). The promise and task of sociology is to understand the relationship between particular individual's biographies and broader patterns produced by the shared experiences of individuals similarly situated—that is, individual's membership in socially constructed groups such as race, class, gender, sexuality, and citizenship. Thus, for example, if I lose my job because of my routine tardiness one could well attribute my job loss to a character failing. Further, if I am routinely tardy because I am a mother who is juggling childcare relying on private resources that aren't adequate to the task that could be just a personal trouble of the milieu. However, if I am one of many such mothers, then my habitual tardiness is not a product of a character failing nor simply a personal trouble, but the public issues of social structure: inequality produced by social norms that structure of who is and is not responsible for the care of children, in terms of gender for example, and how the material costs of that care are funded and by whom, in terms of primary caretakers' unpaid labor for example, and ideas and ideologies about self-sacrificial maternal love as natural rather than socialized, for example. Although there is often common sense awareness and analysis of these issues, for example on the part of women who mother, the task of sociology is to discern and document the social structures that produce, naturalize and often make invisible the power relations driving social facts (Mills, 2004).

For this Latina/o Studies CBL sociology course, then, a core task is to help the students critically reflect on what they think they know about race and racism in their home communities as well as in a particular Latina/o community. That project entails structuring the class so as to recognize, develop and deploy the power of each of the *saberes*: being in the know, know how, ways of knowing, and knowing who is who. Interrogating each one of those knowledges about Hispanic Caribbean Communities in the United States through community-based learning pedagogical strategies—that is, consistently considering not only when and where, but why and how we enter communities ready to learn from and not simply about Latina/os is the mandate of the course.

We Must Stare Into the Ruins—Bravely and Resolutely

I first started teaching this course during my first semester as an assistant professor in the Sociology Department and Latin American and Latino Studies Program at Smith College, my alma mater (Class of 1990). I've always told my students that I teach the course I would have wanted to take when I was an undergraduate Latina student at that predominantly white, wealthy and elite institution located in a predominantly white community (Northampton, Massachusetts), at the heart of the region that was the birth place of White Anglo-Saxonism in the United States (New England). This was a dramatically different place from both my mother's homeland, the Dominican Republic, where I spent large parts of my childhood, and my coming-of-age community of Hudson County, New Jersey which was characterized by its embroidery factories and location on the Hudson River across from Manhattan and by the 1960s where Cuban-American exiles along with a handful of Latinos from other Latin American and Caribbean countries (Prieto, 2009). In both the Dominican Republic and Hudson County, Latina/os and other people of color predominated demographically and whites were largely working class white ethnics—Italians, Irish, and German Americans. Thus, I arrived at Smith and Northampton completely unprepared for the taken for granted wealth and predominant whiteness of the place.

In that elite seven sisters school setting, I often wondered how what I was learning in the classroom was relevant not only to what I had experienced before arriving on campus—near constant residential mobility both within Hudson County and from the United States to the Dominican Republic—but how the insistently non-professional, erudite and highbrow curriculum could in any way prepare me to help my family and my community meet its often-unmet basic needs. I felt as if learning about and training myself in the liberal arts disciplines available at Smith was an exercise in utter selfishness geared toward nothing more than entering the crassly materialistic yuppie culture of conspicuous consumption that characterized the 1980s of my young adulthood. Yet, I was enthralled by my readings for my classes in religious ethics, I relished the debates in and out of the classroom about U.S. foreign policy in Central America, I thrilled in seeing my writing skills steadily improve in both English and Italian, and every so often I managed to relax into the taken-for-granted and unremarked comforts and safety of the campus and the town. Grappling with those tensions between my home and campus worlds took me six years, two exits from and three (re)admissions to Smith; I graduated in 1990 with major in Economics and a minor in Public Policy, rather than 1988 with a degree in English as I'd originally intended. Instead of becoming a print media journalist, "the first Hispanic Barbara Walters" in my mother's parlance, I went on to graduate school in Sociology at the City University of New York Graduate Center.

Along the way, I taught at several junior and senior colleges in the CUNY system and at several of the Rutgers University campuses in New Brunswick, NJ where the majority of my students were first generation, working class, immigrants and students of color from New York and New Jersey. In other words, we were at home both on and off campus. Consequently, when I returned to Smith in the fall of 1999 as a faculty member, I wanted to offer those students who were and did not feel at home there and were grappling with the same issues I had a decade before, both a space where they could feel at home on campus, and the means to understand how and why their education so far from home could make a difference not only in their personal lives, but in their families, in their communities, in the country and eventually at Smith itself. In other words, I want my students to know all the ways that *saber es poder* wherever they find themselves.

The pursuit of higher education often feels like an utterly selfish and self-sacrificial endeavor for first-generation students, particularly those in elite and/or liberal arts colleges (Aries, 2008; Aries & Berman, 2012; Aries & Seider, 2005). Some of the most effective responses to that now well-documented pattern are community-based learning and research (CBLR) courses in which students get the opportunity to make the real time, extensive and intensive connections between the work they are doing in the classroom and the well-being of their families, communities, and countries. (Strand, Marullo, Cutforth, Stoecker, & Donohue, 2003). In other words, when students understand the power of academic knowledge to transform their worlds, their personal investments in their education feel not only much more justified, but absolutely necessary (Daigle-Matos, 2015; Inside Higher Education, n.d.). For Latina/o students, the responsibilities they feel to enact their knowledge as power are multiplied because their citizenship rights are often undermined and disregarded in both their heritage and birth countries.

As Silvio Torres-Saillant (2005) puts it, "[c]itizens become most deserving of the name when they recognize themselves as agents of change responsible for making society more truly human. In that respect, the burden of citizenship usually weighs heavier for members of diasporic communities than for the regular citizenry, since they have more than one society to improve. Among ethnic minorities in the United States, Latinos face this civil overload with distinct acuity" (p. 281). After Chicanos/Mexican Americans, who comprise the majority of Latina/os in the United States, (1,884,000) Cubans, (1,509,000) Dominicans and (4,603,000) Puerto Ricans together comprise the next largest majority (7,996,000).

Although these three groups originate in the Hispanic Caribbean and have a great deal in common in terms of their histories, cultures, economies, politics and societies, they nonetheless also have important differences in terms of when, where and how each have left their islands and entered the U.S. mainland. Each country, and its emigration patterns, offers a case study in how different legacies of colonialism, slavery and imperialism in the Americas structure (im)migrants' incorporation into U.S. society on the mainland. Each begs different, if related, questions whose answers tell us as much about the United States as they do about Cubans, Dominicans and Puerto Ricans themselves.

For example, why is it that Cubans have socioeconomic standing (SES) equal to, or higher than, whites in the United States, while Puerto Ricans have SES equal to and at times lower than African-Americans in the United States, and Dominicans fall somewhere in the middle? Why is it that Puerto Ricans are U.S. citizens by birth since 1917 when the Jones Act imposed US citizenship on the island's residents, and can travel freely from the island to the mainland and any US territory in the world yet are often treated as if they were foreigners on the mainland? Why are over a million of the Dominican Republic's ten million people now living outside the country when a mere fifty years ago there were just over 10,000 Dominicans in the diaspora? Why are Cubans so actively involved in the Republican Party, from holding office at the local level to running for President of the United States, while largely Democratic Puerto Ricans routinely experience voter suppression and Dominicans are deported as alarmingly disproportionate rates? Why are the governments of Cuba socialist, the Dominican Republic putatively an independent democracy, and Puerto Rico a Commonwealth? Why do Cubans—who are most successfully assimilated into mono-lingual, Anglo-normative white U.S. socio-economic structures—speak more Spanish into the third generation than either Dominicans or Puerto Ricans who have been far less able to sustain Spanish-language fluency or bilingualism even into the second generation, despite being highly residentially segregated among co-ethnics? Whether largely Cold War exiles and refugees, colonial second-class citizens or vulnerable immigrants, Cubans, Puerto Ricans and Dominicans exemplify the Latina/o Studies explicatory leitmotif, we are here because you were there.

That is, much, if not all, Latino immigration and migration to the United States mainland is directly or indirectly a result of U.S. intervention in Latin America and the Caribbean. From the Monroe Doctrine of 1823 to the Mexican-American War of 1848, the Cuban—Spanish—American war of 1898, from the Roosevelt Corollary of 1905 to multiple US occupation and military government regimes throughout the Caribbean and Latin America over the course of the 20th century, from the Jones Act of 1917 to Operation Bootstrap in 1954, from to COINTELPRO to the Iran-Contra scandal, from NAFTA to the Panama papers, US policy toward and in Latin America and the Caribbean has been consistently interventionist (Schoultz, 1998). Consequently, U.S. imperialism and colonialism has been a triggering factor in the massive emigration from every single country south of the Rio Grande to the U.S. mainland. How U.S. mainland society has received and structurally incorporated those migrants, refugees, exiles and immigrants, however, has varied dramatically according to the historical moment in which those migrations began, the region of settlement, and to U.S. interests broadly defined: whether Latina/o incorporation occurred because the border crossed them as in the case of Mexicans in the U.S. Southwest when the northern third of Mexicans territory in North America became part of the United States under the terms of the Treaty of Guadalupe Hidalgo in 1848 (Acuña, 2014); or because they were made citizens en masse by virtue of congressional legislation as was the case with Puerto Ricans under the Jones Act (1917) and subsequently recruited as labor migrants for the fields in Connecticut and Hawaii, factories in Philadelphia in New York City, and households in Chicago (Sánchez-Korrol, 1994); or because they were welcomed with open arms as valiant exiles of a Godless Communist Revolution at the height of the Cold War and endowed with millions in public and private funding for professional re-credentialing, homeownership, education and workforce training as in the case of Cubans during the 1960s and 1970s (Masud-Piloto, 1995); or perhaps perfunctorily granted tens thousands of visas by the U.S. Embassy in the aftermath of the April 1965 U.S. military intervention and occupation that installed yet another dictatorial regime as in the case of Dominicans, Latina/o emigrants are the harvest of empire (González, 2000; Hoffnung-Garskof, 2007). In other words, there is a long history behind the personal and community stories of Cubans, Dominicans, and Puerto Ricans on the U.S. mainland.

That history accounts for the immediately discernible differences in SES for each of the three communities, as well as the sometimes similar but mostly different stereotypes attached each. If it is true that Cubans, Dominicans, and Puerto Ricans, are all subject to generalized stereotyping as Hispanics that is, loud, fast talking, colorfully attired, music loving, hip swiveling dancers, passionate and hot tempered folks—then it is also true that each of the three groups are subject to stereotypes unique unto them. Cubans are the least likely to be characterized as unfit for political power and self-representation, as evidenced by the disproportionate representation of Cubans at every level of governance from local to presidential elections (García, 1997). Puerto Ricans and Dominicans alike are routinely stereotyped as drug dealing welfare cheats who see little value in investing in their children's education and contribute and rather than contribute unfairly siphon resources away from hard-working taxpaying Americans (Hoffnung-Garskof, 2007; Irizarry, 2011; López, 2002). And indeed, while Cubans generally are much better off in terms of educational attainment levels, homeownership, wealth, and political participation in formal and electoral politics, Dominicans and Puerto Ricans are overrepresented among the poor, the dropouts, the incarcerated, and single female-headed households. Yet, as Nigerian writer Chimamanda Ngozi Adichie (2009) reminds us, "the problem with stereotypes is not that they are untrue; it is that they are incomplete."

That incompleteness can be addressed through the development of a Latina feminist sociological imagination (Anzaldúa, 1999; Latina Feminist Group, 2001; Sandoval, 1991; Smith, 2005; Torres-Saillant, 2005) that fosters an understanding that there are historical and structural reasons why Cubans have done so much better than Dominicans and Puerto Ricans. For example, even as Cubans have more consistently and avowedly sustained their ethnic distinctiveness, they retain Spanish language use into the third generation, identify as Cuban-American or simply Cuban, and choose residential concentration in predominantly either Cuban or more generally Latin American immigrant and Latino communities particularly in Florida. By contrast, their far less well-off Dominican and Puerto Rican counterparts do not retain the same degree of Spanish-language fluency into the second—much less the third—generation, and find themselves residing alongside co-nationals not by primarily by choice but due to blocked access to housing, jobs and education outside of their urban inner-city neighborhoods. In other words, Cubans have quite successfully incorporated or simulated structurally into mainstream white U.S. society although refusing to give up their *cubanidad*. While Puerto Ricans are castigated for supposedly refusing to assimilate culturally even as their capacity to assimilate structurally has long been blocked by both formal policy and informal discriminatory and racist practices (Black, 2010; Eckstein, 2009; García, 1997). That is to say, developing a sociological imagination enables students to understand intellectually that for these communities' willingness to assimilate, Americanize or pursue the American Dream is not enough.

And We Must See

Moving from stereotype and common sense to intellectual understanding of Hispanic Caribbean communities in the United States based on research literature, however, is insufficient in and of itself. Instead, students with a developed sociological imagination must make the connection between the extensive research literature they read for the course and actual Latina/o communities, including perhaps their own. For it is the case that the Puerto Rican and Dominican students in classes are at times just as inclined as non-Latinos to blame their communities' disadvantaged economic, social and political circumstances on the U.S. mainland on their communities supposed cultural pathologies, rather than on the social structures that condition their community experiences. How do they at once recognize similarities between their own home communities in Boston, New York, Philadelphia, Chicago, Miami, Los Angeles, and the unique particularities of Holyoke's Puerto Rican community? How do they come to learn from and not just about Puerto Ricans in Holyoke and in the United States? In sum, how to train students to use a sociological imagination to see what is hidden in plain sight? Through thoughtfully structured community based learning with the predominantly Puerto Rican community of Holyoke, Massachusetts which is less than ten miles away and yet in many ways is a world apart from the college campus on which they are grappling with these issues.

According to the 2010 Census, there are 37,964 residents in the City of Holyoke, Massachusetts. Of those, 19,313 or 51% are Puerto Rican. Holyoke has the dubious honor of regularly outpacing the much larger, demographically more diverse and geographically more concentrated communities in the Boston metropolitan area in terms of having the highest rates of teenage pregnancy, HIV/AIDs, diabetes and asthma, poverty, unemployment, occupational segregation, incarceration, high school push out and homelessness rates in the state. It also has the lowest educational attainment levels and Latin@ home ownership rates, factors that are intimately related given the property tax-based funding system for public education. That Holyoke is also a predominantly Puerto Rican community is not coincidental to those rankings, nor is the fact that those Puerto Ricans are predominantly children under the age of 18 who live in highly residentially segregated neighborhoods (Gastón, 1994; Granberry & Rustan, 2010; Vasquez, 2003). Consequently, if sadly, Holyoke exemplifies many of the historic patterns and social facts characteristic of Puerto Rican incorporation into U.S. mainland society. In order to intervene in that history and social reality, to offer students a model of sociology in the public interest and to exemplify core Latina/o Studies pedagogy, this course deploys ethically and intellectual rigorous CBL with the Puerto Rican community of Holyoke, Massachusetts.

Smith and Five College students more generally often hear about Holyoke within mere weeks of their arrival on campus by way of word-of-mouth warnings not to visit the city itself, although they are encouraged to go to the Holyoke Mall at Ingleside via the Pioneer Valley Transit Authority (PVTA) bus that serves the Five Colleges. Although the Ingleside Mall bus route takes them through the City's downtown, it largely skirts the lower Ward neighborhoods where Puerto Ricans are concentrated. Nonetheless, whether at the mall or on the downtown streets, many of the Puerto Ricans students encounter at first glance confirm the stereotypes that they are immediately apprised of when they arrive on campus—teenage mothers pushing strollers, the young men hanging out on street corners, stoned drug addicts and alcoholics on the bus talking loudly about their personal troubles of milieu.

That is why I have developed a course that simultaneously introduces students into the Holyoke community and the literature produced within the disciplines of history, sociology, anthropology, political science, education and economics, as well as literature and performance texts. Students read an average of 100 to 150 pages per week of scholarship through which they are introduced to the substantive knowledge they most often lack about Cuba, Puerto Rico and the Dominican Republic, their diasporas and communities on the U.S. mainland. We review and discuss those readings over the course of four to five hours each week, typically over two to three class meetings per week. Beginning in week five, students undertake a four-hour per week internship over the course of ten weeks for a total of 40 internship hours during the semester with a Puerto Rican serving community-based organization in Holyoke. Generally, these organizations respond to community identified needs in the areas of housing, public health, workforce training and economic development, adult basic education, sexual and reproductive rights, family services, environmental justice, and food access. Puerto Ricans themselves founded several of these organizations—the Main Street organizations, Enlace de Familias/Holyoke Family network, Nueva Esperanza, Nuestras Raíces—during the 1980s in response to the arson crisis, but currently the vast majority of these organizations was established and staffed by non-Puerto Rican whites who live outside the City (Bloomgarden, Bombadier, Breitbart, Nagel, & Smith, 2006).

An extensive literature has already documented the fact that student internships not only disproportionately benefit the student intern over the host organization, but in fact constitute a substantial drain on the often-limited resources of nonprofit, community-based, and grassroots organizations. This is largely due to the fact that the host organization necessarily must devote human resources to training, incorporating and supervising a student intern who will commit to the organization very limited hours each week for 14 weeks or less (Hamner, 2002). Often, just at the point at which the student has received enough training to be useful to the organization, she is preparing to leave the organization because the semester is coming to an end. In other words, she obtained valuable human capital and a resume builder without having contributed commensurately to the organization's goals and projects. In order to address that structural dynamic that I have developed long-term sustained relationships with a limited number of CBOs and a process for jointly identifying task-based projects that (1) serve the organizations short term goals, (2) can be broken down into weekly tasks and completed within forty hours over the course of ten weeks and (3) have tangible and measurable outcomes for the host organization.

First, depending on local current events, I select no more than six organizations that I will be working with throughout the semester from a core group of a dozen partner organizations with whom I have established relationships over the years and with whom I am prepared to work at least two years in a row. I meet with the Executive Director and/or with the staff person who will be in charge of student interns at each organization about two to three weeks before the semester begins. This is in response to the fact that I came to learn fairly quickly during my work in Holyoke that neo-liberalism has meant that many, if not most, of the community-based organizations and nonprofits in the city are unable to plan beyond the next three months due to constant funding instability, grant writing pressures, and constantly on jeopardized budgets (Incite! Women of Color Against Violence, 2009). During the pre-semester meeting, which takes from sixty to ninety minutes usually, we identify three to five short-term projects that will directly benefit the work plan strategic plan or short-term agenda of the organization. Past projects have included designing and producing an informational brochure or a newsletter for an organization; collecting federal census or state-generated data and organizing it into the format that the organization can subsequently draw upon for its grant writing or report writing purposes; developing curricula for HIV-AIDS prevention, reproductive and sexual health; developing civic education curricula for English language learners; clearing a rubble strewn lot and preparing the soil for a community garden; researching and contributing to the script for a short informational video; researching assistance for a public history Museum tour; undertaking a walking census of Latino-owned, Main Street business storefronts in support of a Latino Chamber of Commerce economic development initiative; and many, many others.

Once these projects are identified and scopes of work are developed for each of them, representatives from the community-based organizations who will be partnering with the class offer a ten-minute presentation to the class in week three during which they introduce the students to the history, mission and mandate of the organization, as well as to the projects they are willing to host a student intern for. When I first began to teach the course, this meeting took place on Smith campus. However, I soon realized that asking the CBO partners to come to campus for this meeting and presentation placed a substantial burden without compensation for their expertise and time, which was already in short supply. Since then, the meetings have been held on-site in Holyoke, usually hosted by one of the partner organizations. The students travel there together, usually in a college provided van, and in so doing become aware the logistics of travel between Smith and Holyoke. The meetings also offer an invaluable opportunity for the students to navigate the route from Smith to Holyoke by car, to hear directly from the community-based partners, and to ask questions in person about the organizations and about the specific projects. Coincidentally, the collective meeting allows the CBO representatives themselves to hear about what other organizations currently working on in Holyoke. Lack of knowledge about the projects and efforts of other organizations in Holyoke has been a long-standing problem that the Holyoke Unites project has attempted to address since 2000 by establishing a shared calendar and by hosting regular quarterly meetings of all the community-based organizations and nonprofits in the city. However, despite its best efforts, Holyoke Unites has not been able to sustain and reorganize a regular opportunity for community-based organizations and nonprofits to come together and assess or learn about their perspective events, projects, successes and failures.

Having visited the city for a second time (the first is an assigned round-trip by PVTA bus from Main Street, Northampton to Main Street, Holyoke in week three) and heard from the community-based partners about their projects, the students then identify the top three preferred projects within at least two different organizations that they are interested in working with. They prepare application packets that include a cover letter and a resume for each of the three projects, just as they would if they were applying for an internship or paid position at the organization under other circumstances. This packet is due in both electronic and hard copy in class the Monday following the presentations (week four). I then organize the applicant pool for each organization and meet once again with my partners, usually on Tuesday of that week, at which time together we had identified which students will be interning at their organizations and which projects they will be undertaking. No organization hosts more than three students and every organization gets at least two students. The students are informed of their placements by the second or third class meeting of week four, at which point they are asked to sit together during class time and identify several blocks of time during the coming week (week five) when they are available to meet with the host organization as an internship team. Again, the idea is to reduce the time asked of the organization attending to the students, while also beginning to build a team-based identity and ethic among each organization´s interns.

At that first meeting with their project supervisor, the students visit the actual organization for the first time (although they will have usually seen photographs or perhaps a video of the organization during presentation of internship opportunities). They bring with them a very detailed, four-page internship contract I have developed in which the expectations and responsibilities of each party is clearly articulated, including (a) the total number of hours to be worked and the weekly schedule, (b) the start date and end date of the internship, (c) the overall project goal with clearly identified benchmark goals along the way, usually at least one for every from month mid-October to the end of semester which is typically mid-December and (d) specific dates when they will meet formally with their project supervisor to assess the progress they are making towards meeting those benchmark goals and the overall project goal. There is a time sheet attached to the contract and every week they are expected to have their project supervisor initial it to show that they have worked the hours required as scheduled. These internships account for 40% of the course grade and it is the project supervisor who evaluates the work and assigns a grade. They write a two-paragraph assessment of the student intern in which they articulate the rationale for the grade. Clearly stated on the syllabus and again during class on several occasions throughout the semester is that only under compelling extraordinary circumstances have I overridden the project supervisor's grade.

This practice accomplishes two goals. First, it makes clear to the supervisor that he or she is acting as a community-based co-teacher and that therefore they bear certain amount of responsibility not only for training the student intern, but for educating her about the community context within which their work takes place. Second, it clearly conveys to the student that the internship is a serious learning exercise directly related to the work we are doing in the classroom. What they are learning from the organization and the community it is serving is connected to the scholarship we are exploring in our course readings. Further, rigorous community-based learning is formal, progressive and accountability-based and therefore equivalent to the accountability they have for the work they do on campus.

In order to facilitate those connections, the CBL contract also includes a worksheet with a series of prompts that supervisor and the student interns are asked to discuss and document during their monthly check in conversation. Those prompts asked the student and the supervisor to consider how the work they are doing together relates to the literature that the student's reading in class that month, which the students have to explain to their supervisors who are not doing those readings. This exchange is mutually enriching in that the students are sharing their developing knowledge of the scholarship with their supervisors, while also working together with their supervisors to reflect upon how that scholarship relates to, diverges from and/or might enrich the organization's work in the community. In other words, the check-in is an opportunity for reciprocal praxis.

At the end of the semester the community-based organization partners and the student interns come together as a collective once again this time to share with one another the fruits of their collaborative labors. When funding is available, I organize an event at which food is served, guests are invited from the campus and community, and students and partners together present the results of their project work. This is most certainly a highlight of the semester, both because the coming back together after a semester of working part and across the city is in and of itself a pleasure seeing the fruits of their individual laborers together in one space makes manifest their praxis. It also offers their peers and on campus an opportunity to learn about the work they've been doing all semester off campus. Several of these and of semester events have been profiles in local newspapers (Mahoney, 2013).

And Then We Must Act

The third central element of the course is methodological training in feminist ethnographic fieldwork in Latina/o community (Romero, Hondagneu-Sotelo, & Ortiz, 1997; Smith, 2005; Zavella, 2011). Beginning in week two of the semester, students begin to undertake weekly "field assignments" that I have developed over the years intended to foster *verstehen*, or an understanding from within the community of the geographic, political, economic, cultural and social landscape of the community they are interning in. These twelve field assignments include watching one Hollywood produced film that has depicted Cubans, Dominicans, and Puerto Ricans in the United States per month: *Scarface*, *West Side Story*, and *Shaft* (the 2002 remake of the 1971 original). As might be self-evident, the pedagogical goal here is to make clear one source of stereotypes about each community, and to interrogate the relationship between the film's depictions, scholarship on those communities, and students' CBL experiences in Holyoke.

Another field assignment asks the students to research the current minimum wage in Massachusetts, calculate what the net pay would be for a full-time worker earning minimum wage, and to develop a household budget that considers housing, utilities, food, personal grooming, transportation, and childcare costs for one child based on those net wages. A subsequent assignment asks the students to research current Temporary Aid to Needy Families (TANF) and Supplemental Nutrition Assistance Program (SNAP) benefits for that same single-parent, one-child family. With these minimum-wage and TANF housing budgets in hand, I ask the students to actually search for an apartment that is within their budget, to visit that apartment and/or undergo the rental process as far as they can. I also ask students to develop a culturally appropriate meal plan, grocery list, and budget. They then visit a bodega (small Latin@ grocery store), a local supermarket franchise (Stop & Shop) and a farmer's market in order to explore the alignment between their minimum-wage-based and SNAP-benefits based budgets and actual local food costs in each of these venues. Likewise, I ask them to identify jobs available in Holyoke that require at most a high school degree, accept GEDs and/or folks without either a GED or a high school degree, visit the workplaces and inquire about the application process. We also discuss transportation logistics to these available jobs from the Wards Puerto Ricans are largely concentrated in, South Holyoke and the Flats.

Further, since many living in those Ward's reside in public housing do not own cars, I ask students to research how a high school student whose family does not have access to a car gets from the Toepfert Housing complex to Holyoke High School (HHS). They then have to use one of those routes and strategies themselves to make the trip in time to arrive at HHS for the first bell at 7:15 a.m. Likewise, I ask students to get to the Stop & Shop Supermarket on Lincoln Avenue—which is the closest full service supermarket in the city—from the Lyman Terrace Apartments public housing complex without a car. I also ask students to visit the Holyoke Health Center (which was an initiative of the South Holyoke community) and the Holyoke Hospital Emergency room (which is located in one of the City's Upper Wards), engage in two hours of observation in which they compare and contrast both health service provider's publicly visible interaction with Puerto Rican patients and visitors. Finally, I ask students to attend meetings of both the City Council and the Board of Education, and take note of the demographics of both elected officials and constituents present, as well as of the substance and cultural norms of the meetings, including language use. Perhaps not surprisingly, the structural challenges Puerto Ricans face in Holyoke's health, education, housing, food access, the labor market and politics in Holyoke become increasingly clear over the course of the semester.

I began to incorporate these field exercises into the class after having incorporated internships because I came to realize that students were going from the campus to the community-based organization as if in a plexiglass chute, the kind at the bank drive up teller window, and consequently not really understanding the material and social contexts their CBO's navigated and addressed. This lack of exposure to the community beyond the organization often meant that they understood their internships as volunteerism rather than as an opportunity to learn with and from the community about the social problems that each of the community-based organization partners were endeavoring to address—residential segregation, economic inequality, public health challenges, political disenfranchisement and underrepresentation, and a school system that continues to fail Puerto Rican schoolchildren (De Jesús & Rolón-Dow, 2007; Irizzary, 2011; Kidder, 1989).

On average, each of these field exercises field assignments take three to four hours per week to complete. I encourage students to team up on several, if not all, of the assignments because collaborative ethics are critical to the success of community-based learning, and because many of the field assignments are in fact so time consuming as to require division of labor. This is all the more so because the class always draws students from the other four colleges in the Five College consortium—University of Massachusetts at Amherst, Amherst College, Hampshire College, and Mount Holyoke—who also commute to the Smith campus. Since each of those institutions has a unique student demographic and culture, collaborating on the field exercises is further enriched by that as it is by the fact that students often come from a variety of majors: Sociology, Anthropology, History, Government, Latin American and Latina/o studies, Study of Women and Gender, Engineering, English, Spanish and Portuguese, Biology, Psychology, etc. Working together across these institutional, disciplinary and demographic differences allows them to bring to each field assignment talents and skills they have developed from their respective individual academic circumstances. On-going negotiation of these differing positionalities further requires them to consider how their various intellectual orientations can be complementary rather than inherently contradictory or superior, which is a core tenet of Latina/o Studies.

From Saber to Poder

During an end-of-year faculty development workshop series on community based learning and research that I organized in 2008, a recent white, upper middle-class graduate who had taken this class and was presenting as part of a panel of CBLR students from the Five Colleges, opened her comments by stating, "CBL helped me understand that I entered and exited the community indebted to its residents, and not vice versa as I had previously imagined." In other words, she understood not just that "we are here, because you were there" but also that the socio-economic well-being and political power of her community is a product of the economic, political and social disadvantage of communities like Puerto Rican Holyokers (Kleinman & Copp, 2009). She went on to explain how the readings, field assignments and internship together constituted a "boot camp in Latina/o Studies, the sociological imagination and qualitative research methods" that not only inspired her to continue working for social justice in the non-profit sector, but left her feeling confident that she would enter graduate school well-prepared were she to pursue an advanced degree. Equally important, as a middle-class white woman, she felt prepared to be a civically engaged citizen who was informed, conscious, and conscientious about communities that were not her own. In other words, she felt the knowledge and sociological imagination she had developed in a CBL Latina/o Studies class had empowered her to transform her society for the good of all, including those neither near nor necessarily dear to her (Hironimus-Wendt and Wallace, 2009).

Likewise, Latina students who take the class have regularly come to consciousness about how their *latinidad* is not in and of itself sufficient basis for understanding Hispanic Caribbean communities in the United States. Rather, they come to realize that academic learning and scholarly research have a great deal to offer in terms of elucidating and valorizing knowledge not just for knowledge's sake, but for justice's sake (Mahoney, 2013; Marullo & Edwards, 2000). While Stanley Fish and his largely White, heterosexual, U.S. citizen, male, middle class and above cohort argue strenuously that justice concerns corrupt higher education, for first generation, female, of color, and immigrant students, education is rarely a purely intellectual exercise (Daigle-Matos, 2015; Fish, 2012). Likewise, empowerment through education, paradigm shifting and knowledge production are at the heart of Latina/o Studies, which was born of the understanding that a monopoly over knowledge and its institutionalization is a key source of white supremacist, imperialist patriarchal power (hooks, 1992, 1994). Yet with a sociological imagination developed through the practice of rigorous community based learning, feminist ethnography and Latina/o Studies scholarship, *saber* is most definitely *poder*. Ultimately, as Junot Díaz (2011) states, "We must stare into the ruins—bravely, resolutely—and we must see. And then we must act."

References

Acuña, R. F. (2014). *Occupied America: A history of Chicanos* (8th ed.). New York, NY: Pearson.

Adichie, C. N. (2009, July). *The danger of a single story: TED global.* Retrieved from https://www.ted.com/talks/chimamanda_adichie_the_danger_of_a_single_story?language=en

Anzaldúa, G. (1999). *Borderlands/La frontera: The new mestiza* (2nd ed.). San Francisco, CA: Aunt Lute Books.

Aries, E. (2008). *Race and class matters at an elite college.* Philadelphia, PA: Temple University Press.

Aries, E., & Berman, R. (2012). *Speaking of race and class: The student experience at an elite college.* Philadelphia, PA: Temple University Press.

Aries, E., & Seider, M. (2005). The interactive relationship between class identity and the college experience: The case of lower income students. *Qualitative Sociology, 28*(4), 419–443.

Black, T. (2010). *When a heart turns rock solid: The lives of three Puerto Rican brothers on and off the streets.* New York, NY: Vintage.

Bloomgarden, A., Bombadier, M., Breitbart, M. M., Nagel, K., & Smith II, P. H. (2006). Building sustainable community/university partnerships in a metropolitan setting. In R. Forrant & L. Silka (Eds.), *Inside and out: Universities and education for sustainable development* (pp. 105–120). Amityville, NY: Baywood Publishing Company.

Cooper, A. J. (1892). *A voice from the south.* Xenia, OH: Aldine Printing House.

Daigle-Matos, J. M. (2015). La familia: The important ingredient for Latina/o college student engagement and persistence. *Equity & Excellence in Education, 48*(3), 436–453.

De Jesús, A., & Rolón-Dow, R. (2007). The education of the Puerto Rican diaspora: Challenges, dilemmas, and possibilities. *Centro Journal, XIX* (2), 4–11.

Díaz, J. (2011). Apocalypse: What disasters reveal. *The Boston Review.* Retrieved from http://www.bostonreview.net/junot-diaz-apocalypse-haiti-earthquake

Eckstein, S. (2009). *The immigrant divide: How Cuban Americans changed the U.S. and their homeland.* New York, NY: Routledge.

Fish, S. (2012). *Save the world on your own time.* Cambridge, MA: Oxford University Press.

García, M. C. (1997). *Havana USA: Cuban exiles and Cuban Americans in South Florida, 1959–1994.* Berkeley, CA: University of California Press.

Gastón Institute. (1994). *Latinos in Holyoke: Poverty, income, education, employment, and housing.* Boston, MA: Gastón Institute, University of Massachusetts.

González, J. (2001). *Harvest of empire: A history of Latinos in America.* New York, NY: Penguin.

Granberry, P., & Rustan, S. (2010). *Latinos in Massachusetts selected areas: Holyoke, Chicopee, and Easthampton.* Boston, MA: Gastón Institute, University of Massachusetts.

Hamner, D. M. (2002). *Building bridges: The Allyn and Bacon student guide to service learning.* Boston, MA: Allyn and Bacon.

Hironimus-Wendt, R., & Wallace, L. E. (2009). The sociological imagination and social responsibility. *Teaching Sociology, 37*(1), 76–88.

Hoffnung-Garskof, J. (2007). *A tale of two cities: Santo Domingo and New York after 1950.* Princeton, NJ: Princeton University Press.

hooks, b. (1992). *Black looks: Race and representation.* Boston, MA: South End Press.

hooks, b. (1994). *Teaching to transgress: Education as the practice of freedom.* New York, NY: Routledge.

Incite! Women of Color Against Violence (Eds.). (2009). *The Revolution will not be funded: Beyond the non-profit industrial complex.* New York, NY: South End Press.

Inside Higher Education. (n.d.). *Teaching ethics: A key role for educators.* Retrieved from https://www.insidehighered.com/content/teaching-ethics-key-role-educators?utm_source=Inside+Higher+Ed+Notifications&utm_campaign=300887650a-Teaching_Ethics_20151022_Email2&utm_medium=email&utm_term=0_b7c36aa67a-300887650a-198814249

Irizarry, J. (2011). *The Latinization of U.S. schools: Successful teaching and learning in shifting cultural contexts.* New York, NY: Paradigm Publishers.

Kidder, T. (1989). *Among schoolchildren.* Boston, MA: Houghton Mifflin.

Kleinman, S., & Copp, M. (2009). New Yorker social harm: Students' resistance to lessons about inequality. *Teaching Sociology, 37*(3), 283–293.

Latina Feminist Group. (2001). *Telling to live: Latina feminist testimonios.* Durham, NC: Duke University Press.

López, N. (2002). *Hopeful girls, troubled boys: Race and gender disparity in urban education.* New York, NY: Routledge.

Mahoney, P. (2013, January 23). Smith College sociology students learn from GED students at Holyoke Community College. *Hampshire Daily Gazette.*

Marullo, S., & Edwards, B. (2000). From charity to justice: The potential of university-community collaboration for social change. *American Behavioral Scientist, 43*(5), 895–912.

Masud-Piloto, F. (1995). *From welcome exiles to illegal immigrants: Cuban migration to the U.S., 1959–1995.* New York, NY: Rowman & Littlefield.

Mills, C. W. (2004). The promise of sociology. In D. Kauzlarich (Ed.), *Sociological classics.* Upper Saddle River, NJ: Pearson/Prentice Hall.

Prieto, Y. (2009). *The Cubans of Union City: Immigrants and exiles in a New Jersey community.* Philadelphia, PA: Temple University Press.

Romero, M., Hondagneu-Sotelo, P., & Ortiz, V. (Eds.). (1997). *Challenging fronteras: Structuring Latina and Latino lives in the U.S.* New York, NY: Routledge.

Sánchez-Korrol, V. (1994). *From colonia to community: The history of Puerto Ricans in New York City.* Los Angeles, CA: University of California Press.

Sandoval, C. (1991). U.S. third world feminism: The theory and method of oppositional consciousness in the postmodern world, *Genders, 10*, 1–24.

Schoultz, L. (1998). *Beneath the United States: A history of U.S. policy toward Latin America.* Cambridge, MA: Harvard University Press.

Smith, D. (2005). *Institutional ethnography: A sociology for people.* Lanham, MD: Alta-Mira Press.

Strand, K., Marullo, S., Cutforth, N., Stoecker, R., & Donohue, P. (2003). *Community-based research and higher education: Principles and practice.* New York, NY: Jossey-Bass.

Torres-Saillant, S. (2005). Racism in the Americas and the Latino scholar. In A. Dzidzienyo & S. Oboler (Eds.), *Neither enemies nor friends: Latinos, Blacks, Afro-Latinos* (pp. 281–304). New York, NY: Palgrave Macmillan.

Vasquez, D. W. (2003). *Latinos in Holyoke, Massachusetts.* Boston, MA: Gastón Institute, University of Massachusetts.

Zavella, P. (2011). *I'm neither here nor there: Mexicans' quotidian struggles with migration and poverty.* Durham, NC: Duke University Press.

Section III

Expanding the Media and Cultural Power of Communities

11. *Media Literacy as Civic Engagement*

JILLIAN M. BÁEZ

Media literacy is arguably one of the most important skills to master as a citizen in the 21st century. Media literacy is the ability to critically engage with media and involves four elements: accessing media, analyzing media content, evaluating the messages encoded in media and creating media (Aspen Institute, 1993). In a media-saturated society, media literacy is a necessary skill, empowering individuals with a toolkit to not only decipher media images, but also facilitating advocacy for media policy issues which affect who owns and produce media along with the type of content that is created and how it is distributed. In addition, media literacy is a form of social justice for marginalized communities who otherwise might not have formal spaces to critically engage with media. Furthermore, in emphasizing how media are produced and under what political and economic conditions, media literacy encourages civic engagement by encouraging consumers to view themselves as actors within the media production and regulation processes.

In this reflective chapter, I consider media literacy as a form of civic engagement for Latina/o communities. Among media literacy scholars and practitioners, it is agreed that one of the potential outcomes of media literacy programs is increased civic engagement since one will become not only more critical of media messages, but also more aware of media policy (Hobbs, 1998a; Hobbs, 1998b; Kellner & Share, 2005). Media literacy is understudied among Latina/o communities and this chapter focuses on how media literacy can be a form of civic engagement for Latina/os, especially with limited access to modes of production and regulation. Based on several years of research in various contexts working closely with Latina/o audiences, I call attention to issues of media inequality and offer strategies for developing media literacy skills and advocacy in intergenerational Latina/o communities.

In particular, I emphasize the need for media literacy curriculum both inside and outside the classroom that addresses not only mainstream media, but also Spanish-language and ethnic media because most Latina/o audiences encounter these multiple forms of media on a daily basis. Media literacy as a form of civic engagement involves not only learning how to deconstruct media texts, but also understanding oneself as a player within the media system who can advocate and/or contest media production, ownership, and content (Hobbs, 1998a; Kellner & Share, 2005; Kellner & Share, 2007; Silverstone, 2004). This process involves teaching students to understand longstanding patterns of representations of Latina/os in various media forms, introducing students to regulation, particularly how the Federal Communications Commission (FCC) operates, and exposing them to organizations that advocate for media reform such as the National Hispanic Media Coalition, Free Press, and the National Association for Latina/o Independent Producers.

Media, including television, film, radio, newspapers, magazines, and social media platforms, are important sites where each of us obtain information and seek entertainment. Who is represented in both production and content reflects the larger power structures and hierarchies in our society. Put differently, it matters who is behind the camera as much as it matters who is on camera (Bobo, 1998; Negrón-Muntaner, Abbas, Figueroa, & Robson, 2014). As such, I consider media to be an important part of the public sphere where important issues, values, and beliefs are engaged and debated in our contemporary society (Amaya, 2013). Given that we are bombarded by media messages in our daily lives, researchers and teachers have embraced media literacy as a way for ordinary people to foster awareness about, question, and sometimes challenge media images. Many schools and non-profit organizations currently teach media literacy for students in K-12. In fact, some states such as Massachusetts and North Carolina include media literacy in their state education standards. In most colleges and universities, there is at least one media literacy course in the catalog. Additionally, there are major national non-profit organizations, such as the Center for Media Literacy and National Association for Media Literacy Education, that advocate for media literacy education and provide curricular support for educators and community organizations.

While media literacy is growing as a dynamic field with various philosophical strands and approaches (Hobbs, 1998a; Hobbs, 1998b; Hobbs & RobbGrieco, 2013), most media literacy programs do not take into account the media consumption habits of Latina/o audiences (Boske & McCormack, 2011; LeGrande & Vargas, 2001; Vargas, 2006, 2009). Most media literacy curricula focus on mainstream, English-language media. Latina/os are often bicultural and bilingual and regularly encounter mainstream,

Spanish-language, and ethnic (both Latina/o and African American) media. In addition, most media literacy programs target youth and it is difficult to find curricula designed for adults. Finally, except for the work of Bondy and Pennington (2016), LeGrande and Vargas (2001), Boske and McCormack (2011), and Vargas (2006, 2009), there are few studies that examine media literacy among Latina/os.[1]

In this chapter, I focus on media literacy about and for Latina/os within informal and formal educational contexts. First, I explore my experience designing and piloting a media literacy program for a community-based organization that serves Latina girls and women in Chicago. Then, I compare that experience with my experiences teaching undergraduate students in colleges and universities, largely in the Northeast. In doing so, I elucidate what is at stake for diverse Latina/o populations and the media. I discuss two cases of Latina/os learning about media literacy: working class and low-income girls in a pilot media literacy program and college-students in a course on Latina/os and the media. Then I offer some strategies to facilitate media literacy among Latina/o communities. In short, because Latina/o audiences are often denied access to media literacy education, they also face inequality with regards to producing and consuming media content. The lack of media literacy also limits the forms of civic engagement Latina/os can enact due to a lack of education about how media systems operate, function, are regulated and can be changed. In other words, media literacy is a form of social justice, which can enable civic engagement among Latina/o communities.

Media Literacy With Latina Girls in a Community-Based Organization

It was a hot, humid day in the predominately Mexican neighborhood of Pilsen in the Lower West Side of Chicago. Two staff members and I led (or perhaps more accurately dragged) fifteen pre-teen girls to the backside of the building to set up for our first media literacy workshop. We told the girls to sit in a circle while we set up the large Post-it easel board and the screen projector. While we prepared for the workshop, I overheard conversations about the latest telenovela while other girls looked at a teen celebrity magazine. A few of the girls struggled to poke their heads out of the small window at the end of the room and whispered that they saw some boys from school across the street. I also noticed two of the girls showing off their American Girl doll—Marisol, the latest addition to the line that happened to be Mexican American from Chicago—to their peers. One of the staff members signaled to the girls that it was time to get started. As we began, the girls seemed bored and listless. When I asked, what was going on, they in turn asked me if I was Puerto Rican. I responded yes and they asked if I was from the Northside of Chicago.[2] I told them that I do live on the Northside, but that I am originally from New York. This tidbit seemed to fascinate the girls. One girl touched my hair and said, "oooh, such curly hair! How do you get it like that?" Before I could respond another girl yelled, "because she's Puerto Rican, you dummy." One of the staff members then intervened telling the latter girl not to call anyone stupid. Now animated, the girls seemed focused and excited about starting the workshop. One of the quietest girls kicked off the session asking, "so, what is media again?"

This vignette illustrates some of the complicated racial and ethnic dynamics within media literacy. On the one hand, my presence as a Puerto Rican woman in a predominately Mexican setting disrupted the expectations and norms of the girls. The two staff members I worked with were of Mexican origin as were most of the staff and members of the organization. As such, the girls had rarely interacted with anyone non-Mexican at the organization. Coupled with their limited interaction with non-Mexican Latina/os at the organization, school and their neighborhood, the girls also drew on local perceptions of Puerto Ricans by Mexicans in Chicago. These perceptions included assumptions of Puerto Ricans as lighter-skinned with some markers of Afro-descent such as textured hair and wider noses. Mexicans, on the other hand, were viewed as generally having darker skin and more indigenous physical traits. In the particular case of women, Puerto Rican women were viewed as sassier, more assertive, and more cosmopolitan than Mexican women.[3]

Initially, drawing on these stereotypes the girls cast me as the Other, but as the media literacy workshops continued over the course of two months, the girls exoticized me less and found some commonalities with me. These similarities included my bilingual competency in English and Spanish (though I am certainly more of an English-dominant speaker) and my personal experiences navigating generational differences (i.e., my father migrated from Puerto Rico). Also, as we moved through the workshops and talked more about how Latinas are represented in mainstream media, the girls became more aware that non-Latina/os might not see the nuances and differences between Mexicans and Puerto Ricans. As such, I believe that my specific background as the facilitator shaped much of the dynamic of the workshop. Following the reflexive turn in anthropology that urged ethnographers to examine the role of their presence in the research process, some scholars have explored the role of the facilitator or teacher in media literacy programs.

For example, in her ethnography *Producing Dreams, Consuming Youth,* Vicki Mayer (2003b) reflexively discusses her presence as a white ethnographer and facilitator of a media production program for Mexican American youth at a community-based organization in San Antonio. In her study of a media literacy program for Latina teens in North Carolina, Lucila Vargas' (2009) has a different relationship with her participants given her history as a Mexican migrant working with many girls who also migrated from Latin America to the U.S. In both cases, the facilitators' insider and outsider statuses (based on race, gender, age, and class) enabled them to have different degrees of access to the communities they worked with. My experience also suggests that who the facilitator is, and all of the social and cultural baggage they bring with them into the classroom, matters greatly in terms of how audiences, particularly from historically marginalized groups, will engage in media literacy programs.

I volunteered to pilot a media literacy program for low-income and working class Latina girls after meeting a representative from a community-based organization in Chicago that serves Latinas. At a university panel the representative reported that women at their organization faced many challenging issues, the most important being: access to quality healthcare, adequate housing, domestic violence, and lack of media literacy. I was struck that amongst pressing day-to-day issues of health, housing and domestic violence, the representative also considered media literacy to be essential to the women's well-being. As a media scholar, I certainly see the value in media literacy, but sometimes media literacy education is viewed as an important, but nonessential skill, in community-based organizations with limited resources who are focused on helping members meet basic needs. I introduced myself to the representative after the panel discussion and she noted that there were little resources available at her organization to develop Latinas' media literacy skills. The representative added that there are virtually no curricula on Spanish-language media, which was heavily consumed by some of their older members of the organization. In particular, there was a need for an intergenerational media literacy program that would address the hybrid media consumption patterns of the girls and young women they served along with the largely Spanish-language media use of the mothers and grandmothers participating in the organization. Given my expertise a media scholar, particularly of Latina/o media and audiences, I volunteered to help the organization develop a media literacy program.[4]

After consulting with a few media literacy practitioners, including one who developed a program for Latina girls in another part of the country, I began developing a curriculum for the girls and women at the non-profit organization. I also consulted with several staff members at the organization as I designed the curriculum. Initially, I planned to hold separate workshops for the girls and the adult women because the staff indicated that their media consumption habits might differ. For example, the adult women—many of them immigrants—were more likely to consume Spanish-language media almost exclusively while the girls tended to consume a mix of English and Spanish-language media. However, because we were not working under a grant and had very limited resources, I was only able to create and facilitate a series of four media literacy workshops for girls between the ages of 12 and 14.

After consulting with staff members and some girls in their youth program, I designed and implemented a four-part workshop. The workshops were focused on the (a) language of media (i.e., visual and sonic aesthetics, types of narratives, etc.) (b) stereotypes of Latinas (c) body image and (d) political economy of the media. The first workshop on the language of media entailed teaching the girls various visual (i.e., color, setting, positioning, and framing), sonic (i.e., music and sound effects) and narrative (i.e., types of storytelling) techniques commonly deployed in media. The second workshop introduced the prevailing stereotypes of Latinas (i.e., female clown, spitfire, and the maid). The girls were asked to apply the skills they learned the prior week on the language of media to specific images of Latinas in film and television clips along with print advertisements and magazine covers. The third workshop explored how media might shape one's body image which included an exercise where the girls were paired up and traced each other's body shapes on large sheets of paper. They then talked about how they felt about their bodies and their ideal body image. The girls noted that their body image ideals came from family, friends, and both English-language and Spanish-language media. The last workshop entailed a discussion about media policy, particularly in regards to the FCC's governance of broadcast media and how one might actively participate in the process of regulation.

As in the tradition of most media literacy programs, we ended the series with a production unit where the girls brainstormed making a zine that reflected their interests. A zine is a self-published work that might include both original and appropriated text and images that are distributed on a small scale. I chose this type of project because we did not have access to camera equipment and the majority of the girls did not own smart phones. In addition, the girls had limited access to computers with a high-speed Internet connection outside of school and the organization. A zine would be easy to create by hand and on a computer and could easily be copied at the organization. In addition, zines have been productive in some feminist media literacy programs (Moscowitz & Carpenter, 2014). The girls did lose interest in this project after the brainstorming stage noting the laborious and tedious nature of the production process. I want to emphasize here although no final product was produced, this collaborative project did introduce the girls to the production process and made them more aware of the choices (i.e., editorial decisions, what artwork to include, etc.) involved in creating media.

The workshop series was conducted primarily in English because although most of the girls were bilingual, most of them preferred to speak in English. The first workshop began by asking the girls to define media and when I asked the girls to share their favorite media, I was surprised that few of the girls mentioned mainstream television and film. Only a handful of the girls were very familiar with Latinas visible in contemporary general market media (i.e., Jennifer Lopez, Salma Hayek, Eva Longoria, Eva Mendes, etc.). Instead, the girls were more familiar with teen magazines, pop and Latin music, toys (i.e., dolls), and *telenovelas*.[5] While the girls tended to consume magazines, music, and toys alone or with their peers, they watched *telenovelas* with their families. In consultation with the staff at the organization (whom I assumed would know the girls' media consumption habits better than me), I actually designed the workshops to be more focused on Latina representations within mainstream media, particularly film and television, assuming that as second and third generation Latinas the girls would consume more general market, English-language media. In doing so, I was following other standard media literacy models that were hinged on mainstream media. However, as Suzanne LeGrande and Jocelyn Vargas Geligas (2001) note, it is not always appropriate to start with mainstream media because marginalized communities may not have as much familiarity with general market media, especially in immigrant communities. Early on in this chapter I suggested that my background shaped my access to this community and the dynamic that was cultivated in the group—so did my assumptions as a media studies scholar trained to be most attuned to mainstream media. Hence, I reproduced the assumption that mainstream media mattered most in a community where in fact media consumption was much more complicated, and included both English-language teen media and Spanish-language family media.

Two full-time adult staff members at the organization attended all of the workshops and assisted me with managing the logistics. These two staff members seemed much more interested in the workshop content than the girls, particularly in the workshop focused on the political economy of media. The staff members were bilingual women, in their twenties, of Mexican origin. In particular, the staff members admitted to not knowing that broadcast media are regulated by the federal government. Furthermore, they were fascinated that ordinary citizens can make complaints to the FCC. They were especially surprised that the Spanish-language television stations, *Univisión* and *Telemundo*, were under the auspice of the FCC. The staff members assumed that Spanish-language media in the U.S. was out of purview of any supervision or regulation because Spanish-language media is viewed as foreign because it is not in English. This is an excellent example of how and why Latina/os historically have been uninvolved (or unrecognized) in media policy. Many Latina/os do not know that they have rights to broadcast media so they do not organize around media policy issues (Castañeda, 2008, 2014). Media policy is often eclipsed because our media system is private and part of the corporate sector. This is partly due to media industries' and regulators' construction of the televisual public sphere as English-speaking, white, and middle class (Perlman & Amaya, 2013). It is also historically tied to a lack of visibility of Latina/o leaders in U.S. media policy to Latina/o communities.

My experience working with girls at a community-based organization mirrors some of the issues I encounter teaching courses that emphasize media literacy at the college-level. In particular, I noticed a similar gap in media literacy curriculum and activities addressing ethnic or alternative media when teaching my Latina/os and the Media course. I have taught iterations of Latina/os and the Media at several types of institutions that include a research-intensive university, selective liberal arts college, and a comprehensive university. I have taught in predominately white classrooms as well as more racially and ethnically diverse classrooms. Most of the students I currently teach are working class or lower middle class, but when I taught at a selective liberal arts college I also worked with students from very wealthy, privileged backgrounds. Latina/os and the Media was a cross-listed course (i.e., between Communications and Sociology, Cinema Studies, and/or American Studies) at all of the institutions I taught it at, and students enrolled in my course tended to take it as an elective for their majors. Regardless of the type of institution and its student population, a third of all of the enrolled students were Latina/o.

Media Literacy Among Latina/o College Students

Similar to the girls in the community media literacy program, many Latina/o college students—many of whom were working class and second to third generation—were not that familiar with mainstream images of celebrity Latinas. However, upon viewing mainstream images of Latina/os, the students, especially Latina/o students, were often appalled or outraged at the stereotypes still prevalent in the news, television, and film. Some of these stereotypes included Latinos as criminals (i.e., as drug lords or gang bangers), Latinas as hypersexual spitfires, and as illegal immigrants draining U.S. economic resources. Although it was not the first time that students viewed images like these, their outrage seemed to stem from the repetition of these stereotypes over time and in various media outlets. In other words, students assumed that when they confronted those media stereotypes that they were random and isolated representations (e.g., as being in only one film or one news report) as opposed to what Patricia Hill Collins (2000) calls controlling images or depictions that circulate widely over space and time and legitimize the oppression of marginalized groups. Equipping students with required readings that provide historical overviews of Latina/o media representation in the U.S. (Ramirez Berg, 2002; Valdivia, 2010) enabled them to contextualize images we analyzed in class. This, along with a toolkit embedded in lectures, discussions, and activities to decode media images in terms of visual, sound, and narrative elements, facilitated students' ability to critically engage with Latina/o representations in media.

Most people do not know much about U.S. media policy, so it was unsurprising that like the staff members at the community-based organization, students also knew very little about media policy. However, Latina/os' limited knowledge of media policy might impact this community more than others in two ways. First, many Latina/os regularly consume Spanish-language television and radio which are deregulated in terms of ownership (Castañeda, 2008; Castañeda Paredes, 2003) and also in terms of content (i.e., decency, children's programming, etc.) despite being under the same regulation set by the FCC for English-language media. In particular, Latina/o and non-Latina/o students alike had no idea that Spanish-language television networks are under the purview of the FCC. In addition, although the Latina/o and the Media class is often a 200 or 300 level course, this is often the first-time students encounter Latina/o media content in the classroom.

Many of the students, particularly the Latina/o students, are familiar with some forms of Latina/o media outside the classroom, but these media texts have never been the object of study. Some of the media texts I include in the class range from mainstream media representations (i.e., the film *Selena* and the television series *Jane the Virgin)* to Spanish-language (i.e., *telenovelas* airing on *Univisión* and *Telemundo* and New York City's *El Diario* newspaper) and ethnic and alternative media (i.e., *Latina* magazine and independent films like Alex Rivera's *Sleep Dealer*, 2008). As mentioned earlier, I also require students to read historical overviews of Latina/o representation in media. To reinforce this overview in a more accessible way, I also screen the documentaries *Latinos Beyond Reel: Challenging a Media Stereotype* (2012) and *The Bronze Screen* (2002). *Latinos Beyond Reel* juxtaposes interviews media makers and scholars with various clips of Latina/o representations in media across time. *The Bronze Screen* is focused exclusively on cinema, but also provides both interviews with experts and key scenes from germinal films. Both films enable students to situate media representations of Latina/os historically.

During the first two-weeks I also review pertinent conceptual frameworks in media studies, including theories of representation (Hall, 1997), political economy (especially deregulation, conglomeration, and consolidation), race, gender, and transnational studies. Every class also includes case studies, media texts, organizations (i.e., *Univisión*, *Telemundo*, and the advertising firm LatinWorks), and media producers (i.e., film directors Gregory Nava and Alex Rivera) in order to apply the theories. Students are also required to apply theories learned in class to a text of their own choosing in a formal paper. In order to make connections between theory, praxis, and social justice, I also introduce students to media advocacy through organizations such as Free Press, the National Hispanic Coalition, and the National Association of Latino Independent Producers. After the course is done, some students do report reaching out to these organizations and volunteering in various capacities. Given that most of the students that enroll in this course aspire to be media makers, students also partake in activities that apply concepts to media projects.

For example, students have created advertising campaigns targeted to Latina/os that attempt to depart from commonly deployed stereotypes. Alternatively, students also worked collaboratively to pitch a magazine for Latina/os. For Latina/o college students preparing to be media professionals, media literacy should especially be focused on ethics since many of the participants will be creating media for a wider public. Following Roger Silverstone's (2004) call for the need to create a critical culture within media industries through media literacy, my experience teaching Latina/os and the Media suggests that media literacy can train students to not only critically reflect on media, but also begin to envision how to produce more transgressive media representations.

It takes students at least a few weeks to begin to engage with the media texts and apply theoretical concepts used within media studies not only the mainstream media students are analyzing in other courses, but also to Spanish-language and ethnic media. It should be noted that the media encountered in the course includes English and Spanish-language media. I found it especially challenging for students to seriously engage with Spanish-language media. For example, one Latina student majoring in Communications last semester reported, "I didn't know that I could see these media in a critical way." Many of these students, as second generation Latina/os, reported being very familiar with Spanish-language television, having viewed it in their home with family, but because this programming is not covered in their other media courses they did not consider them as a significant media form. Hector Amaya (2013) argues that Spanish-language media in the U.S., particularly television, is positioned as a marginal and separate public sphere when compared to English-language media. Latina/o students internalized this marginalization perceiving Spanish-language media as outside the field of proper analysis within Communications. Thus, even for students who are majoring in Communications and have taken other media studies courses, Latina/o media are initially viewed as outside the purview of the field.

Conclusion

Overall, my experiences with implementing media literacy pedagogies within a Latina/o context suggest that media literacy is an arena that needs to be considered as a space of inequality. Although Latina/os increasingly comprise a large segment of the media audience, there is a lack of media literacy curricula that takes into account Latina/os' hybrid media consumption patterns (Vargas, 2005). In both cases presented in this chapter, Latina/os consumed both English and Spanish-language media. For college students, it was difficult for them to view Spanish-language media as worthy of study. Spanish-language media was perceived as separate from and inferior to English-language media. As a result, students were initially less critical of Spanish-language media than English-language media. Media literacy educators should be mindful of this bias and attend to explaining the significance of Spanish-language media within the global media landscape. In addition, media literacy educators also should emphasize that Spanish-language media, like its English counterpart, reproduces and circulates ideologies about race, class, gender, and sexuality to large audiences across the hemisphere. In addition, media literacy programs implemented for Latina/o communities must hone in on issues of regulation since media policy is an arena that Latina/os historically have had uneven access (Castañeda, 2014).

The Latina/o gap in media literacy is a form of inequality because it disempowers Latina/o communities from substantively understanding, engaging with and challenging media. Based on my experiences facilitating media literacy education, I suggest that media literacy is a form of civic engagement because it can encourage Latina/o audiences to read media images critically and demand equality within the media. For the girls at the community-based organization, the workshops gave them a primer on the language of media through both critical analysis and the production process. The staff members at the organization gained awareness of broadcast regulation and now know where to find more information and how to organize their own community around media policy issues. College students gained these insights along with a deeper historical trajectory of Latina/o media representation.

Whereas media industries construct Latina/os largely as consumers (Báez, 2014), media literacy positions Latina/os as citizens. Ultimately, media literacy is about social justice and consciousness-raising encouraging audiences to think critically about the world around them and its stratification along lines of race, class, and gender—through a media lens. My hope is that by becoming more media literate, people will increase their participation in the public realm, understanding the root problems of media inequality as a reflection of inequalities in society.

Notes

1. Notable exceptions include the work of Boske and McCormack (2001), LeGrande and Vargas (2001), Mayer (2003a), Vargas (2006, 2009), and Yosso (2002).
2. Historically, most Puerto Ricans in Chicago have settled and resided on the Northside of Chicago.
3. There is quite a bit of ethnographic research that explores intra-Latina/o relations among Mexicans and Puerto Ricans in Chicago, including how both groups stereotype one another in terms of race, gender, class, and citizenship. See De Genova and Ramos-Zayas (2003) Garcia and Rúa (2007), Pérez (2003), and Rúa (2001, 2012).
4. I was not paid for any part of the process.
5. These media consumption patterns are consistent with Lucila Vargas' (2006, 2009) study of Latina teens in a media literacy program in North Carolina. The girls tended to consume music and toys. Studying Latina/o youth in Austin, Vicki Mayer (2003a, 2003b) finds that Latina teens consume *telenovelas* fairly regularly. Both Vargas and Mayer find that Latina/o youth interpret media through the lens of hybridity drawing on both U.S. and Latin American cultural standards to interpret content. Although Vargas also found that Latina teens were very familiar with black media, the girls in the media literacy workshops I facilitated did not indicate regular consumption of African American content.

References

Aspen Institute. (1993). *National leadership conference on media literacy: Conference report.* Washington, DC: Aufderheide, Patricia.

Amaya, Hector. (2013). *Citizenship Excess: Latino/as, Media, and the Nation.* New York: New York University Press.

Báez, J. (2014). Latina/o audiences as citizens: Bridging culture, media, and politics. In A. Dávila & Y. Rivero (Eds.), *Contemporary Latina/o media: Production, circulation, politics* (pp. 267–284). New York, NY: New York University Press.

Bobo, J. (1998). *Black women film & video artists.* New York, NY: Routledge.

Bondy, J. M., & Pennington, L. K. (2016). Illegal aliens, criminals, and hypersexual spitfires: Latin@ youth and pedagogies of citizenship in media texts. *The Social Studies, 107*(3), 102–114.

Boske, C., & McCormack, S. (2011). Building an understanding of the role of media literacy for Latina/o high school students. *High School, 94*(4), 167–186.

The Bronze Screen. (2002). Directed by N. De Los Santos & A. Domínguez. Distributed by Tela Latina.

Castañeda Paredes, M. (2003). The transformation of Spanish-language radio in the United States. *Journal of Radio Studies, 10*(1), 5–16.

Castañeda, M. (2008). The importance of Spanish-Language and Latino Media. In A. Valdivia (Ed.), *Latino/a communication studies today* (pp. 51–66). New York, NY: Peter Lang.

Castañeda, M. (2014). The role of media policy in shaping the U.S. Latino radio Industry. In A. Dávila & Y. Rivero (Eds.), *Contemporary Latina/o media: Production, circulation, politics* (pp. 267–284). New York, NY: New York University Press.

Collins, P. H. (2000). *Black feminist thought: Knowledge, consciousness, and the politics of empowerment* (2nd ed.). New York, NY: Routledge.

De Genova, N., & Ramos-Zayas, A. Y. (2003). *Latino crossings: Mexicans, Puerto Ricans, and the politics of race and citizenship.* New York, NY: Routledge.

Garcia, L., & Rúa, M. (2007). Processing Latinidad: Mapping Latino urban landscapes through Chicago ethnic festivals. *Latino Studies, 5*(3), 317–339.

Hall, S. (1997). *Representation: Cultural representations and signifying practices.* Thousand Oaks, CA: Sage.

Hobbs, R. (1998a). Building citizenship skills through media literacy education. In M. Salvador & P. Sias (Eds.), *The public voice in a democracy at risk* (pp. 57–76). Westport, CT: Praeger Press.

Hobbs, R. (1998b). The seven great debates in the media literacy movement. *Journal of Communication, 48*, 9–29.

Hobbs, R., & RobbGrieco, M. (2013). *A field guide to media literacy education in the United States.* Philadelphia, PA: Temple University. Retrieved from http://mediaeducationlab.com/sites/mediaeducationlab.com/files/Field%20Guide%20to%20Media%20Literacy%20.pdf

Kellner, D., & Share, J. (2005). Toward critical media literacy: Core concepts, debates, and organizations, and policies. *Discourse: Studies in the Cultural Politics of Education, 26*(3), 369–386.

Kellner, D., & Share, J. (2007). Critical media literacy is not an option. *Learning Inquiry, 1*(1), 59–69.

Latinos Beyond Reel: Challenging a Media Stereotype. (2012). Directed by M. Picker & C. Sun. Distributed by Media Education Foundation.

LeGrande, S., & Vargas, G. J. (2001). Working together: Multicultural media literacy and "the community." *Journal of Film and Video 53*(2/3), 77–92.

Mayer, V. (2003a, September). Living telenovelas/telenovelizing Life: Mexican American girls' identities and transnational novelas. *Journal of Communication, 53*(3), 479–495.

Mayer, V. (2003b). *Producing dreams, consuming youth: Mexican Americans and mass media*. New Brunswick, NJ: Rutgers University Press.

Moscowitz, L., & Carpenter, M. B. (2014). Girl zines at work: Feminist media literacy education with underserved girls. *Girlhood Studies, 7*(2), 25–43.

Negrón-Muntaner, F., Abbas, C., Figueroa, L., & Robson, S. (2014). *The Latino media gap: A Report on the state of Latinos in U.S. media*. Retrieved from http://www.columbia.edu/cu/cser

Pérez, G. (2003). "Puertorriquenas recorosas y Mejicanas sufridas": Gendered ethnic identity formation in Chicago's Latino communities. *Journal of Latin American Anthropology, 8*(2), 96–125.

Perlman, A., & Amaya, H. (2013). Owning a voice: Broadcasting policy, media ownership, and Latina/o speech rights. *Communication, Culture, & Critique, 6*(1), 142–160.

Ramirez Berg, C. (2002). *Latino images in film: Stereotypes, subversion, and resistance*. Austin, TX: University of Texas Press.

Rúa, M. M. (2001). *Colao* subjectivities: PortoMex and MexiRican perspectives on language and identity. *Centro, 13*(2), 116–132.

Rúa, M. M. (2012). *A grounded identidad: Making new lives in Chicago's Puerto Rican neighborhoods*. New York, NY: Oxford University Press.

Silverstone, R. (2004). Regulation, media literacy and media civics. *Media Culture Society, 26*(3), 440–449.

Sleep Dealer. (2008). Directed by A. Rivera. Distributed by Maya Entertainment.

Valdivia, A. N. (2010). *Latina/os and the media*. Malden, MA: Polity.

Vargas, L. (2009). *Latina teens, migration, and popular culture*. New York, NY: Peter Lang.

Vargas, L. (2006). Transnational media literacy: Analytic reflections on a program with Latina teens. *Hispanic Journal of Behavior Sciences, 28*(2), 267–285.

Vargas, L. (2009). *Latina teens, migration, and popular culture*. New York, NY: Peter Lang.

Yosso, T. J. (2002). Challenging deficit discourse about Chicana/os. *Journal of Popular Film and Television, 30*(1), 52–62.

12. "I Exist Because You Exist": Teaching History and Supporting Student Engagement via Bilingual Community Journalism

Katynka Z. Martínez

The first issue of the bilingual San Francisco newspaper, *El Tecolote*, was published on August 24, 1970 and includes a mission statement that highlights its commitment to advocacy journalism. The words *Canto de la Calle* (Song of the Street) and the drawing of an owl (*tecolote*), depicted in Mesoamerican tradition, are inscribed above the mission statement. The English and Spanish language mission statements begin by directly addressing the reader and speaking of a reciprocal relationship between *El Tecolote* and the person who holds the newspaper in their hands: "I exist because you exist and because others have forgotten us. My role is a simple one—to inform and to create for us an identity." The mission statement ends with the following promise: "together we will examine community problems and issues because a well-informed people are a progressive people" (*Canto de la Calle*, 1970, p. 1).

El Tecolote was created after the five-month San Francisco State College student-led strike (1968–1969) that led to the establishment of the College of Ethnic Studies. Two years after the end of the strike, Juan Gonzáles created and taught a Raza Journalism class in the newly formed Raza Studies department. The young Stockton, California native was fresh from graduating from San Francisco State University (SFSU) with a B.A. in Journalism when he and his students created *El Tecolote* in August of 1970. Nearly forty years later, I was hired to teach media classes in the department of Latina/Latino Studies at SFSU and have been teaching the course, Latina/Latino Journalism, since 2007. The partnership between my class and *El Tecolote* has been quite smooth. I met the newspaper editor prior to beginning my post at San Francisco State University, and in 2009 I was invited to join the board of Acción Latina, the non-profit organization that is the fiscal sponsor of the newspaper.

This chapter focuses on the ways in which I have drawn from *El Tecolote* to expand my civic engagement efforts within a class on Latinas/Latinos in California that I teach every spring semester. I begin the chapter by defining community journalism and describing the role that community service learning plays within *El Tecolote*, which is based out of San Francisco's Latino Mission District neighborhood. I then highlight course references to the history of the ethnic press, student contributions to *El Tecolote* and student projects that draw from the newspaper's archives. The chapter ends by returning to the original mission statement of *El Tecolote* and reflecting on current community building efforts in the neighborhood that serves as the newspaper's home.

Community Journalism and Community Service

Sociologist Morris Janowitz conducted one of the first studies of community journalism during the early 1950s. His book, *The Community Press in an Urban Setting*, is the result of systematic content analysis, survey research, and interviews with both readers and non-readers of Chicago community newspapers. Janowitz identifies the following as the main elements that comprised the way Chicago residents viewed the community press.

1. The community press is generally perceived as an auxiliary not as a competing news source with the daily press.
2. The community press is not generally perceived as a medium which is "commercialized."
3. The community press is not generally perceived as political or partisan but rather as an agent of community welfare and progress.
4. The community press is generally perceived as an extension of the reader's personal and social contacts because of its emphasis on news about voluntary associations and local social and personal news. (Janowitz, 1952, p. 154)

Published thirty years after Robert E. Park's, *The Immigrant Press and Its Control*, Janowitz's study includes surprisingly little about the immigrant press. He argues that a decline in the number of foreign-born residents in Chicago coupled with the relocation of immigrant residents outside of ethnic enclaves resulted in the immigrant press becoming a regional or national ethnic newspaper that no longer focused on local community news.

While not a history of the Chicago Mexican press, Gabriela Arredondo's *Mexican Chicago* fills a gap between the projects of Park and Janowitz. She notes that Spanish-language newspapers of the 1920s and 1930s provided local news, announced social gatherings, shared information regarding employment opportunities, and addressed community concerns. For example, Arredondo references a 1928 article in *México* that tells readers they can avoid anti-Mexican prejudice and abuse by not participating in local Fourth of July celebrations (Arredondo, 2008). The history of the Latino press, and the examples included in Arredondo's study indicate that being non-partisan or non-political is a luxury not afforded to Latino community newspapers. These newspapers were often created to monitor and challenge mainstream news media reports about Latinos. By doing this, the newspapers create a forum for Latinos to discuss everything from local racial violence to American expansionism (González & Torres, 2011; Gutierrez; 1977; Rodriguez, 1999; Subervi-Vélez, 2008).

Kevin Howley presents a definition of community media that is expansive enough to address the activist history and advocacy journalism orientation of the Latina/Latino press. He describes community journalism being composed of "locally oriented, participatory media organizations that are at once a *response* to the encroachment of the global upon the local as well as an assertion of local cultural industries and socio-political autonomy in the light of these global forces" (Howley, 2005, p. 40). While this definition brings us closer to accounting for the activism of the Latino press, the question now becomes whether all Latino community newspapers are by default radical newspapers. Christopher Anderson's study of the participatory journalistic field helps answer this question. Anderson analyzed the publications of diverse journalistic organizations to assess whether they qualify as radical community newspapers. He considered the level of participation, adherence to journalistic norms, and ties to radical social movements (Anderson, 2010). Applying this type of analysis to *El Tecolote* results in the newspaper being classified as community media but remaining outside of the radical newspaper category. The volunteer-run newspaper has high levels of community participation, engages in advocacy journalism, and does not adhere to journalistic norms such as the privileging of official sources or the principle of objectivity and impartiality. However, the newspaper is not directly tied to radical social movements.

El Tecolote was born out of San Francisco State College's five-month strike but it was not directly tied to the student movement. The founder of the newspaper, Juan Gonzáles, began teaching in the newly created department of Raza Studies in 1970 and was transformed by what he refers to as “the whole political sentiment that was on the campus—that the college needed to serve the community” (Gonzáles, 2014, n.p.). He agreed that departments in the College of Ethnic Studies “all had to have a component of service to the community. And then when it came down even further—what are you going to do for your community. That was all part of that whole social movement on the campus. It was hard to divorce yourself from that” (Gonzáles, 2014, n.p.).

The connection between San Francisco State and *El Tecolote* has continued since Gonzáles left the university in 1984. Students enrolled in a community service learning class intern at *El Tecolote* for a minimum of thirty hours per semester and write biweekly journal entries that make links between their work with the newspaper and the readings and discussion from another Latina/Latino Studies class. Students have contributed articles, photos, and artwork for the newspaper and many have continued working with the newspaper after completing their community service hours. Three of my former students have served as either photo editor or editor in chief of *El Tecolote* after graduating from SF State. In addition, one former student served as the Cultural Arts Manager of Acción Latina.

Newspapers and the History of Latinas/Latinos in California

Most *Tecolote* volunteers are students from my Latina/Latino Journalism class but more are coming from my Latinas/Latinos in California class due to my incorporation of the newspaper within this class' curriculum. On the first day of class I introduce myself and tell students that we will be drawing from newspapers and other forms of media and art throughout the semester. I continue with a discussion of the 1848 Treaty of Guadalupe Hidalgo, which ended the Mexican-American War, resulted in the annexation of formerly Mexican territories, and promised the “enjoyment of all the rights of citizens” to Mexicans who continued living in present day California, New Mexico, Texas, and parts of Utah, Nevada, and Colorado (Menchaca, 1995, p. 25). I link journalism and the Mexican-American War by informing students that the invasion of Mexico was the first armed conflict covered by the penny press. This is significant because it was the first American war fought on foreign soil and the first time that U.S. forces occupied a foreign capital. I present examples of articles that were filled with stereotypes of Mexicans that clearly demonstrate the ways in which the penny press promoted the project of manifest destiny which benefitted homesteaders (González & Torres, 2011). For example, the New York *Sun* called for the release of lands at the lowest possible prices for homesteaders and the Philadelphia *Public Ledger* declared that the “mission” of the United States was to extend "political Christianity" across the continent "under federal democracy" (Saxton, 1984, p. 230).

After reviewing the syllabus, I lead a class icebreaker through which students see images of birds and are asked to provide the names of these creatures. Most students can identify a humming bird, a woodpecker and an owl. I then ask if anyone can identify these birds using languages other than English. Students offer *chuparosa* for humming bird and *buho* or *lechuza* for owl. Rarely do students use the *Nahuatl* word, *tecolote*, to refer to the owl. I then show them the cover of a recent issue of *El Tecolote* that presents an image of an owl in its masthead. I ask students why a *Nahuatl* word might have been chosen as the name of a newspaper that is printed in Spanish and English. Students familiar with the editorial slant of the newspaper note that pride in their own indigenous heritage is central to the project of decolonization and often informs leftist Latina/Latino ideologies (Anaya, 1991; Mariscal, 2005). This is used as a starting point from which to discuss how the concept of whiteness operated during early California statehood.

The first course readings focus on the end of the Mexican-American War and the ambivalence that this generated among the new Anglo ruling class regarding how to categorize Mexicans in relation to African Americans, Chinese immigrants, and Native Americans that also lived in California (Almaguer, 1994; Pitt, 1970). For example, the Catholic religion was not deemed pagan as were the practices of Native Americans and Chinese Buddhists. Some Anglos converted to Catholicism and married fair-complexioned women of the Mexican elite without challenging anti-miscegenation statues. These economically advantageous unions illustrate that Anglos recognized class-based status differences among Mexicans. The mestizo working class was often categorized as Indian and this was used to deny rights that were supposed to be granted to Mexicans according to the Treaty of Guadalupe Hidalgo (Almaguer, 1994). I emphasize that governing forces like the Supreme Court of the state of California and the California Land Commission were not the only agents making these categorizations. Everyday people were contributing to the discussion of how Mexicans were to be categorized. This is evidenced by the publication of goldrushers' letters within the pages of east coast newspapers and in travelogues (Stillson, 2006).

Hubert Howe Bancroft, often recognized as the first California historian, drew from the work of popular historians, journalists, and journal writers to compile what is today presented as the history of mid to late 19th century California. Bancroft is cited in many of the readings that I assign for the Latinas/Latinos in California class (Almaguer, 1994; Castañeda, 1990; Kropp, 2006) and most Bay Area students are familiar with the historian's name since

Bancroft Avenue is a large thoroughfare that cuts through the cities of Oakland and San Leandro. The composition of my classes are mainly Latinas/Latinos and the students often become incensed when reading excerpts from Bancroft's 1888 tome *California Pastoral* that describes Mexicans as "droves of mongrels" deriving from a "turgid racial stream." Bancroft concludes that Mexicans were "not a strong community either physically, morally, or politically." Rather, he posits that Mexicans lived a life in California wherein "to eat, to drink, to make love, to smoke, to dance, to ride, to sleep seemed the whole duty of man" (Castañeda, 1990, p. 10). Such descriptions were attempts to support hierarchical relations of group inequality through which California land commissions and the courts invalidated Mexicans' property rights and local school boards provided Mexican children with segregated and substandard schools.

It is not uncommon for students to quickly make connections between these inequities, Bancroft's attitude, and xenophobic discourse and legislation that currently circulate at the national, state, local and interpersonal level. Upon learning that Bancroft was originally from Ohio and arrived in San Francisco when he was 19 years of age, many Bay Area students who have witnessed gentrification in their own neighborhoods respond by leveling their frustration at Bancroft the individual. When this happens, I try to direct the conversation back toward course readings and a discussion of the political and economic structures at play during the early to mid-1800s. We discuss the role newspapers played to fuel the anti-Indian policies of President Andrew Jackson's westward expansion and the endorsement that newspapers provided for American filibuster movements in Mexico and Central America (González & Torres, 2011).

While this history of the U.S. press is addressed in class, I make a conscious decision not to solely focus on the racist depictions of Mexicans that filled the pages of English-language Gold Rush California newspapers. Instead, I ask students to reflect on the ways in which Latinas and Latinos have been omitted from histories of early California and also consider the ways in which we have historically utilized the ethnic press as a way to create visibility and merge activism and community formation in the U.S. in the face of erasure. One of our early course readings is the article "A Gold Rush Salvadoran in California's Latino World" (2009) by David Hayes-Bautista, Cynthia Chamberlin, and Nancy Zuniga. This article focuses on a letter to the editor that was written by a Salvadoran man named Ángel Mora and published in 1857 in the Los Angeles-based Spanish-language newspaper *El Clamor Público*. The authors use this letter to draw attention to the personal, economic, and geopolitical reasons that Central Americans came to California during the

Gold Rush and why many of them, like Mora, ultimately chose to leave California and the United States. Mora's reasons for leaving California are vague but the authors surmise that he left the state defeated because he was unable to gain the riches necessary to marry a woman he loved.

I include this article in the course reader for a couple of reasons. First, I want to highlight the fact that a U.S. Latino literary heritage can be traced to the farewell letters that were published in California's gold rush-era Spanish-language newspapers as well as to the broadsheets, pamphlets and declarations that challenged the Spanish monarchy during the early 1800s (Coronado, 2013; Hayes-Bautista et al., 2009). Secondly, I assign this article to highlight the fact that Salvadorans did not first arrive in San Francisco during the 1980s as a consequence of El Salvador's Civil War. Rather, Salvadorans were among the gold rush migrants who came from places that include but are not limited to the East Coast of the United States, Mexico, Chile, and China (Pitt, 1970; Sisson, 2008).

Most students had never considered Salvadorans among the people who migrated to California during the gold rush, largely because normative historical records have consistently described gold rush migrants as people coming from the east coast of the United States. In fact, one of the exercises that my students do early in the semester calls for them to free associate words and phrases that come to mind when they hear the words gold rush. The word "Salvadoran" has never emerged. Common terms that have been proposed include: mining, traveling, wealth, forty-niners, displacement, economic boom, manifest destiny, environmental disasters, sprawl, opportunity, unjust, false advertisement, new people.

Student Voices Amid a Digital Gold Rush

As part of my ongoing introduction of *El Tecolote* to the class I show the students the 2014 issue of the *SF Weekly* newspaper that awarded *El Tecolote* the title of "Best Community Newspaper in the City." I do this to generate excitement for student engagement in the newspaper and also to highlight that this particular issue of the *SF Weekly* links San Francisco's gold rush era to the city's current boom generated through the location of companies such as Facebook, Apple and Google in Silicon Valley and their workforce in San Francisco. I then ask students to read the *Los Angeles Times* article "San Francisco Split by Silicon Valley's Wealth" and the *Tecolote* article "Locals Protest Tech Bus Invasion of Public Bus Stops" (Christopher, 2014; Guynn, 2013). The *Los Angeles Times* article references a "digital gold rush" that is sweeping through San Francisco. The *Tecolote* article focuses on the direct actions that

Bay Area residents have taken to protest the fact that the mayor of San Francisco has permitted private buses to utilize public bus stops without paying fees to the city. I ask the students to complete a reflection paper in which they answer the following sets of questions related to the articles that describe shuttle buses offered by Apple, Facebook, Google and other major Silicon Valley companies.

1. In your opinion, how might these shuttles impact the relationship riders have to San Francisco residents? How might these shuttles impact the relationship riders have to the city of San Francisco?
2. Describe your commute to San Francisco State University. How does this commute impact the relationship you have to San Francisco residents? How does this commute impact the relationship you have to the city of San Francisco?

This reflection is important because it aims to direct the conversation around transportation toward a discussion of the encroachment of private interests on public spaces and how this may impact the development of community. San Francisco State University is a commuter school. Most students use public transportation and many of those who drive are experts in navigating parking options in the residential neighborhoods that surround campus. The students are familiar with parking restrictions, rising bus and subway fees, and the high cost of on-campus parking permits.

I ask the class if they feel their plight as students has been adequately chronicled in the local press. One activity we engage in is to try to imagine what a future historian may understand about San Francisco if they pick up *El Tecolote* 150 years from now. Would the students feel like their experiences and observations are adequately represented? If not, how can we address that during the semester? I ask students these questions because our earlier discussion of late 1800s newspapers and travelogues illustrate the agenda setting power of newspapers. I want everyone in the class to recognize how they can impact the narratives presented in their local newspaper.

Students receive copies of *El Tecolote* on a bi-weekly basis and are encouraged to attend editorial meetings, which are open to the public. I share with them previous students' articles on topics that range from the impact that high asthma rates have on the education of youth of color, to a story on the extended family created through an Aztec dance troupe, to a profile of a Latino immigrant who owns and operates a bike shop. Students are also presented with the option of assisting Acción Latina on projects not directly related to the newspaper. For example, one student organized the Acción Latina photo archives during the semester that she was enrolled in my Latinas/Latinos in

California class. Under the guidance of the executive director, she reviewed *Tecolote* news stories and identified articles on Latina/Latino youth. She then compiled photos of Latina/Latino youth of the 1980s and constructed a photo display for the San Francisco History Expo. She told me she was honored to contribute to the exhibit and attend the event especially since Acción Latina was one of only a handful of organizations dedicated to preserving and presenting the history of San Francisco's communities of color.

After completing this project, the student began assisting Acción Latina on another archiving project. This project shared photos via the online platform of Historypin, a website that provides a user-generated archive of historical photos, videos and documents that are overlaid on interactive maps. The student posted photos from the Acción Latina archive to a map of San Francisco and I often refer to these interactive maps within my class lectures. I also regularly draw from the Acción Latina archive to share photos of Bay Area locations that the students are familiar with. For example, when we discuss the 1970 Los Angeles Chicano Moratorium, I explain that this was just one of many protests against the war in Vietnam. I then share a 1984 photo from Acción Latina's archive and emphasize that the banner with the words "No Viet Nam War in El Salvador" visually demonstrates that the organizing and themes of Chicano Moratoriums has extended to address issues like U.S. military aid during El Salvador's Civil War. This photo was taken in San Francisco's Dolores Park, which has recently been referred to as a "landfill for the privileged" with empty bottles of high-end alcohol and remnants of designer pastries found throughout the park after a sunny weekend (Blei, 2015, n.p.). Most students are unaware that this park was once a place where Latino families gathered and musicians came together for conga jam sessions.

I Exist Because You Exist: Continuing the Dialogue Through El Tecolote

Just as most students did not know that political demonstrations and Latino music once filled the space of Dolores Park, they can also not imagine a time when San Francisco did not serve as a refuge for queer individuals attempting to escape persecution in their hometowns and/or within their families. To contextualize this historical geography, I assign the work of Horacio Roque Ramirez on the migration of queer Latinas/Latinos to the Bay Area. I also provide students with copies of two articles that were written by members of the Gay Latino Alliance (GALA) and published in *El Tecolote* in 1976 and 1977. I ask the students to answer the following questions after reading the *Tecolote* articles: (a) how do the authors emphasize that they are committed to the struggle of all exploited people? (b) who do you think is the intended audience(s) of this article? What is your assessment based on? (c) could you imagine this article being published in a Latina/Latino newspaper today. Why or why not? and (d) how would this article need to be updated to be relevant today? Through answering these questions, I want students to recognize that intersectionality led GALA members to engage in both the struggle for the rights of lesbian and gay San Francisco Latinas/Latinos and also organize against U.S. military intervention abroad. The GALA articles reference the War in Vietnam, racism in the U.S., and the reproduction of violence and discrimination within communities of color. The authors seamlessly draw from the language, ideologies and allegiances that were prevalent in the liberation movements that were occurring within Latin America, Africa, and Asia during the 1970s.

While we review the GALA 1976 and 1977 articles as historical documents within my class, the articles were recently invoked in *Tecolote* articles on hate crimes that were leveled against the Mission District gallery, Galeria de la Raza. This Latina/Latino art space was founded in 1970 and in 1974 the gallery inherited the billboard space that is located on the northern facing wall of their building. Since then they have used the billboard to post murals related to the artwork on display within the gallery. In the past, the gallery has utilized the billboard to address topics such as gentrification and displacement, police shootings, and violence against women. On June 13, 2015 Galeria de la Raza's billboard showcased the mural "Por Vida," which depicts two men embracing, one woman caressing another woman's face, and a trans man with visible post-surgery scars along his chest. The mural, by Manuel Paul of the Maricón Collective, was defaced with black spray paint within a week of being installed. Galeria de la Raza volunteers took down the defaced mural twice and reinstalled it twice. On June 29, 2015, the mural was set on fire, and on July first hundreds of community members rallied in front of the mural to support the Maricón Collective and Galeria de la Raza.

The cover story of the July 2 issue of *El Tecolote* quoted Viviana Paredes who has lived in the Mission District for the past forty years and was one of the founding members of the Gay Latino Alliance. The issue of the newspaper also included a staff editorial that referenced the 1976 and 1977 GALA authored articles that were printed in *El Tecolote*. The staff editorial referenced homophobic threats against the mural that circulated online prior to the arson attacks. The staff reiterated their support for Galeria de la Raza, which "has always been at the vanguard, be it in Chicano/Latino art or in the fight for social justice. Like Galeria, El Tecolote has for 45 years stood for what it believes is right, providing a voice for the voiceless and promoting equality and freedom of expression through art" (El Tecolote Stands, 2015, p. 4).

The staff editorial shared the page with a letter to the editor that came from the Calle 24 Council, a consortium of Mission District residents, merchants, service providers, and arts organizations that are located along the 24th Street corridor between Mission Street and Potrero Avenue. The letter is titled "Stand for Unity" and reads,

> together we fought and marched for Alex Nieto, against police brutality, against the displacement of residents and business and the destruction of our arts and culture. We stand by our youth and our seniors. We stand not for violence or division, but for dialogue so that we can move forward together as a community, at a time when we see injustice everywhere in the Mission. Straight or gay we are your brothers and sisters, your aunts and uncles, your mothers and fathers. Only as a true family can we move forward. Let's create that dialogue. (Letter to the Editor, 2015, p. 4)

The letter references the work that the Calle 24 Council has been involved in since it was originally created as the Lower 24th Street Merchants and Neighbors Association during the tech boom of 1999. Over the years, the volunteer group has organized to halt construction of market rate housing along 24th Street and to fast-track affordable housing projects planned for the Mission District. The group was also among the community groups that participated in marches and demanded investigations immediately following the 2014 police shooting of Alex Nieto. The 28-year-old Mission District resident and security guard died after four San Francisco police officers fired fifty-nine shots at him. The police officers claim they mistook his taser gun for a pistol and were found not guilty of using excessive force. This police shooting is especially poignant for long-time Mission District residents who have identified the key role that police violence and aggressive gang injunctions play within the displacement of communities of color from gentrifying neighborhoods.

The letter from the Calle 24 Council is in many ways similar to the mission statement that was published in the first issue of *El Tecolote.* Like the letter to the editor, *El Tecolote's* 1970 mission statement spoke directly to the reader and asserted:

> I exist because you exist and because others have forgotten us.
>
> My role is a simple one—to inform and to create for us an identity.
>
> Who are the people of the Mission District? What are we? Where are we going? With your help, I shall make the worth of our community known.

> With your help, my own worth will be to keep you informed about community services, social events, club meetings, political functions, and other community activities, large or small.
>
> But more importantly, together we will examine community problems and issues because a well-informed people are a progressive people.
>
> Finally, I exist to create a better understanding of one another and to bring us closer together.
>
> I am El Tecolote. I am the people. I am yours. (Canto de la Calle, 1970, p. 1)

This mission statement and the letter from the Calle 24 Council are recognizing bonds that are rooted in a commitment to social justice and the well-being of a community. Both statements recognize that dialogue is essential to establish trust and unity. As a professor, I have found that the dialogue among students is often so much richer than any PowerPoint or prepared notes that I can bring to the class. However, the students must first feel that their contributions are welcome. They must first see themselves in the histories of California.

By interrogating California newspaper coverage of Latinas/Latinos and reading counter-narratives in the ethnic press students can link their own acts of resilience and organizing to a legacy of self-determination. However, to do so it is not enough for students to simply read a book written by an historian. They must also be able to see how that book drew from texts and discourses that circulated among everyday people. We begin this discussion by considering the sources that Hubert Howe Bancroft drew from. Later in the semester I identify the course readings written by scholars that have turned to *El Tecolote* to gain insight into Latina/Latino experiences in San Francisco. I highlight the works of Cary Cordova (2006), Jason Ferreira (2011), Nancy Mirabal (2009), Horacio Roque Ramírez (2003), and Tomás Summers Sandoval (2003), and I tell students that this research exists because they, students who choose to enroll in a Latinas/Latinos in California class, exist. The students are implicated in the histories presented by these scholars and by the civic engagement work they do in my class—work such as writing articles for *El Tecolote*, organizing the Acción Latina photo archive, and preparing a photo display for the San Francisco History Expo. The students are now part of a dialogue that exists between scholars, within the pages of newspapers, and among community historians, archivists and researchers. The original mission statement of *El Tecolote* asked: "What are we? Where are we going?" These are questions that the students are answering and will continue to engage with well after my course.

References

Almaguer, T. (1994). *Racial fault lines: The historical origins of white supremacy in California*. Berkeley, CA: University of California Press.

Anaya, R. A. (1991). Aztlan: A home without boundaries. In R. A. Anaya & F. Lomeli (Eds.), *Aztlan: Essays on Chicano homeland* (pp. 230–241). Albuquerque, NM: University of New Mexico Press.

Anderson, C. (2010). Analyzing grassroots journalism on the web. In C. Rodriguez, D. Kidd, & L. Stein (Eds.), *Making our media: Mapping global initiatives toward a democratic public sphere* (pp. 47–69). Cresskill, NJ: Hampton Press.

Arredondo, G. (2008). *Mexican Chicago: Race, identity and nation*. Chicago, IL: University of Illinois Press.

Blei, D. (2015, March 24). Dolores Park is becoming a landfill for the privileged. *The Bold Italic*. Retrieved from https://thebolditalic.com/dolores-park-is-becoming-a-landfill-for-the-privileged-the-bold-italic-san-francisco-d80ba3a317de#.stiiczmd3

Canto de la Calle. (1970, August 24). *El Tecolote*. San Francisco, CA.

Castañeda, A. I. (1990). Gender, race, and culture: Spanish-Mexican women in the historiography of frontier California. *Frontiers: A Journal of Women Studies, 11*(1), 8–20.

Christopher, J. (2014, January 16–29). Locals protest tech bus invasion of public bus stops. *El Tecolote*. San Francisco, CA.

Cordova, C. (2006). Hombres y mujeres muralistas on a mission: Painting Latino identities in 1970s San Francisco. *Latino Studies, 4*(4), 356–380.

Coronado, R. (2013). *A world not to come*. Cambridge, MA: Harvard University Press.

El Tecolote stands with Galería de la Raza. (2015, July 2–15). *El Tecolote*. San Francisco, CA.

Ferreira, J. (2011). "With the soul of a human rainbow": Los Siete, Black Panthers and third worldism in San Francisco. In C. Carlsson (Ed.), *Ten years that shook the city: San Francisco 1968–1978* (pp. 30–47). San Francisco, CA: City Lights Books.

Gonzáles, J. (2014, August 4). Personal Interview.

González, J., & Torres, J. (2011). *News for all the people: The epic story of race and the American media*. New York, NY: Verso.

Gutierrez, F. (1977). Spanish-language media in America: Background, resources, history. *Journalism History, 4*(2), 34–68.

Guynn, J. (2013, August 22). San Francisco split by Silicon Valley's wealth. *Los Angeles Times*. Los Angeles, CA.

Hayes-Bautista, D. E., Chamberlin, C. L., & Zuniga, N. (2009). A gold rush Salvadoran in California's Latino world, 1857. *Southern California Quarterly, 91*(3), 257–294.

Howley, K. (2005). *Community media: People, places, and communication technologies*. Cambridge, UK: Cambridge University Press.

Janowitz, M. (1952). *The community press in an urban setting*. Glencoe, IL: The Free Press.

Kropp, P. (2006). *California vieja: Culture and memory in a modern American place.* Berkeley, CA: University of California Press.

Letter to the Editor: Stand for unity. (2015, July 2–15). *El Tecolote.* San Francisco, CA.

Mariscal, G. (2005). *Brown-eyed children of the sun: Lessons from the Chicano movement, 1965–1975.* Albuquerque, NM: University of New Mexico Press.

Menchaca, M. (1995). *The Mexican outsiders: A community history of marginalization and discrimination in California.* Austin, TX: University of Texas Press.

Mirabal, N. R. (2009). Geographies of displacement: Latina/os, oral history, and the politics of gentrification in San Francisco's Mission District. *The Public Historian, 31*(2), 7–31.

Pitt, L. (1970). *The decline of the Californios: A social history of the Spanish-speaking Californians, 1846–1890.* Berkeley, CA: University of California Press.

Rodriguez, A. (1999). *Making Latino news: Race, language, class.* Thousand Oaks, CA: Sage.

Roque Ramírez, H. N. (2003). "That's my place!": Negotiating racial, sexual, and gender politics in San Francisco's Gay Latino Alliance, 1975–1983. *Journal of the History of Sexuality, 12*(2), 224–258.

Saxton, A. (1984). Problems of class and race in the origins of the mass circulation press. *American Quarterly, 36*(2), 211–234.

Sisson, K. J. (2008). Bound for California: Chilean contract laborers and "patrones" in the California gold rush, 1848–1852. *Southern California Quarterly, 90*(3), 259–305.

Stillson, R. T. (2006). *Spreading the word: A history of information in the California gold rush.* Lincoln, NE: University of Nebraska Press.

Subervi-Vélez, F. A. (2008). *The mass media and Latino politics: Studies of U.S. media content, campaign strategies and survey research 1984–2004.* New York, NY: Routledge.

Summers Sandoval, T. F. (2013). *Latinos at the golden gate: Creating community and identity in San Francisco.* Chapel Hill, NC: University of North Carolina.

13. *Hashtag Jóvenes Latinos: Teaching Civic Advocacy Journalism in Glocal Contexts*

Jessica Retis

This chapter examines the process of implementing critical pedagogy in teaching journalism to bilingual and bicultural college students in California. Based on the principles of civic advocacy journalism and communication for social change, this approach utilizes liberatory pedagogies, community engagement, and service learning approaches to (a) prepare journalism students to become engaged citizens (b) train students in critical analysis of the news media practices and (c) incorporate the consciousness of social injustices when covering diversity and minorities (Boyer, 1990; Butin, 2007; Freire, 1973, 1994; Giroux, 1992,1997, 2010; Gumucio & Tufte, 2006; Massey, 1998; Schaffer, 1996; Tufte & Mefalopulos, 2009; Waisbord, 2008, 2009; Wilkins, Tufte, & Obregón, 2014). This essay reviews a two-semester project that prepares students to analyze contemporary history of underserved minorities and the role of mainstream and ethnic media in portraying them and/or serving these groups. Students start in Fall semester with a lecture course. Part of them continues during Spring semester in a laboratory/production class.

This chapter reflects on three main questions. How can journalism courses incorporate elements of civic advocacy journalism and communication for social change in the work of undergraduate students? How can students connect with community organizations as main rather than alternative sources of news stories? How can community-oriented journalism courses facilitate stories to be told by, for and with young Latinos in the U.S.? The first part of this chapter surveys journalism practices moving beyond traditional journalism to incorporate social consciousness in news coverage practices. The second part examines the implementation of liberatory pedagogies in teaching journalism. The third part presents a lecture course where students are exposed to critical analysis of Latinos and the media. Fourth section describes a TV production/lab class where students work with community organizations and community members as main sources of their video reporting. Assessment of these practices is discussed in the last part of this chapter.

Civic Advocacy Journalism: Why Labels?

In recent decades, journalism practitioners and educators have been developing new labeled journalism practices. The main idea behind these approaches is, paradoxically, to return to the origins of what journalism was about: serving their communities. There have been back and forth movements from citizens and community organizers to journalists to producing and publishing stories on social inequities (Castells, 2009; Downing, Ford, Gil, & Stein, 2001; Ostertag, 2006; Rodriguez, Kidd, & Stein, 2010). Part of these experiences has been echoed in college classrooms.

As John Hochheimer (1992) noted in the early nineties, teaching is not value-neutral but a dynamic course of action that interacts with the forces of the times. In this context, education can facilitate a process of liberation where the role of the educator is to enter into a dialogue with the students in order to provide them with the instruments to teach themselves. Freire's liberatory educational practice implies the transition from a hierarchical method to a more dialogic approach, demonstrating ways in which students can become active participants in their own education. How can we implement this dialogic approach when instructing journalism students? Durham (1998) emphasizes that the foundation of Freire's philosophy is the notion of *conscientização*, which refers to the development of a consciousness of social, political and economic contradictions in order to take action against injustices (Freire, 1994). In this pedagogical model, the awareness of inequity is the first step (Durham, 1998). According to Hochheimer (1992),

> the difference between "reporting about" and "understanding with," and the personal transformation of the student, are similar to what Martin Buber sees as the difference between an "I-It" and an "I-Thou" relationship: in the first students see themselves apart from the world they describe; in the second they engage it actively, critically, as parts of what they seek to comprehend. Thus, this method of journalism education is a practical attempt to merge Buber's philosophy with Freire's liberating pedagogy: it is dialogic journalism with a social conscience. (p. 6)

This dialogic approach demands to move beyond traditional journalism practices and look for different ones. Since the nineties numerous scholars have analyzed a wide range of movements, naming them as civic journalism, advocacy journalism, participatory journalism, community journalism, alternative journalism, or citizen journalism, among others. Some of these have been implemented in the classrooms by college professors. The study and exercise of these types of labeled journalism promoted the formation of groups-of-interest in academic and professional organizations.[1]

There have been numerous efforts to incorporate social consciousness in journalism practices and instruction. Some authors argue that civic journalism finds it roots in investigative journalism, an approach that emphasizes exposure of corporate and governmental fraud that would not abandon either investigative reporting or compelling news narrative but supplement them with a news report framed to stimulate public deliberation on pressing community issues (Lambeth, 1996; McDevitt, 2000; Simon & Sapp, 2006). Others remind the old discussion back in the 1920s between Walter Lipmann and John Dewey. It was Lipmann's not Dewey's view that became part of the underlying philosophy of journalism education for most of the twentieth century. According to Voakes (2004),

> the emergence of the Lipmann-endorsed trustee model brought about not only investigative reporting but, with its admiration of professional expertise, the "beat" reporting system. This in turn enhanced the journalist's First Amendment role as watchdog on government officials. But the negative impact of the ascendance of the trustee model, according to Carey, is that the public became a passive observer of the public life. (p. 26)

In their efforts for turning the public into active participant of the public life, journalists, civil society members and community organizers have promoted the inclusion of alternative voices. As Morris Janowitz (1975) notes, advocacy journalism assigns journalists the role of active interpreters who speak on behalf of certain groups. Silvio Waisbord (2008) proposes to go beyond this advocate-journalist concept to the civic model of advocacy journalism: "it refers to organized groups that use the news media to influence reporting, and ultimately, affect public policies" (p. 371). It belongs to forms of civic mobilization that seek to increase the visibility of political and social issues (Waisbord, 2009).

Since the emergence of the civic journalism movement in the 1980s, critics and advocates centered the debate on maintaining the principles and practices of traditional journalism. Additionally, a half-step approach has emerged as a third perspective in which elements of traditional and new journalism co-exist within many newsroom and individual journalists (Anyaegbunam &

Leland, 2003). Harcup (2011) discusses the relationship between forms of journalistic activity that might be labeled alternative while expressions of citizenship might be labeled active, and thus proposes to understand alternative journalism as active citizenship (p. 16). Yet this relationship may be regarded of marginal interest in academia given the powerful structure of mainstream media, although it is one of the various alternative ways of producing journalism that has survived over the years (Harcup, 2011; Keeble, 2009).

As Waisbord (2008) explains, while advocacy journalism has found supporters among European publishers and journalists, mainstream US press has vigorously criticized it. Europeans approached news reporting as a way to get politically involved and to promote viewpoints generally associated with political parties. In the United States the adoption of objectivity as the normative ideal of professional reporting displaced advocacy journalism to the margins of the press system. He further argues that neither in the North nor in the global South is contemporary journalism limited to the journalist model. The recent growth of the civic model of advocacy has been significant and unlike the journalist model, which expresses the political interests of journalists, the civic model represents advocacy efforts by civic groups that promote social change.

> Civic advocacy journalism is driven by the notion that the news media should be a tool of social change. Because the press contributes to both raising awareness among the public and setting policy priorities and agendas, civic actors aim to shape news coverage. (Waisbord, 2008, p. 375)

How can we teach civic advocacy journalism? One first step is the introduction of the principles of communication for social change. Tufte and Mefalopulos (2009) remind us how this approach pursues a more dialogical communication rather than linear communication. Since the 1990s, it has focused on structural inequality and social transformation. As the Communication for Social Change Consortium explains:

> [communication for social change] is a process of public and private dialogue through which people themselves define who they are, what they need and how to get what they need in order to improve their lives. It utilizes dialogue that leads to collective problem identification, decision making, and community-based implementation of solutions to development issues. (Tufte and Mefalopulos, 2009, p. 2)

Thus, civic advocacy journalism and communication for social change become pillars when preparing journalism students to become engaged citizens, and training them in critical analysis of the news media practices, and to incorporating consciousness of social injustices when covering diversity and minorities.

There is a sort of consensus in the scholarship (and in the industry) that contemporary journalism is experiencing new challenges when reporting and producing stories since the beginning of the digital revolution. It is crucial then to examine how to implement these new approaches to training journalists envisioning a comprehensive understanding of social injustices in the digital age. On the one hand, we can find ways to implement critical pedagogies and experimental learning theories that foresee pedagogical spaces challenging traditional Euro-centric models of education. We can advocate for creating learning opportunities that incorporate students' cultural knowledge and expertise and link to relevant community action and reflection experiences (Shadduck-Hernández, 2006). On the other hand, we can implement social justice approaches and community engagement or service learning approaches aiming to awaken students to injustice and catalyze action (Boyer, 1990; Butin, 2007; Mather & Konkle, 2013).

In my courses, my students and I examine and develop a deeper knowledge of the contemporary history of Latinos and Latino media in the U.S. in order to address the following questions: How and why Latinos became a vital part of the U.S.? Why is it important to explore the past, understand the present, and examine the future of demographics with political, economic and cultural perspectives? Why is it important to understand structural inequities from hyperlocal and transnational perspectives? What role does mainstream media plays in the public understanding of diversity and ethnic minorities? What role has Spanish-language and Latino-oriented media played in conforming a counter flow of information and communication? How do new technologies and convergence as well as media industries new formations are affecting journalism in the digital age? How and why do Latino journalists need to incorporate elements of civic advocacy journalism when entering as practitioners in different news media outlets in English or Spanish?

Teaching Journalism From an Inclusive Perspective

There have been several studies on the issue of social inclusion in news reporting and the ways in which diversity is taught in Journalism and Mass Communications programs in the United States. Most of these studies demonstrated the lack of coverage of Latinos and their stereotypical representation in mainstream media (Dávila, 2001). They also claim the need of hire and promote more diversity in newsrooms. Some studies found that the examination of race, gender, and social justices became less important in the ethics curriculum (Lambeth, Christians, Fleming, & Lee, 2004; Smith, 2008). Other studies have demonstrated that Latinos are made invisible in the mainstream media or they are represented in a misinformed way and with a greater negative connotation than other ethnic minorities (National Council of La Raza, 1997; Santa Ana, 2013). In the 1990s, the amount of national news concerning Hispanics represented only 1% of all news produced (National Council of La Raza, 1997), which was even less than the amount of news covering African-Americans or Asians/Asian-Americans (Entman & Rojecki, 2000).

The Network Brownout Report showed that in the case of TV news, the representation margin was less than in the printed news media outlets (National Association of Hispanic Journalists [NAHJ], 2006). Only 0.83% of broadcast stories by ABC, CBS, and NBC in 2005 covered Hispanics. This low percentage was, paradoxically, an increase from previous year, when the average was 0.72%. Santa Ana (2013) analyzed over 12,000 stories broadcast in 2004 by the four top American networks (ABC, CBS, NBC and CNN) and found that less than 1% of these stories addressed Latino issues, and that "given that Latinos comprised 14% of the United States population at the time, the nation's understanding of Latinos from network news programs was and remains wholly inadequate" (Santa Ana, 2013, p. xvii). Even though diversity has increased in newsrooms over the past decades (from 3.95% in 1978 to 12.76% in 2015), one can find only 4% of Hispanics in American newspaper newsrooms (ASNE, 2015). In this context, how can we instruct bilingual and bicultural Latino students willing to enter into the news industry? Over the years, I have engaged with liberatory pedagogies in order to most effectively teach civic advocacy journalism and communication for social change. When I started instructing bilingual and bicultural students in California I encountered new challenges and opportunities in doing so.

Some journalism educators found that while students in the early stages of their professional preparation might support the goals of public or civic journalism, connections to such goals tend to erode by the increasing importance of autonomy that comes with professional identification (McDevitt, 2002). Others found that a combination of traditional journalism instruction and civic education appeared to produce favorable learning outcomes (Simon & Sapp, 2006). Scholars such as Chaffee and McDevitt (1999) have experimented with innovative instructional models to make students experience and critically reflect on the principles and practices of traditional and civic journalism as ordinary citizens of a community and as journalists operating in that community. For instance, Anyaegbunam and Leland (2003) implemented John Dewey's concept of reflective thought to encourage "reflective thinking as part of the critical thinking process, help learners analyze and make judgments about what has happened, and support them in the transition from being learners to becoming practitioners in a dynamic environment that demands autonomy and innovativeness" (p. 66).

Other instructors such as Smith (2008) propose to step away from the presumption that diverse workforce is the only key to the solve media's diversity problem. Rather, a professional's cultural environment also plays a critical role in developing diverse news content. She examines how determining whether "featuring diversity as critical journalistic responsibility (alongside basic broadcast news 'skills' such as photography, editing, story organization, and interviewing techniques) translates into inclusive stories among collegiate broadcast journalism students" (Smith, 2008, p. 185). Smith argues that by infusing the curriculum with discussions about race and social responsibility, professors can create a climate of inclusion that leads to greater sources of diversity. Moreover, scholars such as Shadduck-Hernández (2006) argues that universities can only become democratic center when the exclusion of diverse communities ends: "such positions beckon educators to go against the grain of traditional education and experiment with alternative models that support action, experience, reflection, and multiple forms of knowing" (p. 73).

Since 2008 I have been trying to implement the pillars of communication for social change, civic advocacy journalism and liberatory pedagogies into teaching/learning environments in California. This chapter examines the experience of a two-semester academic year (2013–2014) that prepares students to analyze contemporary history of underserved minorities and the role of mainstream and ethnic media in portraying them and/or serving these groups. Students started in Fall semester with a course titled Spanish-language News Environment (SLNE). Part of them continue in the Spring semester lab/production course, Spanish-language TV (SLTV). Student reflective essays and video stories were produced in these lecture and skills sequence courses in the Spanish-language Minor in Journalism at California State University Northridge.

These classes aim to advance learning and community development and promote multiple forms of students' written, visual, and performative narrative by implementing strategic and cultural resources that every individual possesses (Giroux, 1997; Shadduck-Hernández, 2006; Velez-Ibañez & Greenberg, 1992). For instance, some students have a deeper knowledge of the Spanish-language while others are very adept at using media technologies. As a consequence, I team-up students in order to promote peer-to-peer learning activities. In this context, my role is less of an instructor and more of a facilitator: students learn from the instructor, instructor learns from students, and students learn from each other. Lecture and production classes aim to understand and practice civic advocacy journalism as it "contributes to widening news coverage by spotlighting issues and featuring voices that are typically ignored by mainstream media. In doing so, it makes positive contributions to democratic debate" (Waisbord, 2008, p. 378). The implementation of these courses has not been a smooth road. Therefore, it is important to assess successes and challenges.

Critical Pedagogy in the Analysis of Latinos and the Media

The design and implementation of this two-semester project pursue the completion of an analytical corpus conformed from research published by Latino communication scholars and Latin American critical researchers. The main objective of this project is to provide students with the instruments to teach themselves and become active participants of their own education. While teaching this class, like other instructors and researchers such as Reyes and Ríos (2005), I found myself identifying with the students and working to help them understand how our own backgrounds and experiences interface with our society. Moreover, I wanted my students to better grasp how our personal and professional experiences influence the way we perceive the world as journalists, researchers, students, instructors, and also as human beings (Reyes, 2003).

The greater part of SLNE students are majors in journalism, while other participants take this course driven by their interest in learning about Latinos and the media.[2] Since the very first class, I explain to students that throughout the semester we will build up parallel sequences to generate discussions on (a) the contemporary history of Latinos and international Latino immigrants in the U.S., and (b) the contemporary history of Latino and Latino-oriented media. By creating a scholarly map of how these two concomitant and coexistent phenomena influence each other, students are encouraged to analyze a variety of topics from critical perspectives They are expected to attain competency in the ability to (1) analyze contemporary Latino diasporas and the history of Latino communities in the U.S., (2) examine historical development and current trends of Latino and Latino-oriented media in the U.S., and (3) compare news coverage of Latino communities in mainstream, Latino and Latino-oriented media.

The course textbook is *Harvest of Empire* by Juan González (2011). Each chapter provides historical perspective that help students better understand U.S.-Latin American international relations over the last two centuries. Class meets twice a week. The first class session of each week entails discussions of historical information with current data (from the U.S. Census Bureau or the Pew Hispanic Center) and selected academic essays or book chapters. In the second weekly class session, students review the role of mainstream and ethnic media in portraying U.S. Latinos or Latino immigrants, and in serving Spanish-language and bilingual communities. A selection of academic essays, book chapters and reports inform class discussions. Throughout these parallel discussions students are encouraged to connect concepts and theories learned in each class with journalism professional practices in order "to allow an exploration of their future careers, foster civic/social responsibility, and force them to look critically at their education process within the context of the society in which they exist" (Purmensky, 2009, p. 102).

Additionally, class discussions and assignments provide students with opportunities to learn about social disparities associated with diverse communities as well as "encourage students to examine their personal biases, gain a better understanding of diversity, and critically analyze the perceived realities of social injustices that affect the community" (Simons, Russell, & Bland, 2009, p. 190). At every session, students are seated in a big circle and a group of student volunteers lead class discussions on assigned readings. Participants become familiar with class dynamics that promotes a team-learning environment. In doing so, they are encouraged to engage in critical reflection, which gives students the opportunity to challenge preconceived notions and compare them with a deeper experience in familiar scenarios (Purmensky, 2009). These student-centered teaching practices allow students to learn together while also taking responsibility for their individual learning. Students examine contemporary diasporas, the role of media in transnational contexts, and critical perspectives such as dependency theory and post-colonial studies (Retis, 2007, 2012). They reflect on how "most of us know little of the enormous differences between how the Spanish and English settled America, or how those disparities led after independence to nations with such radically divergent societies" (González, 2011, p. 3). With the introduction to transnational social field perspective students examine why González argues that Puerto Ricans are citizens yet foreigners and how first Cuban immigration flows were treated as special refugees, but not the second or third waves (González, 2011; Levitt & Glick Schiller, 2004). The fact that most students are familiar with the population of transnational families on the west coast and southwest creates the opportunity for comparative perspectives on similarities and differences among the wide-range of Latino groups in the U.S.

With the introduction of post-colonial studies students examine why González argues that Mexicans represent pioneers of a different type (González, 2011; Grosfoguel, 2011). Additionally, by understanding the crucial role of social networks for international immigrants they examine why Central Americans were a negligible presence in the United States until the final decades of the twentieth century (González, 2011; Menjívar, 2009). These discussions encourage students to understand contemporary history of Latinos in the U.S., but also inspire them to share their own personal and familiar experiences. We start structuring a collective mirror where we relate with the images we recreate from the readings from complex perspectives: the classroom mirror. By adding geopolitics to class discussions, participants examine the connection between capital flows and population flows in transnational contexts especially when analyzing the history and current context of Dominicans and Colombians on the East Coast (Retis, 2007). Students then examine why González (2011) assures that the Dominican exodus, unlike that of Puerto Ricans and Mexicans, began largely as refugee flight in the mid-1960s and the role of U.S. officials and entrepreneurs in these processes. By reading González' *Harvest of Empire*, students can relate to his narrative, not only because the author is a Latino journalist speaking about immigration, but also because most of the book's chapters narrate the history of a particular transnational family, including his. Having students and me as the professor seated in a big circle facilitates the conversational aspect of discussion about class readings: we discuss concepts, theories, and case studies, but, most importantly, we relate these readings to our own personal and familiar experiences.

Given the socio-historical framework of the course, we make an effort to concentrate class discussions on the role of media during every other class session. Students begin by exploring origins of Latino newspapers in the U.S. and how Spanish-language press has been conceived in different historical periods and in different forms such as exile press, immigrant press, native press, activists, cultural or social controllers (Gutiérrez, 1977; Kanellos, 2000; Retis, 2013a). Discussions then move to analyzing and understanding the origins and contemporary history of Spanish-language broadcast media in the United States (Castañeda, 2008; Castañeda Paredes, 2001; Moreno, 2011; Retis, 2013a, 2013b; Rodriguez, 1999, 2001; Sinclair, 2003). Students examine not only media, but also the role of individual journalists, Latino pioneers and *cronistas*, such as Francisco P. Ramírez, Pedro J. González, Ignacio López, or Rubén García. They are often surprised as to how much they know about mainstream media journalists, but very little about Latino professionals and the ways in which most of them have worked to serve their communities in different media platforms, including publishing news stories denouncing social injustices (García, 1989, 1995; Gutiérrez, 2000; Parlee, 1984).

Historical perspectives are relevant because they help us to construct a better sense of the major trends regarding international immigration flows, major areas of settlement, second and third generation U.S. Latinos, and the main struggles of Latino communities in different areas. It also provides the opportunity to historically examine the vital role of Latino media and Latino professionals within the broader journalistic field. Once this historical landscape is established we analyze the role of mainstream media in reporting on these specific topics nowadays. Students reflect on main trends such as the portrayal of Latinos in network TV news, and gender and class in media discourses (Correa, 2010; DeSipio & Hofer, 2000; NAHJ, 2006; National Council of La Raza, 1997; Retis, 2012; Santa Ana, 2013; Vargas, 2000). During the last third part of the semester, class discussion focuses on understanding the media portrayal of young Latinos in the U.S. with specific attention to the anti-immigrant metaphor, undocumented students, and the Dreamers fight (Jefferies, 2009; Santa Ana, 1999; Truax, 2013).

Class assignment requires students to get involved with local community organizations that work on issues relevant to Latino groups or journalism professionals working in Latino or Latino-oriented media. As most students know first-hand local organizations working in their own neighborhoods, during the semester they are asked to find out how and why these community-oriented institutions are vital for civic advocacy journalism practices. Organizations' representatives are invited to participate in class panels and students are expected to develop more in depth relationship with organizations and value their role in our society. Students write a reflective essay discussing these experiences. By incorporating liberatory pedagogies, students work collectively with each other to confront their own perspectives (Freire, 1973, 1994). They share their personal or familiar experiences when analyzing specific topics or theories as developed in their report.

We then work together in an online platform where we map community organizations working with and for Latinos. We analyze why their role is important and why we as journalists have to offer them major spaces in media discourses. By confronting mainstream media coverage of Latinos in the U.S. we analyze also why those organizations and not just official administrators or political representatives must be included as main sources of news information. Their attempts and failures in contacting community organizations brings also a discussion on how difficult is for these organizations to give some extra time to journalists. In other words, how demanding these organizations are and why it takes extra effort for reporters to contact them. Sociology of news media practices and political economy of the media approaches are used to explain these trends to students. This is the moment of the semester where students reflect on the importance of cultivate strong relationship with community organizations working with and for Latinos in the area. They learn how and why these community organizers are the ones that know first-hand the main issues when working towards social change. They examine why these organizations should be main and not alternative sources when reporting social inequities. By the end of the semester, students collectively categorize these organizations and value their role in advocacy of Latino and Latino immigrants' human rights. I explain to students that the mapping conducted during the Fall semester is revisited the following semester when we start the production of investigative reporting for SLTV.

To assemble the dynamics of participatory interactions, a series of discussion panels composed of diverse community organizations and journalism professionals are integrated into the classroom environment. Panels such as "Undocumented Students and the Media" include the participation of representatives from organizations such as Dreams to be Heard, National Immigrant Youth, *Los Otros* Dreamers, Queer Undocumented Immigrant Project and Dream Activists California. Another panel is "Current Trends and the Future of Spanish-language Print and Online Media" with the participation of news editors from *La Opinión*, *Hoy* and *Huffington Voces.* Lastly, we have another panel titled, "Current Trends of Spanish-language TV Newscast in Los Angeles," with the participation of news editors from *Univisión*, *Telemundo*, *MundoFox*, and *Estrella* TV.

The class is expected to write a ten-page report where students discuss news media coverage of these topics and present findings during last sessions of the semester. Critical discourse analysis of mainstream and Spanish-language media is implemented in a comparative perspective. Participants share their findings during the last class sessions of the semester. This series of issues, questions and reflections help examine the parameters and contributions from class readings and debates. Students particularly evaluate questions of democracy, diversity, social justice, and social responsibility. Having participated in the panels of community organizations and having interviewed local Latino organizations, students are better able to question and understand their access to public debate.

The dialogic journalism with a social conscience approach of SLNE class encourages students to become active participants in their own education. All inquiries on the role of mainstream and ethnic media in our society result in a rich reflective environment. By implementing liberatory pedagogy approach, class discussions promote dialogic journalism with a social conscience. By understanding socioeconomic and political structural inequities, students comprehend (a) how and why media become a crucial element in communication for social change and (b) how and why civic advocacy journalism contributes to both raising awareness among the public and setting policy priorities and agendas.

Community Organizations as Main Sources of Information: Video Reporting

The main objective of SLTV in the Spring semester is to introduce students to methods and styles of Spanish-language TV and online news video production. It has been designed with particular emphasis on helping students to practice civic advocacy journalism with documentary storytelling forms for contemporary digital media (Wilkin & Ball-Rokeach, 2006). During the semester, class participants also use social media and online tools for researching, reporting, and producing online video stories. Students are expected to (1) examine technical and esthetic elements of Spanish-language TV production, (2) understand and practice multimedia and transmedia storytelling forms for online news video, (3) understand and practice social media for researching, reporting, producing, and publishing online news video, (4) analyze, understand, and practice multimedia forms of civic advocacy journalism and (5) work on a team project covering Latino affairs.

The class starts by reconnecting with reflections from SLNE and reviewing the previous semester's mapping of Latino organizations that will be used for video production during the Spring semester. Weekly sessions are organized into two different segments. During the first part of the class, students participate in a seminar-style session where they discuss main readings for the course project. During the second part of the class, students are trained in video production *en español.* Since the first meeting students are introduced to principles of civic advocacy journalism followed by discussions on understanding youth cultures and relating this sociological approach to youth with reports, as to how young Latinos come of age in the U.S. (Feixa, 1999; Lopez, 2009; Massey, 1998; Reguillo, 2003; Schaffer, 1996; Waisbord, 2008). It also includes issues regarding identity, citizenship and sense of belonging (Lopez & Barrios, 2008; Reguillo, 2000; Suárez-Orozco et al., 2010). By working with selected essays and reports (as cited previously), students discuss trends in education such as understanding trajectories of newcomer immigrant youth, the situation of immigrants in community colleges, and expectations and achievements of undocumented students (Nichols, 2013; Teranishi & Suárez-Orozco, 2011; Truax, 2013). Participants also explore civic engagement of immigrant youth and youth activism (Lopez & Barrios, 2008; Vélez, Huber, Lopez, de la Luz, & Solórzano, 2008). We pay particular attention on mobilizations toward the Latino youth vote and the dynamics of Latino political identity (De la Garza & Jang, 2011; Jackson, 2011; Michelson, 2006). Students also discuss on issues of access to health care and prevention programs relying in the understanding of social medicine

(Anderson, Smith, & Sidel, 2005; Livingston, Minushkin, & Cohn, 2008; Shaibi, Greenwood-Ericksen, Chapman, Konopken, & Ertl, 2010; Vega, Rodriguez, & Gruskin, 2009). These topics are emphasized because they are priorities that emerged during the previous semester by conversations with community organizations and class discussions.

During technical sessions, students are instructed to explore elements of visual anthropology, such as ethnographic documentaries with *cinema vérité* styles. Class discussions help them to understand why more than an observational piece they are encouraged to approach their videos as texts. In other words, as narratives where the subject, the video-maker and the audience are encountered (Hockings, 2003; MacDougall, 1997). We discuss main approaches of visual anthropology and reflect on the basis of communication for social change as “a process of public and private dialogue through which people determine who they are, what they need and what they want in order to improve their lives” (Gumucio & Tufte, 2006, p. xix; Ruby, 2005). Lecture and lab sessions triangulate to include a pedagogical framework that prioritizes community organizations as main sources for the reporting and develops a news media production style oriented to civic advocacy journalism and communication for social change. It also emphasizes long format online video storytelling that utilizes the basis of visual anthropology and new media/social media elements.

As in SLNE, during class dynamics we construct an imaginary mirror where we see stories, and more specifically the struggles and opportunities of being young Latinos in the U.S. Thus, when students pitch their story ideas, the class turns into a safe zone that promotes a process of self-representation from a critical perspective. After a long discussion on the main objective of this class production, for the 2015 Spring semester class, we selected #JóvenesLatinos for our trend in social media and particular hashtags dedicated to specific sub-topics pitched by every team. … The philosophy of this class production is to produce glocally, which means, reporting locally but thinking globally. Thus, students are encouraged to conduct research for these topics from a broader perspective, yet they must also reconnect with local organizations working on these issues so they may find interviewees for these topics. Class dynamics are based on the active participation of students as part of a wider strategy of collective teaching/learning process. As a consequence, students help each other by commenting their own knowledge on the struggles of young Latinos.

Student groups are composed of two or three students, and together they research, report, produce, edit and publish their videos on our YouTube channel. By the end of the semester, selections of the best videos are incorporated into a TV cultural magazine titled *En Otras Palabras* where they invite representatives from the organizations they partnered with to participate on a TV panel. During all these steps, students keep a permanent contact with organizations working in Latino affairs. Class discussions help students learn how relevant these institutions are but also how important is to incorporate them into the social debate. Some of these organizations came to visit our class, some are active within our campus, and others were contacted during the previous semester. All of them work on a variety of projects to improve the quality of life of young Latinos. The main organizations were Youth Speak Collective, Dreams to be Heard, Queer Undocumented Immigrant Project from United We Dream, Homeboy Industries, Joint Advocates on Disordered Eating, and 100 Citizens, among others.

In the process of researching and understanding prior to reporting, students are asked to contact experts such as professors and researchers. Some of these interviews were taped; others were carried out with the solely objective of learning. During editorial sessions, students also shared their own personal experiences, their families' experiences, their friends and family friends' experiences. These learning methods involve participatory processes were the entire class exchange information and learning abilities. Not all students are fully bilingual to write and/or narrate fluently in Spanish; not all the students have all video/editing skills to produce and edit a video package. But this is never an impediment for them to recreate a collective learning environment. The results are that they learn in class from the readings; they learn from class discussions; they learn from the professor's explanations; they learn from their sources and from their own research; but, most importantly, they learn from each other and they learn from these community partners.

Even though this is a very time consuming class, students are willing to collaborate and expend as much time in researching, reporting, producing, and editing. They are challenged to produce multimedia storytelling from a critical perspective. Every week they present their advances and receive criticism from the professor, from the technicians, and from their classmates. Throughout the evolving of the semester, they present final drafts, showing improvement in their reporting and their visual narratives. Stories on education touched challenges and opportunities of being first generation college students and how these students double the efforts to obtain their majors: #Hijosdeimmigrantes. A second one explored the crucial role of immigrant parents in supporting their children to obtain better opportunities in education: #PadresLatinos. A third video touched in first person the struggles of being a young mother and pursuing college education: #PadresJóvenes. Students also produced a video on challenges of having English as a second language: #ESL #Bilingüismo. Stories centering the attention in health produced videos on the necessity of having more sexual education at young ages: #EducaciónSexual. Research on health also oriented students to examine the problem of obesity and diabetes and how community organizations are working to improve Latino families' health: #Diabetes #100citizens.

Class discussions on problems of depression and eating disorders inspired a group of students to research this topic and narrate the story in first person: #DesordenAlimenticio. Three projects oriented their interest in issues on young Latinos' identity. One covered community organizations working after school programs to help Latino students with their academic performance but also through sports programs: #JóvenesDeportistas. Another centered the attention into community organizations working with young Latinos and helping them to abandon gangs by offering job opportunities and education: #ExPandilleros. Class discussions on the Dreamers fight brought the attention of students into the struggles of undocumented students. In previous semester, a panel organized for SLNE brought to campus main organizations working in these affairs, so students reconnected with them in and outside campus, specifically with Dreams to be Heard (D2BH) from CSUN and Queer Undocumented Immigrant Project (QUIP) from United We Dream: #Undocuqueer. Again, these organizations helped them to understand the topic and address with their production the main challenges of undocumented students.

With, for, and by Young Latinos

Teaching is not value-neutral but a dynamic course of action that interacts with the forces of the times. This two-semester project emphasizes precisely in approaching education as a process of liberation where the instructor promotes a constant dialogue with students in efforts to provide them with instruments to teach themselves. When bilingual and bicultural students enter into this dialogic method of understanding social injustices they become active participants in their own education. Students tend to share class discussions with friends and family members. Reflective essays, in-depth interviews with community organizations help them to understand the crucial role of these types of institutions. Service learning approaches and community engagement frameworks enriches their academic and professional training with a better understanding of the society, awareness of social injustices when covering diversity and minorities. These type of community-oriented classes and multimodal production courses allows professional preparation of students with a strong foundation on civic advocacy journalism and communication for social change.

Notes

1. The Participatory Journalism Interest Group began in 1994 during the formative years of civic/public journalism. The Community Journalism Interest Group was established in 2004. Journalists of color have actively engaged in supporting new professional practices that incorporate diversity and human rights in news coverage: National Association of Hispanic Journalists (NAHJ), Asian American Journalists Associations (AAJA), National Association of Black Journalists (NABJ), Association of LGBT Journalists (NLGJA), Association for Women Journalists (AWJ), among others. Non-profit organizations such as the Institute for Justice in Journalism are dedicated to strengthening journalism about social and economic justice issues by providing training and funding projects. There are also other news publications dedicated to reporting on social justice and diversity, such as The Chronicle of Social Change, New America Media or Colorlines, among others.
2. They pursue majors in Chicano Studies, Central American Studies, Political Science or Communication Studies, among others.

References

Anderson, M., Smith, L., & Sidel, V. (2005). What is social medicine? *Monthly Review, 56*(8), 27–34.

Anyaegbunam, C., & Leland, R. (2003). Students as citizens: Experiential approaches to reflective thinking on community journalism. *Journalism & Mass Communication Educator, 58*(1), 64–73.

ASNE. (2015). *ASNE newsroom census.* Retrieved from http://asne.org/

Boyer, E. (1990). *Scholarship reconsidered: Priorities of the professoriate.* Princeton, NJ: The Carnegie Foundation for the Advancement of Teaching.

Butin, D. (2007). Focusing our aim: Strengthening faculty commitment to community engagement. *Change, 39*(6), 34–37.

Castañeda, M. (2008). The importance of Spanish-Language and Latino media. In A. Valdivia (Ed.), *Latino/a communication studies today* (pp. 51–66). New York, NY: Peter Lang.

Castañeda Paredes, M. (2001). The reorganization of Spanish-language media marketing in the United States. In V. Mosco & D. Schiller (Eds.), *Continental order: Integrating North America for cybercapitalism* (pp. 120–135). Lanham, MD: Rowman and Littlefield.

Castells, M. (2009). *Communication power.* Oxford: Oxford University Press.

Chaffee, S. H., & McDevitt, M. (1999). On evaluating public journalism. In T. L. Glasser (Ed.), *The idea of public journalism* (pp. 175–196). New York, NY: Guilford Press.

Correa, T. (2010). Framing Latinas: Hispanic women through the lenses of Spanish-language and English-language news media. *Journalism, 11*(4), 425–443.

Dávila, A. (2001). *Latinos Inc.: The marketing and making of a people.* Berkeley, CA: University of California Press.

De la Garza, R., & Jang, S. (2011). Why the giant sleeps so deeply: Political consequences of individual-level Latino demographics. *Social Science Quarterly, 92*(4), 895–916.

DeSipio, L., & Hofer, J. (2000). Talking back to television: Latinos discuss how television portrays them and the quality of programming options. In C. Noriega (Ed.), *The future of Latino independent media: A NALIP sourcebook* (pp. 59–83). Los Angeles, CA: UCLA Chicano Studies Research Center.

Downing, J. D. H., Ford, T. V., Gil, G., & Stein, L. (2001). *Radical media: Rebellious communication and social movements.* Thousand Oaks, CA: Sage Publications.

Durham, M. G. (1998). Revolutionizing the teaching of magazine design. *Journalism and Mass Communication Educator, 98*, 23–32.

Entman, R., & Rojecki, A. (2000). *The black image in the white mind: Media and race in America.* Chicago, IL: University of Chicago Press.

Feixa, C. (1999). De culturas, subculturas y estilos. In C. Feixa (Ed.), *De Jóvenes, bandas y tribus. Antropología de la juventud* (pp. 84–105). Barcelona: Ariel.

Freire, P. (1973). *Education for critical consciousness.* New York, NY: Continuum.

Freire, P. (1994). *Pedagogy of hope.* New York, NY: Continuum.

García, M. (1989). Mexican-American muckraker. In Ignacio L. López & El Espectador (Eds.), *Mexican Americans: Leadership, ideology, and identity, 1930–1960* (pp. 84–112). New Haven, CT: Yale University Press.

García, M. (1995). *Border correspondent: Selected writings of Rubén Salazar, 1955–1970.* Berkeley, CA: University of California Press.

Giroux, H. A. (1992). Paulo Freire and the politics of postcolonialism. *Journal of Advanced Composition, 12*(1), 15–26.

Giroux, H. A. (1997). *Pedagogy and the politics of hope: Theory, culture and schooling.* Boulder, CO: Westview Press.

Giroux, H. A. (2010). *On critical pedagogy.* New York, NY: Continuum.

González, J. (2011). *Harvest of empire: A history of Latinos in America.* New York, NY: Penguin.

Grosfoguel, R. (2011). Decolonizing Post-colonial studies and paradigms of political-economy: Transmodernity, decolonial thinking, and global coloniality. *Journal of Peripheral Cultural Production of the Luso-Hispanic World, 1*(1), 1–32.

Gumucio, A., & Tufte, T. (2006). *Communication for social change. Anthology: Historical and contemporary readings.* South Orange, NH: CFSC Consortium.

Gutiérrez, F. (1977). Spanish-language media in America: Background, resources, history. *Journalism History, 4*(2), 34–67.

Gutiérrez, F. (2000). Francisco P. Ramirez. *Media Studies Journal, 14*(2), 16–23.

Harcup, T. (2011). Alternative journalism as active citizenship. *Journalism, 12*(1), 15–31.

Hochheimer, J. (1992). Toward liberatory pedagogy for journalism students: Adapting Paulo Freire's praxis to the non-poor. *College Literature, 19*(1), 12–27.

Hockings, P. (2003). *Principles of visual anthropology.* New York, NY: Mouton de Gruyter.

Jackson, M. (2011). Priming the sleeping giant: The dynamics of Latino political identity and vote choice. *Political Psychology, 32*(4), 691–716.

Janowitz, M. (1975). Professional models in journalism: The gatekeeper and the advocate. *Journalism Quarterly, 52*(4), 618–626.

Jefferies, J. (2009). Do undocumented students play by the rules?: Meritocracy in the media. *Critical Inquiry in Language Studies, 6*(1–2), 15–38.

Kanellos, N. (2000). *Hispanic periodicals in the United States, origins to 1960: A brief history and comprehensive bibliography.* Houston, TX: Houston University Press.

Keeble, R. (2009). *Ethics for journalists.* London: Routledge.

Lambeth, E. (1996). A bibliographic review of civic journalism. *National Civic Review, 85*, 18–21.

Lambeth, E. B., Christians, C. G., Fleming, K., & Lee, S. T. (2004). Media ethics teaching in Century 21: Progress, problems, and challenges. *Journalism & Mass Communication Educator, 59*, 239–258.

Levitt, P., & Glick Schiller, N. (2004). Conceptualizing simultaneity: A transnational social field perspective on society. *International Migration Review, 38*(145), 595–629.

Livingston, G., Minushkin, S., & Cohn, D. (2008). *Hispanics and health care in the United States: Access, information and knowledge.* Washington, DC: RWJF/PHC.

Lopez, H. (2009). *Between two worlds: How young Latinos come to age in America.* Washington, DC: Pew Hispanic Center.

Lopez, H., & Barrios, K. (2008). The civic engagement of immigrant youth: New evidence from the 2006 civic and political health of the nation survey. *Applied Development Science, 12*(2), 66–73.

MacDougall, D. (1997). The visual in anthropology. In M. Banks & H. Morphy (Eds.), *Rethinking visual anthropology* (pp. 276–295). New Haven, CT: Yale University Press.

Massey, B. (1998). Civic journalism and nonelite sourcing: Making routine newswork of community connectedness. *Journalism and Mass Communication Quarterly, 75*(2), 394–407.

Mather, C., & Konkle, E. (2013). Promoting social justice through appreciative community service. *New Directions for Student Services, 143*, 77–88.

McDevitt, M. (2000). Teaching civic journalism: Integrating theory and practice. *Journalism & Mass Communication Educator, 55*(2), 40–49.

McDevitt, M. (2002). Civic autonomy in journalism education: Applying expertise to political action. *Journalism & Mass Communication Educator, 57*(2), 152–160.

Menjívar, C. (2009). Salvadorian migration to the United States in the 1980s: What can we learn about it and from it? *International Migration, 32*(3), 371–401.

Michelson, M. (2006). Mobilizing the Latino youth vote. *Social Science Quarterly, 87*(5), 1188–1206.

Moreno, G. (2011). Televisa and Univision, 50 years of media post-nationalism. *Global Media and Communication, 7*(1), 62–68.

National Association of Hispanic Journalists. (2006). *Network brownout report. The portrayal of Latinos and Latino issues on network television news.* Washington, DC: National Association of Hispanic Journalists (NAHJ).

National Council of La Raza. (1997). Out of the picture: Hispanics in the media. In C. Rodríguez (Ed.), *Latin looks. Images of Latinas and Latinos in the U.S. media* (pp. 21–35). Boulder, CO: Westview Press.

Nichols, W. (2013). *The DREAMers: How the undocumented youth movement transformed the immigrant rights debate*. Stanford, CA: Stanford University Press.

Ostertag, J. (2006). *People's movements, people's press: The journalism of social justice movement*. Boston, MA: Beacon Press.

Parlee, L. (1984, December 22–24). Ballad of an unsung hero. *Nuestro*.

Purmensky, K. (2009). *Service-learning for diverse communities. Critical pedagogy and mentoring English language learners*. Charlotte, NC: Information Age Publishing.

Reguillo, R. (2000). *Emergencia de culturas juveniles. Estrategias del desencanto*. Mexico City: Editorial Norma.

Reguillo, R. (2003). Ciudadanías juveniles en América Latina. *Última década, 19*, 11–30.

Retis, J. (2007). *Mass media and Latin American diaspora in Europe: The rise and consolidation of the new Latino media in Spain*. Paper presented at the International Association for Media and Communication Research. Paris, France.

Retis, J. (2012). Immigrant Latina images in mainstream media: Class, race, and gender in public discourse in the United States and Spain. In M. M. Lirola (Ed.), *Discourses on immigration in times of economic crisis: A critical perspective* (pp. 29–58). London: Cambridge Scholar Publishing.

Retis, J. (2013a). Spanish language newspapers in the United States. In C. M. Tatum (Ed.), *Encyclopedia of Latino culture: From calaveras to quinceañeras*. Santa Barbara, CA: Greenwood.

Retis, J. (2013b). Spanish language TV in the United States. In C. M. Tatum (Ed.), *Encyclopedia of Latino culture: From calaveras to quinceañeras*. Santa Barbara, CA: Greenwood.

Reyes, X. (2003). Teachers' (re)construction of knowledge: The other side of fieldwork. *Journal of Latinos and Education, 2*(1), 31–37.

Reyes, X., & Ríos, D. I. (2005). Dialoguing the Latina experience in higher education. *Journal of Hispanic Higher Education, 4*(4), 377–391.

Rodriguez, A. (1999). *Making Latino news: Race, language, class*. Thousand Oaks, CA: Sage Publications.

Rodriguez, A. (2001). Creating an audience and remapping a nation: A brief history of U.S. Spanish language broadcasting 1930–1980. *Quarterly Review of Film & Video, 16*(3–4), 357–374.

Rodriguez, C., Kidd, D., & Stein, L. (2010). *Making our media. Global initiatives toward a democratic public sphere*. Cresskill, NJ: Hampton Press.

Ruby, J. (2005). The last 20 years of visual anthropology: A critical review. *Visual Studies, 20*(2), 159–170.

Santa Ana, O. (1999). "Like an animal I was treated": Anti-immigrant metaphor in U.S. public discourse. *Discourse & Society, 10*(2), 191–224.

Santa Ana, O. (2013). *Juan in a hundred: The representation of Latinos on network news.* Austin, TX: University of Texas Press.

Schaffer, J. (1996). Civic journalism. *Liberal Education, 82*(2), 20.

Shadduck-Hernández, J. (2006). Here I am now! Critical ethnography and community service-learning with immigrant and refugee undergraduate students and youth. *Ethnography and Education, 1*(1), 67–86.

Shaibi, G. Q., Greenwood-Ericksen, M. B., Chapman, C. R., Konopken, Y., & Ertl, J. (2010). Development, implementation, and effects of community based diabetes prevention program for obese Latino youth. *Journal of Primary Care & Community Health, 1*(3), 206–212.

Simon, J., & Sapp, D. (2006). Learning inside and outside the classroom: Civic journalism and the Freedom of Information Act. *Journalism & Mass Communication Educator, 61*(2), 129–148.

Simons, L., Russell, B., & Bland, N. (2009). An exploration of the value of cultural-based service-learning for student and community participants. In B. Moley, S. Billig, & B. Holland (Eds.), *Creating our identities in service-learning and community engagement* (pp. 189–214). Charlotte, NC: Information Age Publishing.

Sinclair, J. (2003). The Hollywood of Latin America: Miami as regional center in television trade. *Television & New Media, 4*(3), 211–229.

Smith, L. (2008). Race, Ethnicity, and student sources: Minority newsmakers in student-produced versus professional TV news stories. *The Howard Journal of Communications, 19*, 182–199.

Suárez-Orozco, C., Gaytán, F. X., Bang, H. J., Pakes, J., O'Connor, E., & Rhodes, J. (2010). Academic trajectories of newcomer immigrant youth. *Developmental Psychology, 46*(3), 602.

Teranishi, R., & Suárez-Orozco, M. (2011). Immigrants in community colleges. *The Future of Children, 21*(1), 153–169.

Truax, E. (2013). *Dreamers. La lucha de una generación por su sueño Americano.* Mexico City: Oceano.

Tufte, T., & Mefalopulos, P. (2009). *Participatory communication. A practical guide.* Washington, DC: The World Bank.

Vargas, L. (2000). Genderizing Latino news: An analysis of a local newspaper's coverage of Latino current affairs. *Critical Studies in Media Communication, 17*(3), 261–293.

Vega, W., Rodriguez, M., & Gruskin, E. (2009). Health disparities in the Latino population. *Epidemol Reviews, 31*, 99–112.

Vélez, V., Huber, L. P., Lopez, C. B., de la Luz, A., & Solórzano, D. G. (2008). Battling for human rights and social justice: A Latina/o critical race media analysis of Latina/o student youth activism in the wake of 2006 anti-immigrant sentiment. *Social Justice, 35*(1), 7–27.

Velez-Ibañez, C. G., & Greenberg, J. B. (1992) Formation and transformation of funds of knowledge among U.S. Mexican households. *Anthropology and Education Quarterly, 23*(4), 313–335.

Voakes, P. (2004). A brief history of public journalism. *National Civic Review, 93*(3), 25–35.

Waisbord, S. (2008). Advocacy journalism in a global context. In K. Wahl-Jorgensen & T. Hanitzsch (Eds.), *The handbook of journalism studies* (pp. 371–385). New York, NY: Routledge.

Waisbord, S. (2009). The "journalist" and the "civic" models of advocacy journalism. In *Conference Papers.* Washington, DC: International Communication Association.

Wilkin, H. A., & Ball-Rokeach, S. J. (2006). Reaching at risk groups. The importance of health storytelling in Los Angeles Latino media. *Journalism, 7*(3), 299–320.

Wilkins, K., Tufte, T., & Obregón, R. (2014). *The handbook of development communication and social change.* London: Wiley Blackwell.

14. *Chicana/o Media Pedagogies: How Activism and Engagement Transform Student of Color Journalists*

Sonya M. Alemán

Over the past twenty-two years, Chicana/o students at the University of Utah have published forty issues of *Venceremos* (We Shall Overcome), a bilingual Chicana/o student newspaper that seeks to counter mainstream news media's abysmal coverage of their Latina/o communities. Half of those forty issues have been crafted in a communication course explicitly designed to support the publication of *Venceremos* by providing academic credit and technological resources to its contributors. I served as the instructor for the *Venceremos* course for eight years, working with over seventy students to publish more than 100,000 copies of *Venceremos.* The students and I connected by our shared desire to examine and improve the production of mediated content about Chicanas/os and Latinas/os. At various points in the publication's history (Marcial, 1993, p. 2; *Venceremos*, 2008, p. 2), students have delineated the newspaper's mission as:

1. exposing and opposing the negative depictions of Chicanas/os which often appear in the media of the dominant culture;
2. filling a cultural void with our voices, to correct what has been incorrectly reported and to tell our stories untold;
3. providing a counter story to the Eurocentric, heterosexist, racist, and xenophobic perceptions that media often perpetuates.

As advisor and instructor, I was able to not only bolster institutional support and resources for the newspaper, but I was also able to serve the social justice goals of both the newspaper and its student producers by reformulating traditional journalism pedagogy in ways that disrupt mainstream media representations of Latinas/os and Chicanas/os.

Together in our classroom/newsroom, my students and I theorized and refined the alternative journalism practice used to counter disparaging mainstream images and discourses about Latina/o and Chicana/o communities. Referred to as Chicana/o journalism (Alemán, 2011) one of its key elements is advocacy, as contributors seek to empower their readers to think critically and engage in activities that have transformative possibilities for their racially and ethnically marginalized communities. While student producers and I have collected survey data at various points to assess *Venceremos'* influence on its readers,[1] this chapter, in contrast, shares data from a project undertaken to assess the impact of the social justice framework of the *Venceremos* course and newspaper have on media consumption and civic involvement after student contributors graduate or move on from the publication. Focus groups were conducted with a dozen former contributors, while another six students completed electronic surveys that allowed them to reflect on these two topics. The data indicated that media consumption among this group of contributors has been affected after enrolling in the *Venceremos* class. Moreover, it revealed that students reoriented their articulation of civic engagement to pivot on a framework of social justice and include many non-conventional forms of activism.

The following four sections flesh out the findings from this study. First, I will briefly introduce the student producers of *Venceremos*, detailing demographic information about who they are. Then, I will outline the pedagogical approach and social justice-based curriculum structuring the *Venceremos* course. Next, I will briefly describe the methods I used to collect information about the long-term impact of producing a campus-community newspaper founded on social justice principles in a classroom model. Lastly, I will share the key findings from the project and lessons learned from engaging with social justice approaches to community based teaching.

The Venceremos *Contributors*

A little over 90% of the seventy-plus students contributing to Venceremos since 2009 have been Latina/o students. They represent a multitude of *Latinidades*, meaning they have ties to multiple Spanish-speaking countries including Mexico, Colombia, Peru, Argentina, Brazil, and Guatemala, to name a few. Only a handful of non-Latina/o students contributed to the newspaper, identifying as Pacific Islander, Black, Filipino, African Muslim, and White. Over half of all *Venceremos* contributors were born and raised in the United States. A dozen are undocumented students, and several are members of families with mixed citizenship status. Even though the paper publishes in both Spanish and English, *Venceremos* contributors are all English dominant writers and speakers, and vary greatly in their levels of Spanish fluency.

Additionally, *Venceremos* editors and staff have been overwhelmingly female. In fact, 12 out of the 14 editors in the last eight years have been women. Two of them were young mothers, often bringing their children with them to the class/newsroom if they had no other options for child-care during meetings or production times. *Venceremos* contributors represent a variety of majors such as engineering, English, political science, graphic design, nursing, sociology, education, and business: only a handful of students are communication majors. Instead, the majority come to *Venceremos* as self-proclaimed leaders or activists for their communities. They are leaders in other organizations on campus; primarily other student of color groups, but not exclusively. Furthermore, a significant number of them have been high academic achievers, enrolled in the Honors College, or with double majors.

All of the students enrolled in *Venceremos* also worked at least part-time while attending college. About 15% of them often would take classes one semester, then take a semester off to work full-time in order to save money to pay for a subsequent semester. Another 20% received some kind of academic scholarship, but still worked to cover other living or family expenses. Fewer than five *Venceremos* undergraduate contributors lived on campus, and the rest resided with their parent's or with other family members. The majority of them relied on public transportation to commute to campus.

All these factors were simultaneously assets and challenges to meeting deadlines and successfully producing and distributing the thousands of copies of *Venceremos* that were distributed free of charge in eight of Salt Lake City's racially and ethnically diverse neighborhoods, as well as on the University of Utah campus. These students lived experiences and daily realities also made the classroom space an exceptional teaching and learning environment. The following section maps out the pedagogical model and content of the *Venceremos* course and the ways in which it both centered and drew from the student's racialized ways of knowing the world.

Pedagogy of Counter-News-Story

As I have documented in previous research, the pedagogy of counter-news-story is the three-phase instructional approach I employ in the *Venceremos* classroom (Alemán, 2014). This process: (1) demystifies the seeming objectivity of mainstream media; (2) identifies majoritarian stories embedded in news reports, and (3) encourages the formulation and practice of an alternative approach called a counter-news-story. It is undergirded by critical race theory. Every semester I teach the course, I orient students to the tenets of critical race theory as a way to equip them with ways to foster and articulate their distinctive alternative journalism practice (Alemán, 2011, 2014). I will list some of critical race theory tenets here, as they also help illuminate the three elements of a pedagogy of counter-news-story. To begin with, racism is permanent and systemic, rather than an aberration rooted in individual acts of prejudice (Parker & Lynn, 2002; Valdes, Culp, & Harris, 2002). Secondly, critical race theory deconstructs concepts like objectivity, color-blindness, neutrality, individualism and meritocracy to reveal the ways they uphold white supremacy (Ladson-Billings, 1998; Ladson-Billings & Tate, 1995). Another key tenet of critical race theory is praxis, or a commitment to social justice that strives toward eliminating racism and all other forms of oppression (Lawrence, 1995; Matsuda, Lawrence, Richard, & Crenshaw, 1993). Additionally, experiential knowledge of those who have been racially oppressed are considered sources of fulfillment, and communal empowerment (Valdes et al., 2002). Lastly, counterstorytelling reveals and interrogates dominant stories of racial privilege, or majoritarian stories, the "bundle of presuppositions, preconceived wisdoms and shared cultural understandings" that reinforce dominant ideology by centering the white, male, heterosexual, middle-class identity as the norm (Delgado, 1995; Delgado & Stefancic, 1993, p. 462; Yosso, 2006).

In the first segment of the pedagogy of counter-news-story, I draw from the central premise of critical race theory that racism is an enduring aspect of U.S. society, as well as the theory's critique of objectivity. For many of the students enrolled in the *Venceremos* course, they already intuit the insidious ways that racial categories, hierarchy and racism constitute society. In the course, they are exposed to scholarship that reveals how racial ideologies—like the one of white supremacy in U.S. culture—are reinscribed in ideological apparatuses like the media (Lewis, 2004). Notably, students start to comprehend how the seeming neutrality of objectivity normalizes a white male experience as a default perspective for journalists, recognizing the role of journalism textbooks to reinforce this standpoint (Alemán, 2011, 2014). Students are thus equipped to deconstruct news reports that present issues dichotomously and the ways in which they are flawed because they not only elide the power differentials between opposing sides, but because they also benefit those with power and privilege. As a result, the first phase of a pedagogy of counter-news-story exposes the constitutive nature of the media industry, particularly its role in preserving a white supremacist hierarchy of socially constructed racial categories under the semblance of balanced reporting.

The second stage of a pedagogy of counter-news-stories helps students distinguish the majoritarian stories embedded in the mainstream news reports. Catalyzed by the ways dominant discourses in mainstream media unfavorably impact representations of communities of color, *Venceremos* interrogates and opposes "the negative depictions of Chicanas/os which often appear in the media of the dominant culture," (Marcial, 1993, p. 2). Class discussions, then, elucidate the decades-long patterns of damaging coverage that have plagued communities of color. For instance, less than 1% of all network broadcast news stories annually, and 1% of newspaper articles, feature Latinas/os (Montalvo & Torres, 2006; Rivas-Rodriguez, 1998; Santa Ana, 2013). When Latina/os are included, reports tend to focus on "crime or festivals," and not unsurprisingly, on immigration as well (Heider, 2000, p. 51; Mize & Geedham, 2000). Accounts of race relations, racism, prejudice, or discrimination, issues central to the lives of racialized communities, are omitted (Poindexter, Smith, & Heider, 2003). Consequently, critical race theory affords *Venceremos'* student producers a language and a framework that affirms their beliefs that the depictions of lazy, immoral, lawless, or promiscuous Latinas/os rampant in the media stem from systems that recurrently celebrate and reproduce whiteness, rather than a cultural or biological pathology inherent in their communities and families. Students also begin to spot the majoritarian stories that situate the cause of disparities in educational achievement, income levels, incarceration rates, or health inequalities as stemming from the culture, morals, or work ethic of communities of color; in order to obfuscate the ways institutional policies and practices advantage white people. Together, these first two stages foster a sensibility similar to oppositional decoding—the manner in which audience members draw on their marginalized cultural, economic, class, racial, gender, religious identities and experiences to reject or resist hegemonic mediated content and messages that minimizes their experiences or reality—as described by Hall (1973).

During the third and final segment of the course, students craft their own counter-news-stories that will be published in *Venceremos*. A signature precept of critical race theory contends that the machinations of race and racism are best discerned through the experiential and embodied knowledge of those systematically subjected to racial and ethnic oppression (Delgado, 1995; Delgado & Stefancic, 2000, 2001; Yosso, 2006). Furthermore, the collective knowledge, strategies, and tactics used by underrepresented communities to navigate, survive and resist the socio-political legacies of oppression are underutilized yet vital sources of empowerment (Matsuda, 1995). *Venceremos* exists to glean these very tales, with its student journalists instinctively referring to their work as a counter to mainstream news, upholding critical race theory's assertion that communities of color rely on this form of storytelling to chronicle the oppressive structures within which they persevere. Moreover, the voices resounding from the pages of *Venceremos* stem from a legacy of Black and brown communities crusading against dismal reporting, challenging barriers to access and production, and producing publications that counter negative depictions (Cortes, 1983; del Olmo, 1971; Escalante, 1991; Gutiérrez, 1984; 1977; Lewels, 1974; Maldonado, 2000; Maxwell, 1988), as well as a radical racialized journalism practice (Bustillos, 1992; del Olmo, 1971; Kennedy, 1969; Rendón, 1974; Rendón & Reyes, 1971; Ruiz, 1977). Thus, in the culminating stage of the pedagogy of counter-news-story, students transition from critiquing mainstream models of journalism to developing and crafting a counter-news-story that seek to engage issues of social justice.

Venceremos students have produced over 300 counter-news-stories for publication, often about their racialized experiences as students of color in higher education, their bicultural and bilingual identities, their personal, collective and familial strategies for resisting systemic oppression, as well as stories about immigration, undocumented labor, cultural products and expressions, and both historical and contemporary legacies of leadership and activism in their communities. A key component of each of the counter-news-stories is to motivate their readers to be inspired by these journalistic testimonies to engage in activities or behaviors that can transform their communities. Oftentimes, for example, counter-news-stories direct readers to meetings, events, resources, or sources of information for them to pursue. This attribute is a source of pride and passion for many of the student contributors, who see the newspaper and classroom space as providing the opportunity for their readers "to be involved with decision-making that affects his or her communities," as one student explained. Another student similarly indicated that *Venceremos* counter-news-stories can empower "the community through journalism that creates revolutionary thinking." Instead of readers who "just see the issue and say, 'well that sucks for them, [it's] not our problem,'" stated one former student contributor, "We want them to say, 'that's not fair—what can we do about it?'" Fortified with a commitment to engendering activism and a critical media literacy through a social-justice oriented ethnic newspaper, the student contributors of *Venceremos* enroll in the course to produce the newspaper as a way to embody the civic engagement and offer alternative media content. This project, however, seeks to determine whether former student contributors sustain this activism or alter their consumption of media after enrolling in the *Venceremos* course, the next sections detail the results of this inquiry.

Measuring Student Impact

Two main methods guided the data collection aimed at measuring student impact. I used focus groups and an electronic survey to ask former *Venceremos* contributors about their experiences after working on the newspaper. Working with a student researcher, I held and conducted two focus groups with a dozen current and past contributors to *Venceremos*. Most had worked with *Venceremos* for at least three to five years, while the other focus group members had been connected to the paper for at least two years. In addition, I offered an electronic survey with closed and open-ended questions for participants who were unable to attend the focus group meeting. An additional nine contributors completed the survey, for a total of twenty-one contributors providing data about their involvement with *Venceremos* between 2008 and 2014.

Close to 70% of the respondents were female, and all identify as Chicana/o or Latina/o. Half of the respondents have continued their education, by either earning a Master's degree or enrolling in a Master's degree program. Both focus group participants and survey respondents to reflect on how their connection to *Venceremos* might have had an effect on their media consumption and the types of activism or civic engagement they have participated in since their involvement with the paper. The focus groups were transcribed and together with the responses from the qualitative and close-ended survey questions, they were analyzed for themes and patterns in how they understood the ways they had been influenced by *Venceremos*.

For example, responses to the questions about media consumption and media literacy were calculated to determine the proportion of students who indicated changed media consumption behavior. Their open-ended responses explaining their new media habits were grouped into themes and presented here as evidence of their changed behavior. Similarly, responses to questions about the types of civic engagement or activism they engage in after completing the *Venceremos* course were tabulated to assess the frequency for these activities. Again, examples of these behaviors, as well as explanations of these actions were categorized thematically and shared here. In the subsequent section, I lay out the key findings from this data.

Media Consumption and Civic Engagement

Analysis of the focus groups and survey responses revealed that as a result of the *Venceremos* course content and their work on the publication, students have altered their news media consumption habits and recast their understanding and performance of civic engagement. Every individual interviewed or surveyed indicated that following their enrollment in *Venceremos*, the quality and quantity of media sources they engage has been impacted, as has their level of engagement with news reports and their surrounding communities. Former *Venceremos* contributors now primarily consume alternative forms of news media consumption, maintain a healthy appetite for information, and actively share the news information they encounter. In addition, *Venceremos* students articulate an understanding of civic engagement fueled by social justice in ways that reflect the praxis of the *Venceremos* classroom/newsroom environment. For instance, non-traditional forms of activism—such as serving as mentors to other youth of color—is characterized as an ideal form of activist work. I will address these two areas separately below.

News Consumption

More than half of the contributors deliberately avoid mainstream media choices, with 70% rarely or ever watching national cable news, 55% rarely or never watching national broadcast news, and 66% rarely or never reading the statewide local daily newspaper. Indeed, 78% of them said they stopped watching, listening, or reading certain mainstream news sources entirely because they no longer trusted them to be accurate and they believe they reproduce mainstream discourses that often are hurtful to communities of color or other marginalized communities. A female focus group participant who was a writer for the publication explained, "because of *Venceremos,* I was aware there were counter narratives or a counter-side to mainstream media or mainstream reporting. I sought those [outlets] out and I think those [outlets] help keep me better informed about what's going on. I see that I try to be more aware of those other counter narratives." Instead, they engage national public radio, or online alternative news sources, like blogs, podcasts, or independent news organizations. One survey respondent who indicated that her preference is to "listen to a lot of public radio." Another male focus group participant who was a former distribution manager indicated, "the type of media I've come to consume a lot of now are podcasts or various YouTube channels. I don't read the local newspaper and I don't like reading things from established national papers." A female former editor who participated in a focus group indicated that she did not use to read, watch or follow news before enrolling in *Venceremos*, but now she regularly tunes into satirical news shows like the *Daily Show* and *The Colbert Report*, as well as reads the *Huffington Post* and other outlets on her social media news feed.

In fact, several students indicated that their news sources are now often those that convey information via social media, as they follow organizations or sites that align with their political and ideological views such as *Colorlines, Democracy Now, and Racialicious.* Those that watch mainstream news broadcasts, do so to keep abreast of the frames and arguments used in the mainstream press about the matters that impact their Latinas/o and Chicana/o community the most. A little more than a third of all former contributors indicated that they purposefully consume this type of media to be aware of the type of rhetoric, discourses, or arguments used to negatively represent social or racial justice issues they care about. After being in the *Venceremos* class, a female editor and writer student shared during the focus group that she "started watching Fox News to get to know another viewpoint, but it makes me feel so annoyed. I stick with it because it helps me articulate arguments against *that* way of thinking." Another female student in a focus group also shared that she uses what she learned in the class to compare the news frames used in the news outlets she consumes, which include CNN and Fusion.

But for the most part, they, like many of their generation, rely on alternative online news sources. Over 55% said they often or always get their news via social media. "I like going for convenience," explained one survey respondent. "For instance, my Instagram and Facebook is what I grab most and it's filled with critical news, alternative media, which was influenced by *Venceremos.*" Another male focus group participant who regularly contributed to *Venceremos* after taking the course stated that "all my news comes via online outlets nowadays." Likewise, another female focus group participant stated, "social media definitely plays a big role in where I get my news and information from." Importantly, students indicated that they visit multiple news sites to stay informed. For instance, one former female contributor indicated in her survey response that she visits "a lot of different news outlets" because "they each have different perspectives so it's nice to look at that and compare and develop your own perspective on how you feel about a topic." This purposeful pursuit of information was common amongst all twenty-one contributors, who similarly reflected that they seek out news in ways they did not before. For instance, if an issue arises that captures their attention, they will go to multiple sources to learn about it, rather than accept a single version of that news item. In fact, almost 70% of former contributors shared that they often go online after hearing a news report from either a friend, social media, or on the television to look for an alternative or additional perspectives to help inform their understanding of that issue.

They also purposefully choose to share news via their social media networks in ways they did not before. Over 65% of former *Venceremos* students share alternative news reports via their own social media accounts when there is a major news story covered in mainstream media that affects the marginalized communities they care about. One participant indicated they had never posted or shared news reports before being enrolled in the *Venceremos* course and only began doing this regularly after his involvement. Social media accounts function as an additional platform for them to make sure friends and family members get access to the alternative sources they feel provide information that is empowering and useful. They also said they appreciate their like-minded friends connecting them with new and alternative sites and voices to stay informed. Additionally, a little over two-thirds of all participants indicated that they advise members of their Latina/o and Chicana/o communities to seek other news sources when they observe that they are consuming a news source that negatively represents racialized communities.

A final impact on news consumption is that all former *Venceremos* contributors claimed that they have a different lens from which to evaluate news content they consume. As a result of the class and publishing the newspaper, they do not view news as neutral or objective, but rather understand it as produced through a specific worldview. For example, one female student stated that "*Venceremos* helped me learn there is no neutral truth or perspective. ... I remember discussions about the holes in mainstream media that were missing out on communities of color. I think those discussions really helped me realize how little media coverage there is and how there is an agenda and knowing that helped me in how I engage in media now." Another male focus group participant who helped to sell advertising for the publication indicated that "one of the things I feel I learned is that news content is based on where you're coming from, what's your perspective; so, I completely have come to disbelieve anybody that tries to tell me that is the truth." Yet another female focus group participant stated, "*Venceremos* basically opened the gateway for me to be able to understand what I'm reading and understand that there are two sides to everything. It helped me realize how biased the media is, in the sense of how negatively they frame our community." Many former students enrolled in *Venceremos* indicate that they have a distaste for news presented as purely objective, preferring instead to consume news reports that acknowledge a particular epistemological stance. Interestingly, a quarter of them indicated they often critique the stereotyping, negative frames or mainstream sources out loud when watching, listening, or reading the news source. Overall, all study participants indicate that they believe their experience producing *Venceremos* in a classroom setting that deconstructs the ideologies informing mainstream news patterns has made them critical news consumers.

Social Justice-Based Civic Engagement

A second prominent finding that emerged was that *Venceremos* contributors recast their understanding of civic engagement since being involved with the newspaper. About half of the focus group and survey participants employed an activist orientation—clearly fused by a commitment to social justice—to define, describe, and explain forms or levels of civic engagement. As one male focus group participant explained that traditional or non-critical forms of civic engagement can include participating "in the system to be a good citizen and what everybody should do—vote, register to vote, campaign for a candidate, or run for office yourself." However, he adds that when fueled by a greater understanding of social justice, your activism is rooted in trying to "change the system, particularly systems of oppression and privilege." This type of "activism advocates for a shift in power" while conventional forms of "civic engagement maintains the status quo." Another female focus group participant also described a social-justice based form of civic engagement as requiring an understanding of the "structural issues that create the conditions in the first place and the experience of marginalization within larger oppressive systems." Activists with this perspective, are often the individuals who organize and create a rally or protest around that issue." Those without this insight, "show up to the event, and but can't articulate a deep understanding of the problem and want a quick fix to the matter." They acknowledge that traditional civic engagement can be a support system for activism rooted in a sense of social justice, but prefer or admire activism that "occurs at a deeper, more critical level." A few expressed frustration with their college student peers who participate in civic engagement activities on campus, indicating that they see many who "show up because it looks good and they can put it on their resume—but will they stay involved after graduation?" For *Venceremos* students, activism fueled by a sense of social-justice should be a life-long commitment and be reflected in the values you live by.

A significant number of former *Venceremos* contributors also gave examples of their social-justice based advocacy efforts since enrolling in the course. For example, about three-fourths of them have marched or attended a public demonstration addressing issues of social justice, with another half of them actually coordinating a public demonstration or meeting about inequities themselves. Approximately 75% of them have become members of formal and informal organizations that advocate for educational equity, immigrant reform, DREAMer rights, and racial profiling. Significantly, all of the participants said they have volunteered with a non-profit two or more times after their work on *Venceremos*. One survey respondent expressed that politically, *Venceremos* "has empowered me to challenge systems that are currently in place for the betterment of the larger population."

Contacting key decision-makers and policy-shapers is another type of social justice-based activism students noted they have consistently pursued frequently following their enrollment in the *Venceremos* course. One former survey respondent said that the class and newspaper helped them "connect to my culture in a way that makes it easier to stand up for what is right when I see oppression." Indeed, half of them have called, emailed and written to an elected official, non-profit organization, government agency, community leader, school official, business leader, or media outlet at least twice since contributing to the newspaper. All participants affirmed that they have signed an online petition in support of social justice causes, or against damaging or discriminatory policies or practices at least twice since being enrolled in the class. Close to 90% used social media to share information about protests, community meetings, letter-writing campaigns, or online petitions with friends, family, and other members of their on- and off-campus communities. Over a third of them have submitted an article, commentary, or feature to a media outlet besides *Venceremos*, after moving on from the class and publication. One student credited *Venceremos* for teaching him "how to communicate and navigate thoroughly in unwelcoming environments," and perspectives. Together, these efforts reveal the ways *Venceremos* contributors embody the principles of the course and newspaper by ensuring their voices are heard by key individuals in crucial spaces of political power.

Moreover, over 50% of these former students are quite philanthropic, donating money to a social justice cause since their enrollment in the course. In addition, a quarter of them indicated they have donated funds to such causes or organizational efforts six or more times. One survey respondent offers an apt explanation for why so many former *Venceremos* students have such a high degree of investment in their communities: "*Venceremos* has personally showed me that you have more control that you think. Developing my critical lens has helped me cope with injustice, and strategies for development. If you don't know where you stand in the picture, you don't understand what you have to overcome. I strongly feel that you need to be in tuned with whatever culture, and/or environment you are in, in order to be a part of the strategies for success for your community."

Notably, a large degree of the participants characterized a couple of uncommon undertakings as forms of social-justice fueled civic engagement. For instance, multiple former *Venceremos* contributors cite their commitment to mentoring youth into the higher education pipeline, towards a more positive racial identity, and towards a critical consciousness as one the most important forms of activism they engage in. Several explained that they feel obligated to pass on the critical awareness they have acquired through *Venceremos* to others. One male student stated, "It's my turn to teach what I know and what I have learned and teach it to people a little younger than me. *Venceremos* was really was the gateway for me to live my life while being an activist. One of the ways I do that is to teach the younger generations how to stand up for themselves and how to fight the good fight." Importantly, 87% of respondents cited their own personal perseverance through higher education as a form of activism. One female student explained that when she "realized higher education wasn't a system made for her, that knowledge helped me see my participation and success in it as a way of actively countering the system." A few indicated that the efforts they made to either maintain or acquire the ability to read and speak Spanish represented a form of activism because it "counters a loss of culture and identity" that has been actively perpetrated "against my people and my community." What this points to is that engagement with alternative media outlet like *Venceremos* has helped these former student contributors develop deep and nuanced understandings of the ways inequities are reinscribed institutionally and, more importantly, how this knowledge can help them dismantle these structures in subversive and sustainable ways.

Implications

This chapter sought to explore the influence a distinctive alternative Chicana/o student newspaper, and the classroom in which it is created, had on its own student producers. As is evident from the focus groups and survey results, the social justice framework of both the *Venceremos* course and newspaper have impacted media consumption and articulations of civic involvement in the following ways (1) students have changed their news media consumption habits, steadily consuming non-mainstream forms of news media and actively sharing the news information they encounter via critical media literacies and (2) students draw from a sense of social justice to inform their active and frequent forms of civic engagement, including non-traditional forms of activism. Both the study and its findings have at least four implications for media and communication scholars and educators.

For one, the study opens up an almost untouched area research about the impact of producing an ethnic student newspaper on college students. Very little scholarship exists on the impact of daily campus student newspapers. This study focused on outcomes beyond determining the percentage of graduates who acquired a job in the media industry, or what skill sets were marketable. Rather, this project investigated how former communication students and students with other majors have learned to engage the micro and macro communication processes that manufacture and dismantle systems of oppression and privilege.

A second point worthy of consideration is that when the media industry has paid attention to this community, it has approached them as consumer market, identifiable by a shared use of the Spanish language, or a generalized Latina/o identity (Astroff, 1988; Dávila, 2001; Gutiérrez, 1990; Levine, 2001; Rodriguez, 1999). The student producers of *Venceremos* correspondingly intuit that this simplistic and profit-driven understanding of Chicana/o and Latina/o communities is short-sighted and underserves this population. Rather than replicating traditional news models in Spanish, media educators should reimagine models that better represent these racialized and bicultural experiences.

Another broader implication to consider is how the students' involvement with *Venceremos* reveals which traditional journalism models that are no longer viable for members of Latina/o and Chicana/o communities. The students who work on *Venceremos* represent an increasingly growing segment of our population of bicultural and acculturated Chicanas/os and Latinas/os whose news choices and habits do not follow traditional models (Poindexter, Heider, & McCombs, 2006). Communication educators should be spurred to reflect about how a social-justice informed pedagogy could be employed in journalism classrooms to cultivate the type of media practitioners who can better serve this increasingly diverse and politically savvy audience that is growing every day, and want their local news to function as a good neighbor rather than a watch dog. Moreover, they should explore how to revamp journalism curriculum so that it can equip media students with a passion and skill set that empowers them to create meaningful media content that honestly and accurately reflects the racialized experiences students like those involved with *Venceremos* are actively seeking to read about.

Lastly, for communication educators who use a critical, social justice-minded, or democratic communication pedagogy, there is some useful data here about how this real-world collective endeavor to publish counter narratives for and about Latinas/os engenders the type of impact those approaches seek to foster. Educators who approach their teaching with a social-justice orientation endeavor to cultivate students who are mindful and active civic agents, who can help to build a vibrant, healthy and just society. The critical media literacy and activist behaviors that result after taking the *Venceremos* course mapped out in this study enact the idealized civically and democratically engaged student critical communication pedagogues desire. Moreover, the *Venceremos* class experiences highlights the social role journalism is meant to fulfill: inspiring participation in civic society, by "stimulating debates on public issues, serving as watchdog against abuse of power" (Costera Meijer, 2010, p. 327). The lack of this type of dynamic democratic participation is one of the lamentations of social justice-minded media scholars and educators who claim that this function of the press has become destabilized and eclipsed by the drive for profit. As such, communication classrooms that help to craft and theorize an alternative journalism practice for disenfranchised communities show utility in cultivating a social justice fueled political engagement in students, as well as a critical media literacy. In conclusion, communication classrooms like the *Venceremos* that draw on social justice-based pedagogies to produce media content laced with social justice goals, have much to offer its multiple stakeholders—educators, media students, and marginalized communities alike.

Note

1. Using a combination of electronic surveys and paper surveys, we have only been able to successfully survey about 100 readers between 2010 and 2014. This small sample has predominantly included on-campus readers, as our off-campus readers have been more difficult to canvas. Of those respondents, over 60% said they were inspired to get involved with an issue after reading about it in *Venceremos*, including emailing a leader or politician (65%), attending a public meeting or protest regarding the issue (50%), and joining an organization addressing that issue (40%).

References

Alemán, S. M. (2011). Chicana/o student journalists map out a Chicana/o journalism practice. *Journalism Practice, 5*(3), 1–18.

Alemán, S. M. (2014). Reimagining journalism education through a pedagogy of counter-news-story. *Review of Education, Pedagogy, and Cultural Studies, 36*(2), 109–126.

Astroff, R. J. (1988). Spanish gold: Stereotypes, ideology, and the construction of a US Latino market. *Howard Journal of Communications, 1*(4), 155–173.

Bustillos, E. (1992). *Chicano journalism, its history and its use as a weapon for liberation.* San Diego, CA: Self published.

Cortes, C. E. (1983). The greaser's revenge to boulevard nights: The mass media curriculum on Chicanos. In M. T. Garcia, F. Lomerli, M. Barrera, E. Escobar, & J. Garcia (Eds.), *History, culture, and society: Chicano studies in the 1980s* (pp. 125–140). Ypsilanti, MI: Bilingual Press/Editorial Bilingue.

Costera Meijer, I. (2010). Democratizing journalism? Realizing the citizen's agenda for local news media. *Journalism Studies, 11*(3), 327–342.

Dávila, A. (2001). *Latinos Inc.: The marketing and making of a people.* Berkeley, CA: University of California Press.

del Olmo, F. (1971). Voices for the Chicano movimiento. *Quill, October*, 9–11.

Delgado, R. (1995). *The Rodrigo chronicles: Conversations about America and race.* New York, NY: New York University Press.

Delgado, R., & Stefancic, J. (1993). Critical race theory: An annotated bibliography. *Virginia Law Review, 79*(2), 461–516.

Delgado, R., & Stefancic, J. (2000). *Critical race theory: The cutting edge*. Philadelphia, PA: Temple University Press.

Delgado, R., & Stefancic, J. (2001). *Critical race theory: An introduction*. New York, NY: New York University Press.

Escalante, V. (1991). In pursuit of ethnic audiences: The media and Latinos. *Renato Rosaldo Lecture Series Monograph, 7*, 29–53.

Gutiérrez, F. (1977). Spanish-language media in America: Background, resources, history. *Journalism History, 4*(2), 65–67.

Gutiérrez, F. (1984). Spanish language media in the U.S. *Caminos, 5*(1), 10–12.

Gutiérrez, F. (1990). Advertising and growth of minority markets and media. *Journal of Communication Inquiry, 14*(1), 6–16.

Hall, S. (1973). *Encoding and decoding in the television discourse*. Birmingham: Centre for Cultural Studies, University of Birmingham.

Heider, D. (2000). *White news: Why local news programs don't cover people of color*. Mahwah, NJ: Lawrence Erlbaum Associates.

Kennedy, D. (1969). The Chicano press. *Missouri Library Association Quarterly, 30*(3), 221–224.

Ladson-Billings, G. (1998). Just what is critical race theory and what's it doing in a nice field like education? *International Journal of Qualitative Studies in Education, 11*(1), 7–24.

Ladson-Billings, G., & Tate, W. (1995). Toward a critical race theory of education. *Teachers College Record, 97*(1), 45–68.

Lawrence, C. (1995). The word and the river: Pedagogy as scholarship as struggle. In K. Crenshaw, N. Gotanda, G. Peller, & K. Thomas (Eds.), *Critical race theory: The key writings that formed the movement* (pp. 336–351). New York, NY: The New Press.

Levine, E. (2001). Constructing a market, constructing an ethnicity: US Spanish-language media and the formation of a syncretic Latino/a identity. *Studies in Latin American Popular Culture, 20*, 33–50.

Lewels, J., & Francisco J. (1974). *The uses of the media by the Chicano Movement: A study in minority access*. New York, NY: Praeger Publishers.

Lewis, A. (2004). "What group?" Studying whites and whiteness in the era of "colorblindness." *Sociological Theory, 22*(4), 623–646.

Maldonado, C. S. (2000). Social and historical context. In *Colegio Cesar Chavez, 1973–1983: A Chicano struggle for educational self-determination* (pp. 9–26). New York, NY: Garland Publishing.

Marcial, G. (1993, Fall). Venceremos is here!, house editorial. *Venceremos*.

Matsuda, M. (1995). Looking to the bottom: Critical legal studies and reparations. In K. Crenshaw, N. Gotanda, & G. Peller (Eds.), *Critical race theory: The key writings that formed the movement* (pp. 63–79). New York, NY: New Press.

Matsuda, M., Lawrence, C., Richard, D., & Crenshaw, K. (1993). *Words that wound: Critical race theory, assaultive speech, and the First Amendment*. Boulder, CO: Westview.

Maxwell, R. (1988). The Chicano movement, the broadcast reform movement, and the sociology of "minorities and media:" A study of cultural hegemony in the United States. *Confluencia, 3*(2), 89–102.

Mize, R. L., & Geedham, C. (2000). Manufacturing bias: An analysis of newspaper coverage of Latino immigration issues. *Latino Studies Journal, 11*(2), 88–107.

Montalvo, D., & Torres, J. (2006). *National Association of Hispanic Journalists Network Brownout Report 2006: The portrayal of Latinos and Latino issues on network television news, 2005.* Washington, DC: National Association of Hispanic Journalists.

Parker, L., & Lynn, M. (2002). What's race got to do with it? Critical race theory conflicts with and connections to qualitative research methodology and epistemology. *Qualitative Inquiry, 8*(1), 7–22.

Poindexter, P. M., Heider, D., & McCombs, M. (2006). Watchdog or good neighbor? The public's expectations of local news. *The Harvard International Journal of Press/Politics, 11*(1), 77–88.

Poindexter, P. M., Smith, L., & Heider, D. (2003). Race and ethnicity in local television news: Framing, story assignments, and source selection. *Journal of Broadcasting and Electronic Media, 47*(4), 524–536.

Rendón, A. (1974). *The Chicano press: A status report on the needs and trends in Chicano journalism.* Washington, DC: Rendón.

Rendón, A., & Reyes, D. N. (1971). *Chicanos and the mass media.* Washington, DC: National Mexican American Anti-Defamation Committee.

Rivas-Rodriguez, M. (1998). *Brown eyes on the web.* Chapel Hill, NC: University of North Carolina Press.

Rodriguez, A. (1999). *Making Latino news: Race, language, class.* Thousand Oaks, CA: Sage Publications.

Ruiz, R. (1977). The Chicanos and the underground press. *La Raza, 3*, 43–44.

Santa Ana, O. (2013). *Juan in a hundred: The representation of Latinos on network news.* Austin, TX: University of Texas Press.

Valdes, F., Culp, J. M., & Harris, A. P. (2002). *Crossroads, directions, and a new critical race theory.* Philadelphia, PA: Temple University Press.

Venceremos. (2008). Editorial: Venceremos is back! *7*(1), 1.

Yosso, T. J. (2006). *Critical race counterstories along the Chicana/Chicano educational pipeline.* New York, NY: Routledge.

15. *Lessons From Migrant Youth: Digital Storytelling and the Engaged Humanities in Springfield, MA*

Rogelio Miñana

In an academic environment currently dominated by market-driven and quantifiable data, the traditional Humanities are suffering from ever-decreasing funding opportunities (internal as well as external) and an equally shrinking pool of potential majors. In times of economic hardship and high tuition fees, literature, philosophy, or history simply don't hold the promise of financial return that business or engineering seemingly guarantee. However, the potential of traditional Humanities to evolve and adapt to new social realities should not be underestimated. Humanistic disciplines do not have to remain stagnant, particularly if we regard social justice as a significant pursuit of the larger humanistic endeavor. Technology and civic engagement offer struggling Humanities departments the opportunity to interact with students and society alike in ways previously unimaginable.

In the end, the alleged crisis of the Humanities combined with new pedagogical and technological tools may persuade some humanists to take to the streets (quite literally) to work with and learn from our communities as we tackle inequality as one of the greatest humanistic challenges of our time. In no academic area may this be more pertinent and necessary than in the languages, and specifically in U.S. Spanish departments. Latinas/os, most of whom prove culturally engaged with their Latino heritage, have become the largest minority in the country. As a highly diverse ethnic group with a significant presence in most areas of the country, their economic, political, and cultural influence continues to grow while mainstream misconceptions stubbornly perpetuate the framing of Latinas/os as second class citizens.

In this chapter[1] I will present and discuss the lessons I and my college students learned from a digital storytelling workshop we carried out with migrant youth, mostly from Guatemala. After I describe the overall project, I will examine in detail our technology-enhanced and community-based methodology. Finally, I will discuss the lessons learned from our migrant partners, and from our own mistakes. In the conclusion, I will situate this course in the aforementioned debate on the crisis of the Humanities, and reframe our class as an opportunity to advance the Humanities and its social justice pursuit in a digital context.

The Promoting Bilingual Literacy Project

In the fall semester of 2014 at Mount Holyoke College in South Hadley, Massachusetts I offered the interdisciplinary and community-based course, Promoting Bilingual Literacy through Digital Storytelling in Springfield, Massachusetts. In order to examine how digital storytelling (DST) may enhance bilingual literacy, the class was articulated around a digital storytelling workshop imparted in Springfield by my long-time community partner, the office of Community Engagement at WGBY (channel 57), Western Massachusetts' public television station. My twelve enrolled students assisted ten Spanish-speaking migrants from Guatemala and Mexico between the ages of 18 and 21 during the completion of the workshop led by Vanessa Pabón, Community Engagement Director, and her team. Classroom-based, theoretical sessions were conducted at Mount Holyoke College and the DST workshop with migrant youth took place at WGBY headquarters in Springfield, Massachusetts.

Built around the hands-on workshop, classroom-based sessions examined the role of digital storytelling in teaching English for Speakers of Other Languages (ESOL), particularly with Latino communities (I will elaborate on this point in the next section). Additionally, and in the context of recent Central American migration into the U.S., my students examined digital storytelling as a space for self-expression and confidence-building for young migrants. This course featured a hands-on and experimental approach that encouraged students to bring their own interests and disciplinary expertise into their projects. It demanded a concurrent, informed, critical, and self-reflective approach in order to evaluate and refine our experimental use of DST to promote bilingualism. Some of the long-term questions we posed include: How can DST most effectively promote bilingual literacy and reading? What research questions and methodologies may best help us evaluate and improve our use of DST with migrant populations?

Given the broadly interdisciplinary scope of this course, which includes Cultural Studies, Latina/o Studies, Educational Studies, and Participatory Action Research, I compiled an annotated bibliography on a number of topics (digital storytelling, community-based digital humanities, bilingual literacy, and action research, among others) that can be articulated, emphasized, and expanded depending on students' interests and disciplinary skills. I will cite several of these studies in the next section. Our class and my long-time community partner at WGBY 57 collaborated with the Massachusetts Migrant Education Program (MMEP) out of Northampton, Massachusetts, to complement their English as a Second Language instruction for Central American migrant youth with our bilingual DST workshop.

Concrete student projects, which could potentially be compiled in e-portfolios, posted on a website, or disseminated via other digital means, included:

1. digital stories produced by migrant youth with assistance from a team of Mount Holyoke students. Authors voluntarily gave us written consent to use their stories for public showcases and online sharing;
2. research projects (a humanistic scholarly paper, a qualitative analysis, or even a digital story or other creative projects) on the digital stories produced by participants or the experimental pedagogy employed in this course;
3. a web-based forum (accessible only to enrolled students) that collectively addressed questions related to digital storytelling and bilingual literacy. This forum intertwined references to required weekly readings with experiences and concrete examples from our on-site work.

With a minimum language requirement of fourth semester of Spanish, this course attracted mostly Spanish, Education, Anthropology, and Sociology majors (Mount Holyoke does not offer a major in Communications). Previous technological skills in DST or ESOL pedagogy were not required. Ultimately, my students gained experience in video production, adult and English as a Second Language education, and participatory action research. Furthermore, they experimented with the use of DST to foster bilingual literacy by creating group activities, monitoring the progress made by workshop participants, and proposing changes (some for immediate application, others for future iterations) to both the workshop and the course structures. We requested and received Institutional Review Board approval to conduct research with human subjects and obtained consent from all our participants to showcase, post, and employ their digital stories for a variety of activist and scholarly purposes. Before I analyze in detail the actual implementation of our project, let me outline a concise history of the digital storytelling activism in Springfield that made our work possible in the first place.

Digital Storytelling in Springfield, Massachusetts: A Brief Overview

Digital stories are generally understood as a two to five-minute recorded voiceover illustrated with still images or video in which the author recounts a significant episode in her or his life story. Edited with non-professional software such as Moviemaker, PhotoVoice, or iMovie, these short videos usually include a soundtrack as well as simple transition effects. The narration features a conversational tone, for the personal pictures and/or symbolic images that illustrate the voiceover aim to elicit an emotional reaction from the viewer (Lambert, 2008, 2013; Ohler, 2006). Over the years, this basic definition has expanded to include slightly different formats and topics, such as videos focusing on community (rather than personal) issues and stories.

The potential for community-building underlying this alternative, participatory, and digital form of storytelling is best appreciated when we consider the variety of its applications and objectives. An educational, therapeutic, and activist tool (Juppi, 2012; Neilsen, 2006), digital storytelling programs spring in communities all over the world with somewhat different goals, formats, and methods, but with a common focus on self-representation and community-building. Both participatory and deeply personal, these initiatives often develop within the context of community activism around issues of language identity, education, youth, and healthcare, among others (Halleck, 2002). In South Africa and Egypt, for instance, digital storytelling programs have been implemented to promote bilingualism at school, while in the U.S. they have supported ESOL curricula (Ajayi, 2009; Hunt, 2007; McGuinnis, 2007; Sadik, 2008), as we did in our own project.

Numerous youth projects out of Chicago (Digital Youth Network), Stanford University (YouthLab), the University of California at Berkeley (Digital Youth Project), and New York (Global Action Project), among others, employ digital storytelling as a tool for self-expression and as means to raise collective awareness on issues such as migration and domestic violence (Juppi, 2012; Lundby, 2008). Although not always, these projects often work with at-risk or under-represented youth (Coryat, 2011; Notley & Tacchi, 2005; Pearson Hathorn, 2005; Wolske et al., 2008). Beyond age groups, many scholars emphasize the potentially therapeutic effects of exercising self-representation and sharing personal stories with others, especially in the case of traditionally marginalized groups as well as trauma victims (Goldfarb,

2002; Neilsen, 2006). For the broader society, digital storytelling has helped promote and enact community health initiatives across the country (Wilkin & Ball-Rokeach, 2006). On a global scale, indigenous media or what John Downing (Downing, Ford, Gil, & Stein, 2001) calls radical media in general, including movements such as the Zapatistas in Southern Mexico, have employed digital storytelling to foster self-expression and educate local populations in computer literacy (Wilson & Stewart, 2008). Beyond community activism, these initiatives also serve another radical and essential purpose, as under-represented groups such as indigenous communities share local issues with global audiences through platforms such as YouTube, websites like Enlace Zapatista, and social media.

Across the country, a number of community media and digital storytelling projects specifically target Latina/o communities in ways that both overlap and differ from the brand of media activism that my community partners in Western Massachusetts practice. Most of these Latino-oriented programs are curricular and/or research-based. Outside the classroom, in her 2006 dissertation Luisa E. Lara examines the role that technology plays in the lives of young immigrant Latinas in an Ohio high school. Although written only a few years ago, the emergence of social media and newer video editing software have since profoundly altered the media landscape described in this study. More up to date, Patricia Ramirez's (2010) unpublished dissertation analyzes a digital storytelling program for Latino immigrant families at the Parents, Children, and Computers project in California. Although methodologically meticulous, this study limits its scope mostly to issues of representation and self-image, which detracts from its potential value towards a deeper understanding of the broader impact of Latina/o community media activism.

A handful of school projects across the country illuminate the curricular potential of technology and digital storytelling for Latina/o organizing and outreach. Already in 1998, a pioneer project in Santa Clara, California, paired Spanish-language and filmmaking students with Sacred Heart Parish residents in the production of short videos on community issues. Due to time and logistical constraints, in the end the student-resident teams produced only one video, which was showcased to the whole community at an event that also included a conversation with faculty, students, and residents involved in the project (Darias et al., 1999). Several of my own recent courses follow a similar methodology, although advances in technology and community-based pedagogy have likely made production and logistics a less arduous process than it was in the late-1990s. Along the lines of her previous work on Latina *testimonios*, Rina Benmayor (2008) employs digital stories in an undergraduate seminar as means for self-expression and empowerment. In a more explicitly community-oriented way, Katynka Z. Martínez (2011) analyzes how a group of high school students enrolled in an animation course in Los Angeles, California, adapt the classic video game Pac-Man to Latina/o-specific interests and surroundings. Students' free-spirited versions introduce such topics as immigration, the Minutemen, homelessness, and poverty in the originally minimal design of the legendary game. In Martínez's reading, the digital remake of Pac-Man enables teenage participants to articulate their own socio-economic and cultural outlook on the local community. Back in Western Massachusetts, Mari Castañeda (2011) offers a seminar in partnership with Natalia Muñoz, founder of *La Prensa del Oeste de Massachusetts*, in which students (most of them non-Latino) carry out a scholarly and ethnographic examination of the landscape of community media in the area. Among other issues, they ponder Internet access, linguistic skills, and political involvement as determining factors in community media's ability to reach local audiences.

Although in partnership with higher learning institutions, Ms. Pabón and her team at WGBY 57 extend their activities well beyond the learning goals, scholarly objectives, and academic calendar of any particular course or research project such as my own class. Outside the constraints of academia, Ms. Pabón's Telling Our Legacies Digitally (TOLD) and the Latino Youth Media Institute (LYMI) projects, without which my work in Springfield could not have been possible, grow out of the community itself and seek long-term interventions across a broad variety of fields that commonly involve multiple partners. Ms. Pabón founded the Latino Youth Media Institute in 2008 with a Corporation for Public Broadcasting Local Service Initiative Grant. She received support from WGBY 57's C.E.O. Russ Peotter and the station's Latino Advisory Board (LAB), a body of some twelve to twenty local leaders in the political, journalistic, educational, and cultural arenas, with significant but not exclusive Latina/o membership. The LYMI's immediate goal is to provide paid internships for young Latinas/os who wish to pursue a career in media. Over the last seven years, approximately eighty Latinas/os have received training and gained significant experience in digital storytelling workshops, video and television production, image and sound editing, as well as in writing, anchoring, and marketing a variety of news segments and community events. Besides LYMI interns, the WGBY 57 Community Engagement office, which Ms. Pabón directs, employs Verónica García (an Ecuadorian with ample experience in journalism and video production) as Community Engagement Assistant.

In tandem with other organizations and partners, the Community Engagement office conceives, develops, and staffs a variety of initiatives mostly related to digital storytelling and mainly directed at the Latina/o communities of Springfield and Holyoke. The first of such projects, Telling Our Legacies Digitally (TOLD), began four years before the LYMI's founding and is still going strong more than ten years later. TOLD trains community residents in digital storytelling through free-of-charge workshops. Ms. Pabón, who holds two associate degrees in web design and graphic arts, and is certified by MIT's Media Lab and the Center for Digital Storytelling as digital storytelling instructor, first launched this project as an outreach and organizing tool in 2004. As Director of Community Engagement at WGBY, she revived and redeveloped the TOLD project in 2010, which to date has collected and hosts with authors' consent over a hundred digital stories on its YouTube channel (see https://www.youtube.com/user/WGBYStories). TOLD/LYMI also organize several community showcases and events every year, and has plans to air more digital stories on WGBY 57.

A generous grant from the Mellon-funded Five College Digital Humanities Program enabled me to offer in the fall of 2014 a digital storytelling course for Central American migrant youth, a fast-growing but commonly transient population settling in Springfield in considerable numbers in recent years. The differences between the predominantly Puerto Rican North End community and Central American migrants are many, chief amongst them the fact that Puerto Ricans, even if born in the island, hold U.S. citizenship by birthright. In contrast, Central Americans enter the country as immigrants—often unauthorized and, in many cases, as unaccompanied minors. At the risk of experiencing double marginalization for their legal status and Central American provenance (the great majority of Latinas/os in the area come from the Caribbean), this budding community of mostly young workers in the agricultural and service industries frequently lacks the means and opportunity to enroll in school, benefit from social programs, or even learn English.

In partnership with other local organizations such as the Massachusetts Migrant Education Program, the Brightwood Clinic, and the Grey House, I applied for funding in 2013 to recruit young migrants for a digital storytelling workshop integrated into my advanced Spanish and Educational Studies seminar on bilingual literacy. Though with great logistical and scheduling challenges, the first iteration of this course proved a resounding success for the five Latina/o participants who completed the course (ten migrants enrolled initially and eight attended multiple sessions as their personal and work schedules allowed). Their stories were shown at WGBY headquarters on December 7, 2014 to an audience of approximately 60 members of the community and other non-profit staffers. Although material benefits may not be measurable or even relevant in this context, participants unanimously described this experience as empowering and life-changing for the following two main reasons.

First, mostly inexperienced in technology other than cell phones, participants learned computer skills such as searching for information online, image and sound editing, video editing, and others. Secondly and most importantly, however, the workshop provided them with a physical and virtual space in which to tell their own stories in the first person. The experience of being heard and seen, as well as the praise they commanded for both their finished videos and extraordinary life stories, proved a powerful and rather novel feeling for all of them. Despite the phenomenal hardships endured by these youth (the oldest participants were only 21 years old), they consistently and forcefully articulated a message of hope and optimism. From different points of view, their WGBY digital stories illustrate how obstacles can be overcome and dreams pursued even in the more adverse of circumstances.

Engaged Scholarship: A Technology-Enhanced and Community-Based Methodology

Recently I summarized the guiding principles of my community-based work in the acronym C.R.E.A.R (which in Spanish means to create or to make). Based on the budding body of literature on the subject and my own experience, I identified Content, Reciprocity, Effort, Awareness, and Responsibility as the key features of my community-based courses and research. Engaged courses build on rigorous academic content; the relationship with the community must be mutually beneficial and rest on the principle of reciprocity; it takes considerable effort to prepare, implement, and advance campus-community projects; awareness of one's as well as others' socio-economic, gender, racial, ethnic, national, cultural, and religious location is critical to the examination of power relations that should sustain any CBL experience; and the responsibility towards the course and the community extends well beyond the classroom walls and the academic term (Miñana, 2016a).

On the basis of these guiding principles, my community-based work, centered around the use of digital storytelling, seeks to initiate what I called elsewhere the cycle of community media activism. We produce digital stories in a collaborative and inclusive way, involving many constituents such as college students, community members, communication professionals, as well as local political, educational, and business leaders. We aim to generate multimedia and multimodal final products that can migrate across multiple media platforms in order to engage various constituents and institutions. Employing different media formats (the Internet, print media, and audio) as well as modes of expression and dissemination (written, sonic, visual) enables community media users to enter the cycle of activism at any time, by different means, and for various purposes. In collaboration with activist, media, and academic partners, we strive to disseminate our work across different public spaces, adapting our ways of delivery and modes of expression to various target audiences. Finally, by making our final products readily shareable, we aim to complete the cycle of media activism by inciting project participants, whether producers or consumers, to take action. Action can potentially take many forms, from simply learning about under-represented groups such as unauthorized migrants to informing the general public of issues that mainstream media neglect to cover or do so in prejudiced or incomplete ways. In the end, community actions and achievements should feed back into the production of new work, thus perpetuating the cycle of community media activism (Miñana, 2016b).

The methodology I employed in my Promoting Bilingual Literacy course draws on the community work and cyclical media activism I outlined above. My direct involvement in many TOLD/LYMI projects positions me as a practitioner of Participatory Action Research (PAR). In this model, scholars and community members address an issue or problem by collectively designing, conducting, and disseminating research with the ultimate goal to take concrete action (McIntyre, 2008, p. 1). Over the last six years I have engaged in several teaching and scholarly projects around digital storytelling in which essential decisions on topics and methodologies have been made in consultation with TOLD/LYMI staff and with explicit consent from community residents. In that regard, my work loosely benefits from what Norman Denzin (2003) calls performative ethnography, which turns the practice of cultural studies into "public pedagogy [that] employs the aesthetic and performative in the effort to portray the interactions connecting politics, institutions, and experience" (Kincheloe & McLaren, 2008, p. 418). The lessons learned from the community and from our own academic and activist experimentation emerge from participant observations of digital storytelling workshops and related events such as community showcases; informal and formal (audio or videotaped) interviews with TOLD/LYMI staff, Mount Holyoke students, faculty members, and Western Massachusetts residents involved in our various projects; and the discourse analysis of the organization's written and digital materials, all of which are discussed in the next section. By emphasizing the cyclical nature of media activism, I seek to initiate a cycle of academic and practical pedagogical conversations around projects such as promoting bilingual literacy.

As I strive to develop a mutual and candid relationship with community members and other activist and academic partners, we cannot assume that any one party in these complex projects has a definitive answer or absolute knowledge on any given topic. Frequently we will all comment on and sometimes correct or nuance each other's proposals and observations. Over time, we developed the ability to make joint decisions even with regards to those aspects of the project over which a party to the partnership claims a greater sense of expertise or responsibility. In this way, we intentionally avoid two major challenges in action research: the model and the insider monopolies, which result respectively in either the domination of the process by academically-trained scholars or "the assumption that the (community) participants are always right" (Greenwood & Levin, 2008, p. 120). While striving to learn lessons from the community, we can never forget that dialogue and a variety of perspectives may well be the best way to enrich our experience and mutually benefit all parties involved in the process.

In this sense, the first lesson I learned from my community projects is the multi-directional nature of the very mission and structure of Vanessa Pabón's TOLD and LYMI projects. Both initiatives seek to include primarily Latina/o community residents' voices, but also incorporate experiences and perspectives from other groups, such as the Central American migrant youth who participated in our workshop. Through their partnership with higher education institutions, moreover, Ms. Pabón and her team foster the kind of "interaction between local knowledge and expert knowledge through a cooperative process" that Davydd Greenwood and Morten Levin (2008) term the co-generative model (p. 123). All TOLD/LYMI projects grow out of collaborations amongst several organizations and individuals that apply local, technological, academic, and media resources towards community-building and problem-solving. Under Ms. Pabón's leadership, project goals, methodologies, and timelines are mapped out collectively from inception to completion. I applied this same model to my digital storytelling course on promoting bilingual literacy.

Learning From the Community (and Our Mistakes)

My community-based work follows and seeks to advance a growing interest on the part of language faculty to interact with local communities that speak languages other than English, and particularly Spanish. Rather than developing long-term research projects, language faculty tend to focus on practical step-by-step course design guidelines such as the C.R.E.A.R. formula I outlined above (for similar models, see Caldwell, 2007; Ebacher, 2013; Tilley-Lubbs, Raschio, Jorge, & López, 2005). A likely reason for this short-term and curricular focus may rest on the understaffing of language departments and almost complete lack of funding for long-term research projects. In all these language-focused projects, pedagogical awareness and self-reflection emerge as necessary conditions for the implementation of engaged courses. In that vein, I want to discuss the lessons learned from my Promoting Bilingual Literacy seminar in the context of engaged language courses and the methodology of action research in a multilingual context.

Perhaps not surprisingly, the general consensus amongst community-based learning practitioners is that on- and off-campus interactions with local residents enhance student learning (Ebacher, 2013; Krogstad, 2008; Tijunelis, Satterfield, & Benkí, 2013). In contrast, the long-term influence of academic institutions on community organizations and residents likely remains the most elusive and under-studied area within the field of community engagement (CE), for we still lack a persuasive body of evidence supporting the notion that communities benefit from these partnerships (Bloomgarden, Bombardier, Breitbart, Nagel, & Smith II, 2006; Stoecker & Tryon, 2009). In my courses, I (somewhat inconsistently, I must admit) gather data on the dissemination of my students' digital stories, from hits on our YouTube channel to presence across other media such as local television and print media as well as at community screenings. Besides overwhelmingly positive course evaluations, the powerful and lasting effect of CE experiences on my students' social and academic consciousness reveals itself in the number of independent studies and other digital storytelling projects (a couple of which received major Davis Peace Project grants[2]) they have undertaken over the last four years. Through my main community partners, the LYMI and the MMEP in my latest project, or sometimes also personally, I keep track of the impact of our stories on specific individuals and projects, although in an anecdotal, not scientific manner. Lastly, and to the extent possible, I funnel resources from either my institution (Mount Holyoke College at the time) or my own research funding towards my partner organizations in the form of stipends, project-specific grants, and donated equipment.

Since quantifying the benefits of this project for the community is somewhat outside the purview of this chapter, below I will focus on the three main pedagogical and methodological lessons learned from our 2014 digital storytelling workshop. These lessons are consequential for the way I now view both my academic and social location as college professor as well as the nature of campus-community partnerships.

Project-Based, Open-Ended, and Engaged Design

Content for this course included a number of readings on topics such as digital storytelling as a community-building and pedagogical tool, some of which

I reviewed above: the history and current state of Latinas/os in Massachusetts and in Springfield in particular; and recent Central American migration into the U.S (for instance, we analyzed clips from cable news programs and journalistic websites). While anchoring classroom-based instruction in these issues, critical to both the seminar and my own research on digital storytelling, I designed the class around an experimental workshop with migrant youth. We wanted to test whether and how digital storytelling could complement an ESOL course that migrant youth had just taken through the Massachusetts Migrant Education Project. Needless to say, a project-based course in a real-life environment such as this quickly proves both open-ended and unpredictable.

Despite the extensive preparation this course required, including a myriad of logistical and pedagogical challenges, it became evident from the first day that the workshop would have a life of its own. To begin with, and contrary to my initial impression, the English-language skills of our workshop participants soon proved inadequate for digital storytelling. In spite of our disposition to aid with their English, all participants chose to write the script for their stories in Spanish, and used very few English words either in their stories or throughout the ten-week workshop. The activities and research projects we had sketched to test the effectiveness of digital storytelling in ESOL instruction had to adapt to the linguistic abilities of our participants. For many, *Mam* was their native language (most came from Southwestern Guatemala), and several struggled to varying degrees with the Spanish language.

While choosing Spanish to tell their stories, however, they all emphasized the importance of learning English as a way to fulfill their migrant version of the American dream. Consistently, they longed to learn English to more ably navigate the labor market and life in the U.S. In this unexpected context, my students quickly adapted their role in the workshop and their research projects to the linguistic and cultural realities of our participants. We shifted the focus of our open-ended inquiry to technology as a vehicle for migrants to tell their life's story in a way that could be easily shared with wider audiences. On the premise that digital storytelling served as a tool for self-expression for a community either invisible or negatively portrayed in mainstream media, my students undertook a number of interdisciplinary projects that I detail in the next section.

Interdisciplinary Collaborations

As I have mentioned before, my students came from a variety of humanistic and social science majors. I encouraged cross-disciplinary research projects conducted in groups of one to three students that included to the extent possible different methodological approaches to their topic of choice. Two papers (written individually by two Spanish majors) focused on how digital storytelling improved the technological abilities of our workshop participants; two more examined how migrant youth deployed in their videos cultural citizenship as well as self-advocacy; and yet two more reflected on digital storytelling as a vehicle to express belonging to transnational communities and to their local environment (Springfield, Massachusetts in this case). As a whole, these essays employed a variety of methods and bibliography from disciplines such as Psychology (a test of self-efficacy and self-confidence), Anthropology (participant observations and ethnographic surveys), and more traditionally humanistic methods (linguistics and discourse analysis with particular attention to visual, stylistic, and sonic elements).

While the workshop produced five digital stories by migrant youth, the class yielded six interdisciplinary research papers written by a total of twelve students. As a third layer of scholarly production, this course took a broader approach and a longer view to our campus-community partnership and the efficacy of digital storytelling in ESOL instruction. Having worked with my community partner for several years on projects similar to mine, Smith College Psychology Professor Phil Peake attended most of the ten sessions of our workshop with three of his students, as well as several of my classroom-based sessions at Mount Holyoke. I will briefly describe his project, intertwined with my course, in the next section.

Action Research and True Partnership

Ultimately, and while still conceived, coordinated (mostly), and overseen by me, this course spread the responsibility of the different project components amongst our various participants: my students, community partners, research partners, and workshop participants (the migrant youth). We all ended up actively engaging each other and producing results that fulfilled different goals and aspirations. The dissemination of our participants' digital stories online and through showcases enhanced their sense of belonging and self-worth while simultaneously giving true meaning to the work of both my students and the community organizations involved in this project. The action research project conducted by my students and my research partner, Smith Professor Phil Peake, provided our community partners with further accountability metrics and a rather objective, data-based source of feedback. My class and Prof. Peake's students worked closely, under his leadership, to develop a detailed survey for workshop participants on their technological skills, English-language proficiency, and sense of belonging to a community.

Participants took this web-based survey on the first and last day of our collaboration, and the results gave us an approximate sense of the workshop's impact and efficacy. Prof. Peake is currently analyzing the results of his research for a future publication, but overall, data suggests participants felt extremely positive about the workshop. They experienced significant gains in technology proficiency and sense of belonging, and to a lesser extent in their English abilities. The survey was conducted before the community showcase of their work, in which several of the ten workshop participants addressed an audience of around sixty in both Spanish and English. This culminating experience may have had an impact as well on their sense of self-confidence and belonging to the community, but the survey would have not documented it.

Conclusion: Crisis or Opportunity for the Engaged Humanities?

While hardly radical in associated fields such as Latina/o Studies, this type of courses and research are still highly unusual in language (and I'd say other humanities) departments. Project-based, interdisciplinary, and engaged courses present challenges that often feel unsurmountable, whether because of lack of resources, institutional recognition, and/or methodological and pedagogical skills on the part of faculty. As graduate schools and language faculty members across the country continue to make strides in engaged pedagogy and scholarship, however, we need to carefully think about how to better fulfill our obligations as academic partners to community organizations and residents alike (Jay, 2010). The lessons learned from this project point to the need to do the following.

1. Devise long-term, far-reaching partnerships and not solely individual courses or mere volunteer opportunities.
2. Implement action research projects to keep track of whether and how our campus-community partnership benefits both our communities and our students.
3. Make engaged work count at our institutions for tenure, promotion, research support, and merit-based raises.

In the end, the most important lesson I learned from this project is the urgent need for us, academics, to interact and learn from our communities. The Humanities and Social Sciences face renewed scrutiny in a neoliberal academic environment that prioritizes economic over intellectual value. However, our communities, and particularly those in the margins and the shadows, teach us that social justice and equity demand a humanistic approach. In the intersection of social progress and knowledge sharing, the Humanities can find new points of connection with both students and society at large. By updating our methodologies and truly engaging our communities, the Humanities will remain a critical catalyst for social justice.

Notes

1. This chapter builds on, expands, and complements Miñana (2016a) (on establishing community partnerships and course design) and Miñana (2016b) (on the cyclical nature of Latino community media activism from production to dissemination and action).
2. Mika Weissbuch founded in the summer of 2011 the Managua-based (and ongoing) Podcasts for Peace. In the summer of 2012, Hilary Pollan imparted the Educational Image Project workshop for adult GED students in Holyoke, Massachusetts.

References

Ajayi, L. (2009). English as a second language learners' exploration of multimodal texts in a junior high school. *Journal of Adolescent & Adult Literacy, 52*(7), 585–595.

Benmayor, R. (2008). Digital storytelling as a signature pedagogy for the new humanities. *Arts & Humanities in Higher Education, 7*(2), 188–204.

Bloomgarden, A., Bombardier, M., Breitbart, M. M., Nagel, K., & Smith II, P. H. (2006). Building sustainable community/university partnerships in a metropolitan setting. In R. Forrant & L. Silka (Eds.), *Inside and out: Universities and education for sustainable development* (pp. 105–120). Amityville, NY: Baywood Publishing.

Caldwell, W. (2007). Taking Spanish outside the box: A model for integrating service learning into foreign language study. *Foreign Language Annals, 40*(3), 463–471.

Castañeda, M. (2011). ¡Adelante!: Advancing social justice through Latina/o community media. In J. Pooley, S. C. Jansen, & L. Taub (Eds.), *Media and democracy: Critical media scholarship and social justice* (pp. 115–130). New York, NY: Palgrave Macmillan.

Coryat, D. (2011). A youth media agenda for social justice. *Working guide trend papers on arts for change: Animating democracy.* Retrieved from http://animatingdemocracy.org/working-guide-abstracts#coryat

Darias, T., Gómez, A., Hellebrandt, J., Loomis, A., Orendain, M., & Quezada, S. (1999). Community video: Empowerment through university and community interaction. In J. Hellebrandt & L. T. Varona (Eds.), *Construyendo puentes (building bridges): Concepts and models for service-learning in Spanish* (pp. 149–169). Washington, DC: American Association for Higher Education.

Denzin, N. (2003). *Performative ethnography: Critical pedagogy and the politics of culture.* Thousand Oaks, CA: Sage Publications.

Downing, J. D. H., Ford, T. V., Gil, G., & Stein, L. (2001). *Radical media: Rebellious communication and social movements.* Thousand Oaks, CA: Sage Publications.

Ebacher, C. (2013). Taking Spanish into the community: A novice's guide to service-learning. *Hispania, 96*(2), 397–408.

Goldfarb, B. (2002). *Visual pedagogy: Media cultures in and beyond the classroom.* Durham, NC: Duke University Press.

Greenwood, D. J., & Levin, M. (2008). *Introduction to action research: Social research for social change.* Thousand Oaks, CA: Sage Publications.

Halleck, D. (2002). *Hand-held visions: The impossible possibilities of community media.* New York, NY: Fordham University Press.

Hunt, G. (2007). Failure to thrive? The community literacy strand of the additive bilingual project at an Eastern Cape community school, South Africa. *Journal of Research in Reading, 30*(1), 80–96.

Jay, G. (2010). The engaged humanities: Principles and practices for public scholarship and teaching. *Journal of Community Engagement and Scholarship, 3*(1), 51–63.

Juppi, P. (2012). Digital storytelling as a tool for adolescent participation and identity-building. In J. Krappe, T. Parkkinen & A. Tonteri (Eds.), *Moving in! Art-based approaches to work with the youth* (pp. 63–79). Turku: Turku University of Applied Sciences Press.

Kincheloe, J. L., & McLaren, P. (2008). Rethinking critical theory and qualitative research. In N. K. Denzin & Y. S. Lincoln (Eds.), *The landscape of qualitative research* (pp. 403–456). Thousand Oaks, CA: Sage Publications.

Krogstad, A. (2008). Community as classroom: Service learning in the foreign language classroom. *The International Journal of Learning, 15*(1), 37–41.

Lambert, J. (2008). *Digital storytelling: Capturing lives, creating community.* London: Routledge.

Lambert, J. (2013). *Seven stages: Story and the human experience.* Berkeley, CA: Digital Diner Press.

Lara, L. E. (2006). *Communities and technologies: New immigrant young Latinas in the new millennium* (Unpublished doctoral dissertation). The Ohio State University.

Lundby, K. (2008). *Digital storytelling, mediatized stories: Self-representations in New Media.* New York, NY: Peter Lang.

Martínez, K. Z. (2011). Pac-Man meets the Minutemen: Video games by Los Angeles Latino youth. *National Civic Review, 100*(3), 50–57.

McGuinnis, T. A. (2007). Khmer rap boys, X-Men, Asia's fruits, and Dragonball Z: Creating multilingual and multimodal classroom contexts. *Journal of Adolescent & Adult Literacy, 50*(7), 570–579.

McIntyre, A. (2008). *Participatory action research.* Thousand Oaks, CA: Sage Publications.

Miñana, R. (2016a). Beyond the classroom wall: Guidelines for engaging local communities in multilingual contexts. *ADFL Bulletin, 43*(2), 27–38.

Miñana, R. (2016b). The cycle of Latina/o community activism. In M. E. Cepeda & D. I. Casillas (Eds.), *The Routledge companion to Latina/o media* (pp. 186–200). New York, NY: Routledge.

Neilsen, P. (2006). Digital storytelling as life-writing: Self-construction, therapeutic effect, textual analysis leading to an enabling "aesthetic" for the community voice. In R. Vella (Ed.), *Speculation and innovation: Applying practice-led research in the creative industries.* Queensland, Australia: Queensland University of Technology. Retrieved from www.speculation2005.qut.edu.au/papers/Neilsen.pdf

Notley, T., & Tacchi, J. (2005). Online youth networks: Researching the experiences of "peripheral" young people in using new media tools for creative participation and representation. *3C Media Journal of Community, Citizen's and Third Sector Media and Communication, 1*, 1–10.

Ohler, J. (2006). *Digital storytelling in the classroom: New media pathways to literacy, learning, and creativity.* Thousand Oaks, CA: Corwin Press.

Pearson Hathorn, P. (2005). Using digital storytelling as a literacy tool for the inner city middle school youth. *The Charter Schools Resource Journal, 1*(1), 32–38.

Ramirez, P. (2010). *Digital storytelling: A window into the lives of Latino immigrant families in the United States* (Unpublished doctoral dissertation). University of California, Santa Barbara.

Sadik, A. (2008). Digital storytelling: A meaningful technology-integrated approach for engaged student learning. *Educational Technology Research and Development, 56*(4), 487–506.

Stoecker, R., & Tryon, E. (Eds.). (2009). *The unheard voices: Community organizations and service learning.* Philadelphia, PA: Temple University Press.

Tijunelis, V., Satterfield, T., & Benkí, J. R. (2013). Linking service-learning opportunities and domestic immersion experiences in U.S. Latino communities: A case study of the "En Nuestra Lengua" Project. *Hispania, 96*(2), 264–282.

Tilley-Lubbs, G. A., Raschio, R., Jorge, E., & López, S. (2005). Taking language learning into the real world. *Hispania, 88*(1), 160–167.

Wilkin, H. A., & Ball-Rokeach, S. J. (2006). Reaching at-risk groups: The importance of health storytelling in Los Angeles Latino media. *Journalism, 7*(3), 299–320.

Wilson, P., & Stewart, M. (Eds.). (2008). *Global indigenous media: Cultures, poetics, and politics.* Durham, NC: Duke University Press.

Wolske, M., Ayad, M., Budhathoki, N. R., Kowalski, C., Nam, C., Ritzo, C., … Bruce, B. C. (2008). Youth community informatics: Using new digital media to foster personal growth and community action. In L. Stillman (Ed.), *Proceedings of the Prato CIRN community informatics conference—ICTs for social inclusion: What is the Reality?* Prato, Italy: Monash University, Centre for Community Networking Research.

Contributors

EDITORS

Mari Castañeda is Professor and Chair of the Department of Communication at the University of Massachusetts Amherst, and affiliated with the Center for Latin American, Caribbean and Latina/o Studies. Her fields of study include Latinx/Chicana communication, academic labor, and digital media policy. Her engaged scholarship has appeared in various journals/monographs and she has two co-edited books: *Telenovelas and Soap Operas in the Digital Age: Global Industries and New Audiences* (Peter Lang, 2011), and *Mothers in Academia* (Columbia University Press, 2013).

Joseph Krupczynski is Director of Civic Engagement and Service-Learning and Associate Professor of Architecture at the University of Massachusetts Amherst. A designer, public artist and educator, his creative work and scholarship promotes reciprocal community partnerships and creates participatory processes to explore equity and social justice within the built environment. Professor Krupczynski is a founding director of the design resource center, The Center for Design Engagement (CDE) in Holyoke, MA (www.designengagement.org).

SECTION I

CHAPTER 1

Antonieta Mercado, Ph.D. is Assistant Professor of communication and social justice at the University of San Diego Communication Studies Department. Her areas of study are cosmopolitan citizenship, advocacy journalism, media and conflict resolution, communication and social justice, immigrant media, transnational indigenous movements, decolonization, and indigeneity. Her work has been published in *Journalism, Theory, Practice and Criticism*, *Journal of Border Studies*, *Comunicación y Sociedad*, and other interdisciplinary outlets dedicated to communication, citizenship, and social justice research.

CHAPTER 2

Joseph Krupczynski is Director of Civic Engagement and Service-Learning and Associate Professor of Architecture at the University of Massachusetts Amherst. A designer, public artist and educator, his creative work and scholarship promotes reciprocal community partnerships and creates participatory processes to explore equity and social justice within the built environment. Professor Krupczynski is a founding director of the design resource center, The Center for Design Engagement (CDE) in Holyoke, MA (www.designengagement.org).

CHAPTER 3

Claudia A. Evans-Zepeda, Ph.D. is Assistant Professor of Communication at California State University, Fullerton. Her research program focuses on the communicative intersections of culture, social justice, and race within the context of social justice. Prior and current research projects focus on the rhetorical protest practices of undocumented youth, and how DREAMers communicate their identity given the vitriolic anti-immigrant discourse. Engaging the fields of communication studies, critical race theory, and Latino Studies, her research appears in numerous journals and edited collections.

CHAPTER 4

Marisel Moreno, Ph.D. is Associate Professor of Latino/a Literature in the Department of Romance Languages and Literatures at the University of Notre Dame. Her first book, *Family Matters: Puerto Rican Women Authors on the Island and the Mainland* (U Va P.), was published in 2012. In 2011, she received the Indiana Governor's Award for Service-Learning and in 2016 she received the prestigious Sheedy Excellence in Teaching Award given by Notre Dame's College of Arts and Letters.

CHAPTER 5

Clara Román-Odio is Professor of Spanish and Director of Latino/a Studies at Kenyon College. Author of *Sacred Iconographies in Chicana Cultural Productions* (2013), and *Octavio Paz en los debates críticos y estéticos del siglo*

XX (2006), she has published extensively on modern/postmodern aesthetics and feminisms of color. Her most recent engagements include spearheading the Kenyon Community Engaged Learning Initiative and the creation of the public humanities project *Latinos in Rural America.*

Patricia Mota is a Fulbright ETA based in Veracruz, Mexico. She recently graduated cum laude from Kenyon College with a BA in Spanish Literature and International Studies. From her internship at *Mil Mujeres,* an immigration law firm in Chicago, to her work at Kenyon, Patricia's experiences have fostered a deep commitment towards educational equity and community development. Next year, she will teach bilingual education in Dallas ISD. She intends to pursue a Ph.D. in Hispanic Literature in the near future.

Amelia Dunnell is in her final semester at Kenyon College, pursuing a BA in Spanish and Women's and Gender Studies. Amelia has held leadership roles at Kenyon's civic engagement organizations and has interned at the *City Bar Justice Center*, a legal non-profit in New York City, where she worked within the Immigrant Justice Project unit. Upon graduation, Amelia intends to pursue a career in immigration law in the non-profit world.

SECTION II

CHAPTER 6

Jonathan Rosa is Assistant Professor in the Graduate School of Education, Center for Comparative Studies in Race and Ethnicity, and, by courtesy, Anthropology and Linguistics, at Stanford University. He collaborates with communities to analyze the interplay between racial marginalization, linguistic stigmatization, and educational inequity. His work has appeared in scholarly journals such as the Harvard Educational Review, American Ethnologist, American Anthropologist, and the Journal of Linguistic Anthropology, as well as media outlets such as MSNBC, NPR, CNN, and Univision.

CHAPTER 7

Judith Flores Carmona is Assistant Professor in the Department of Curriculum & Instruction and in the Honors College at New Mexico State University. Her teaching and research interests include Chicana/Latina feminisms, critical multicultural education, critical race theories, oral history, social justice education, and testimonio methodology and pedagogy. Her work has appeared in *Equity & Excellence in Education*, *Race Ethnicity and Education* and in *Chicana/Latina Studies: The Journal of MALCS.*

CHAPTER 8

J. Estrella Torrez is Associate Professor in the Residential College in the Arts and Humanities at Michigan State University. Dr. Torrez's scholarly interests include critical pedagogy, community engagement, multicultural education, Indigenous education, Xicana studies, and sociocultural literacies. She is particularly interested in the role of language and culture in sustaining community-based knowledge, particularly among rural Latino families and urban Indigenous youth.

CHAPTER 9

Celeste González de Bustamante is Associate Professor in the School of Journalism at the University of Arizona and an affiliated faculty member of the Center for Latin American Studies. Her research interests include history of news media, and the U.S.-Mexico borderlands. She is the author of *"Muy buenas noches," Mexico, Television and the Cold War* (University of Nebraska Press, 2012), and the co-editor of *Arizona Firestorm: Global Immigration Realities, National Media, and Provincial Politics* (Rowman and Littlefield, 2012).

CHAPTER 10

Ginetta E. B. Candelario is a Brooklyn-born, Jersey-raised transnational Dominican anti-racist feminist single mother. She has been a faculty member in Sociology and Latin American & Latin@ Studies at Smith College since 1999. As a Smith professor, her teaching and scholarship focus on race, gender, class and belonging in the Hispanic Caribbean and U.S. She is currently working on a history Dominican feminist thought and activism, tentatively titled *Voices Echoing Beyond the Seas: Dominican Feminisms, from Trans-atlantic to Transnational, 1882–1942.*

SECTION III

CHAPTER 11

Jillian M. Báez is Assistant Professor of Media Culture at the College of Staten Island-CUNY. Báez specializes in Latina/o media, audience studies, and transnational feminisms. She has published her research in *Critical Studies in Media Communication*, *Women's Studies Quarterly*, *Journal of Popular Communication*, *Centro: Journal of the Center for Puerto Rican Studies*, and several anthologies. Báez is author of the forthcoming book *Consuming Latinas: Audiences and Citizenship* (University of Illinois Press). She is also co-editor of *WSQ* (formerly *Women's Studies Quarterly*).

CHAPTER 12

Katynka Z. Martínez is Associate Professor of Latina/Latino Studies at San Francisco State University. Her published work has focused on Latina/Latino community journalism as well as Latina/Latino-oriented television, women's magazines, and video games. Since 2008, the students in her Latina/Latino Journalism class have contributed articles, photography, and artwork to the bilingual newspaper *El Tecolote*. She also encourages student involvement with *El Tecolote* through her other classes such as Latina/Latino Visual Culture, Latinas/Latinos and the Media, and Latinas/Latinos in California.

CHAPTER 13

Jessica Retis is Associate Professor at CSUN in the Journalism Department. She studied Communications at the Universidad de Lima, Peru; Masters in Latin American Studies from UNAM, Mexico; and Ph.D. in Contemporary Latin America from Universidad Complutense de Madrid, Spain. She worked for almost twenty years as a journalist in Peru, Mexico and Spain. Her areas of research are contemporary diasporas and the media, political economy of the media, cultural industries, and Hispanic media in the US, Europe, and Asia.

CHAPTER 14

Sonya M. Alemán is Associate Professor at the University of Texas at San Antonio in the Mexican American Studies program. She studies the representations and manifestations of race, racism, and whiteness in the media. Her work reimagines journalism pedagogy to better reflect the lives and experiences of communities of color and investigates media representations produced by communities of color. She also is invested in improving the educational experiences of students of color.

CHAPTER 15

Rogelio Miñana is Professor of Spanish and Head of Global Studies and Modern Languages at Drexel University. His research centers on the role of classic cultural icons, particularly *Don Quixote*, in 21st century political and social justice discourse. In both his scholarship and pedagogy, he specifically explores the interplay between the traditional humanities, youth organizations, and digital storytelling. His latest book project is tentatively entitled *Living Quixote:* Don Quixote, *Politics, and Social Justice in 21st-century Spain and the Americas.*

Index

A

B

C

D

E

F

G

H

L

M

N

X

Y

Z

Yolanda Medina and Margarita Machado-Casas
GENERAL EDITORS

Critical Studies of Latinos/as in the Americas is a provocative interdisciplinary series that offers a critical space for reflection and questioning what it means to be Latino/a living in the Americas in twenty-first century social, cultural, economic, and political arenas. The series looks forward to extending the dialogue to include the North and South Western hemispheric relations that are prevalent in the field of global studies.

Topics that explore and advance research and scholarship on contemporary topics and issues related with processes of racialization, economic exploitation, health, education, transnationalism, immigration, gendered and sexual identities, and disabilities that are not commonly highlighted in the current Latino/a Studies literature as well as the multitude of socio, cultural, economic, and political progress among the Latinos/as in the Americas are welcome.

To receive more information about CSLA, please contact:

Yolanda Medina (ymedina@bmcc.cuny.edu) &
Margarita Machado-Casas (Margarita.MachadoCasas@utsa.edu)

To order other books in this series, please contact our Customer Service Department at:

(800) 770-LANG (within the U.S.)
(212) 647-7706 (outside the U.S.)
(212) 647-7707 FAX

Or browse online by series at:

WWW.PETERLANG.COM